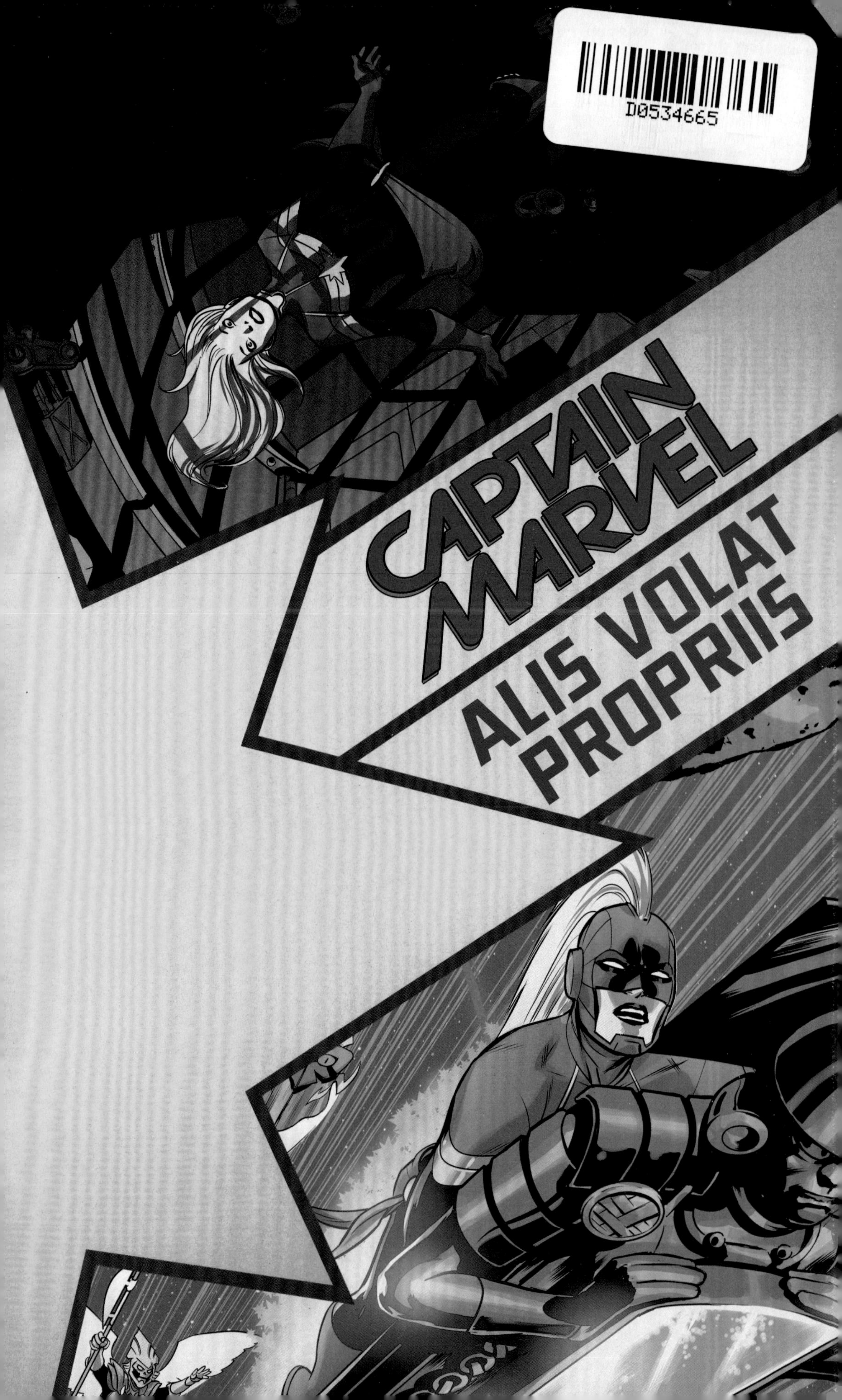
CAPTAIN MARVEL
ALIS VOLAT PROPRIIS

CAPTAIN MARVEL VOL. 3: ALIS VOLAT PROPRIIS. Contains material originally published in magazine form as CAPTAIN MARVEL #12-15. First printing 2015. ISBN# 978-0-7851-9841-3. Published by MARVEL WORLDWIDE, INC., a subsidiary of MARVEL ENTERTAINMENT, LLC. OFFICE OF PUBLICATION: 135 West 50th Street, New York, NY 10020. Copyright © 2015 MARVEL No similarity between any of the names, characters, persons, and/or institutions in this magazine with those of any living or dead person or institution is intended, and any such similarity which may exist is purely coincidental. **Printed in Canada.** ALAN FINE, President, Marvel Entertainment; DAN BUCKLEY, President, TV, Publishing and Brand Management; JOE QUESADA, Chief Creative Officer; TOM BREVOORT, SVP of Publishing; DAVID BOGART, SVP of Operations & Procurement, Publishing; C.B. CEBULSKI, VP of International Development & Brand Management; DAVID GABRIEL, SVP Print, Sales & Marketing; JIM O'KEEFE, VP of Operations & Logistics; DAN CARR, Executive Director of Publishing Technology; SUSAN CRESPI, Editorial Operations Manager; ALEX MORALES, Publishing Operations Manager; STAN LEE, Chairman Emeritus. For information regarding advertising in Marvel Comics or on Marvel.com, please contact Jonathan Rheingold, VP of Custom Solutions & Ad Sales, at jrheingold@marvel.com. For Marvel subscription inquiries, please call 800-217-9158. **Manufactured between 6/26/2015 and 8/3/2015 by SOLISCO PRINTERS, SCOTT, QC, CANADA.**

10 9 8 7 6 5 4 3 2 1

WRITERS KELLY SUE DeCONNICK (#12-15)
& WARREN ELLIS (#12-13)
ARTIST DAVID LOPEZ
COLOR ARTIST LEE LOUGHRIDGE
LETTERER VC's JOE CARAMAGNA
COVER ART DAVID LOPEZ
ASSISTANT EDITORS DEVIN LEWIS & CHARLES BEACHAM
EDITOR SANA AMANAT
SENIOR EDITOR NICK LOWE

COLLECTION EDITOR: JENNIFER GRÜNWALD
ASSISTANT EDITOR: SARAH BRUNSTAD
ASSOCIATE MANAGING EDITOR: ALEX STARBUCK
EDITOR, SPECIAL PROJECTS: MARK D. BEAZLEY
SENIOR EDITOR, SPECIAL PROJECTS: JEFF YOUNGQUIST
SVP PRINT, SALES & MARKETING: DAVID GABRIEL

EDITOR IN CHIEF: AXEL ALONSO
CHIEF CREATIVE OFFICER: JOE QUESADA
PUBLISHER: DAN BUCKLEY
EXECUTIVE PRODUCER: ALAN FINE

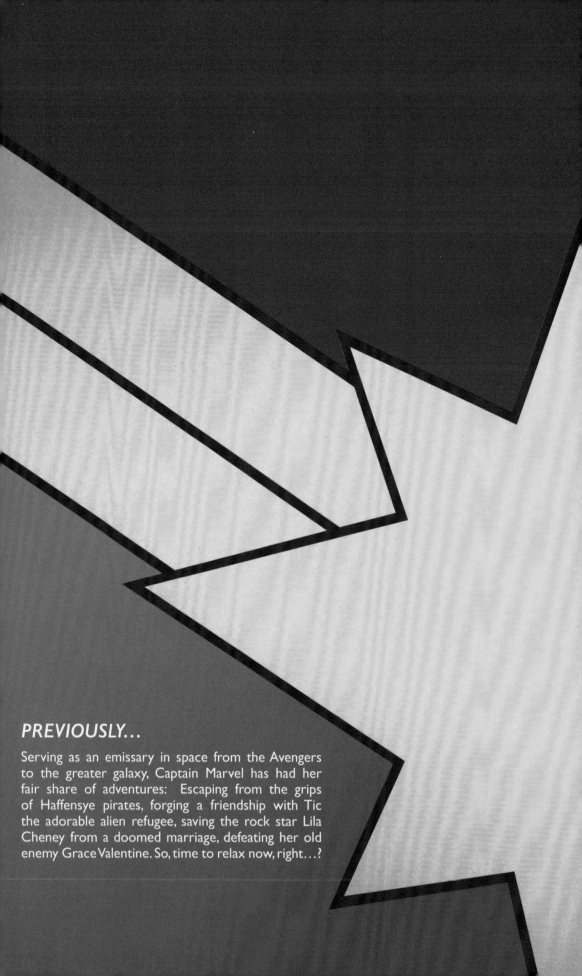

PREVIOUSLY...

Serving as an emissary in space from the Avengers to the greater galaxy, Captain Marvel has had her fair share of adventures: Escaping from the grips of Haffensye pirates, forging a friendship with Tic the adorable alien refugee, saving the rock star Lila Cheney from a doomed marriage, defeating her old enemy Grace Valentine. So, time to relax now, right...?

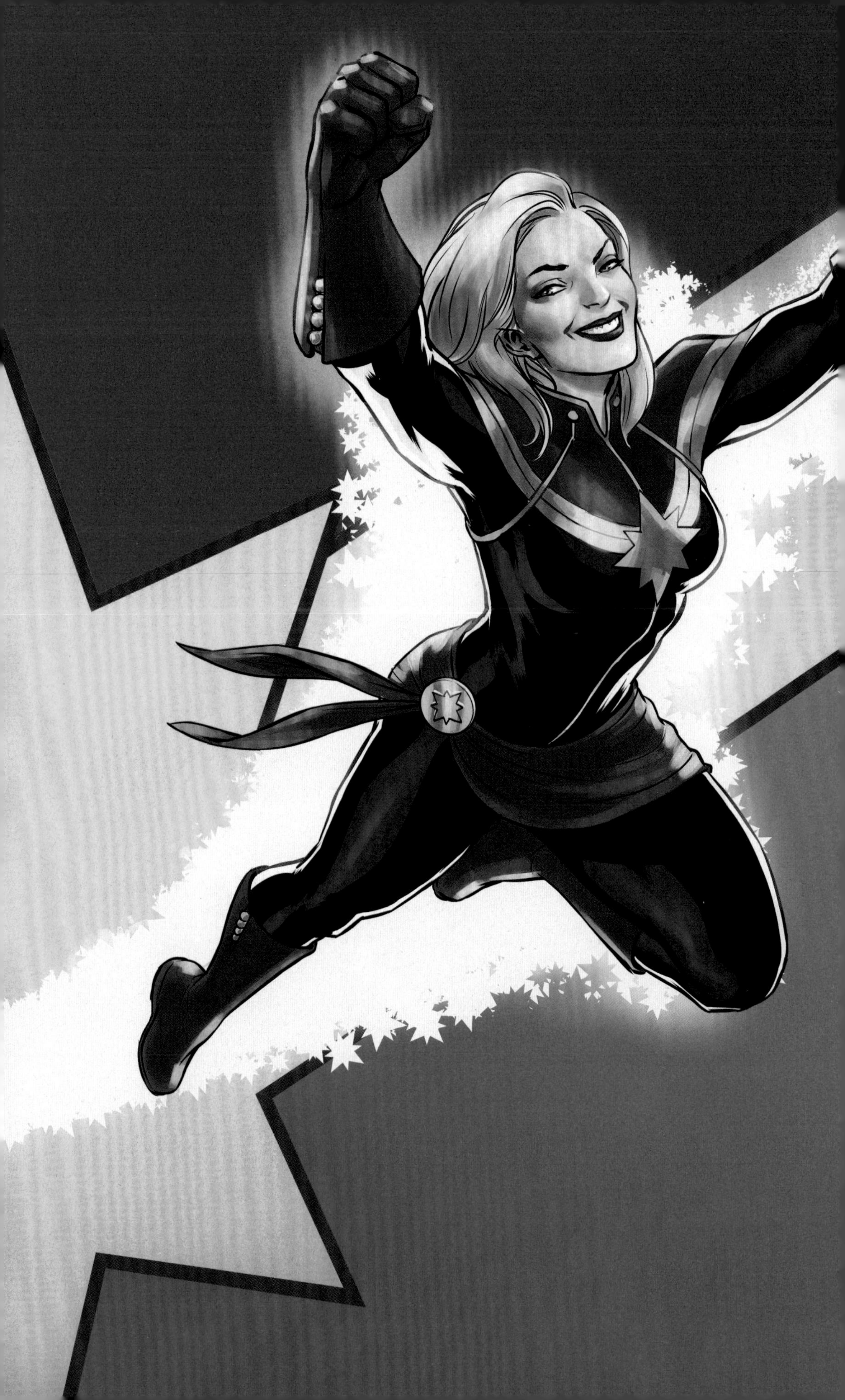

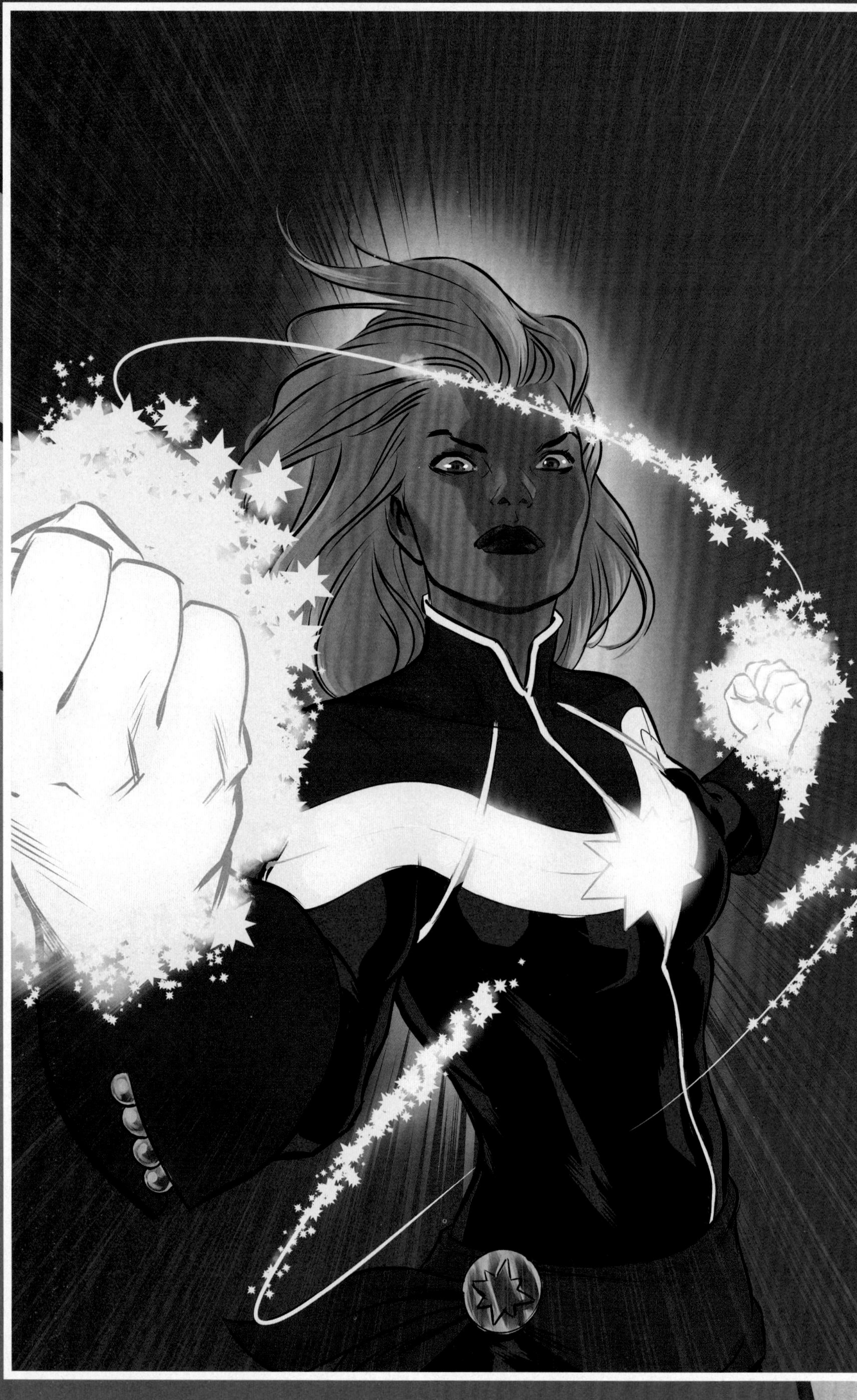

TWELVE THE 7 SECONDS BEFORE YOU DIE PART 1

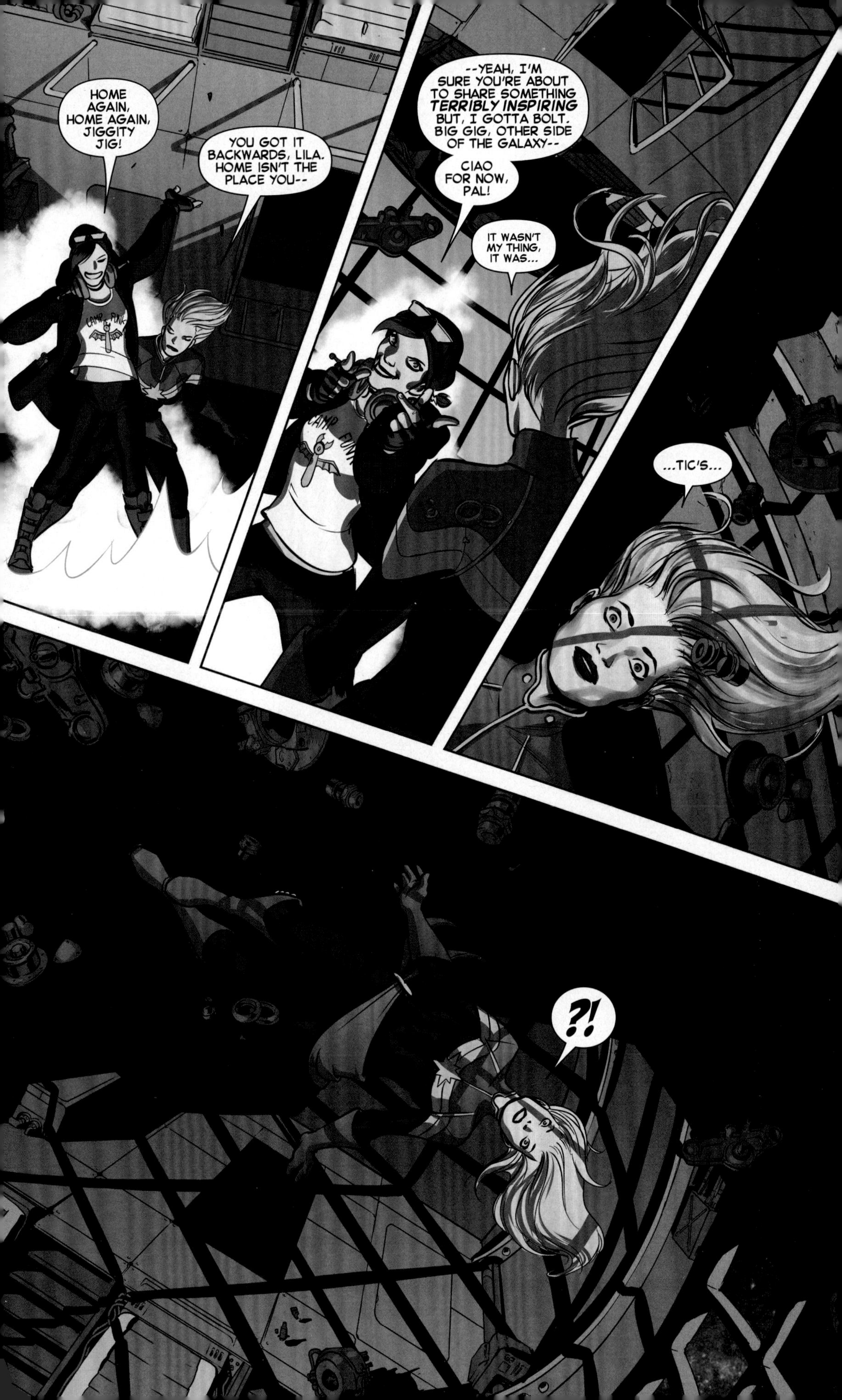
HOME AGAIN, HOME AGAIN, JIGGITY JIG!
YOU GOT IT BACKWARDS, LILA. HOME ISN'T THE PLACE YOU--
CAMP FUNK
--YEAH, I'M SURE YOU'RE ABOUT TO SHARE SOMETHING *TERRIBLY INSPIRING* BUT, I GOTTA BOLT. BIG GIG, OTHER SIDE OF THE GALAXY--
CIAO FOR NOW, PAL!
IT WASN'T MY THING, IT WAS...
CAMP FUNK
...TIC'S...
?!

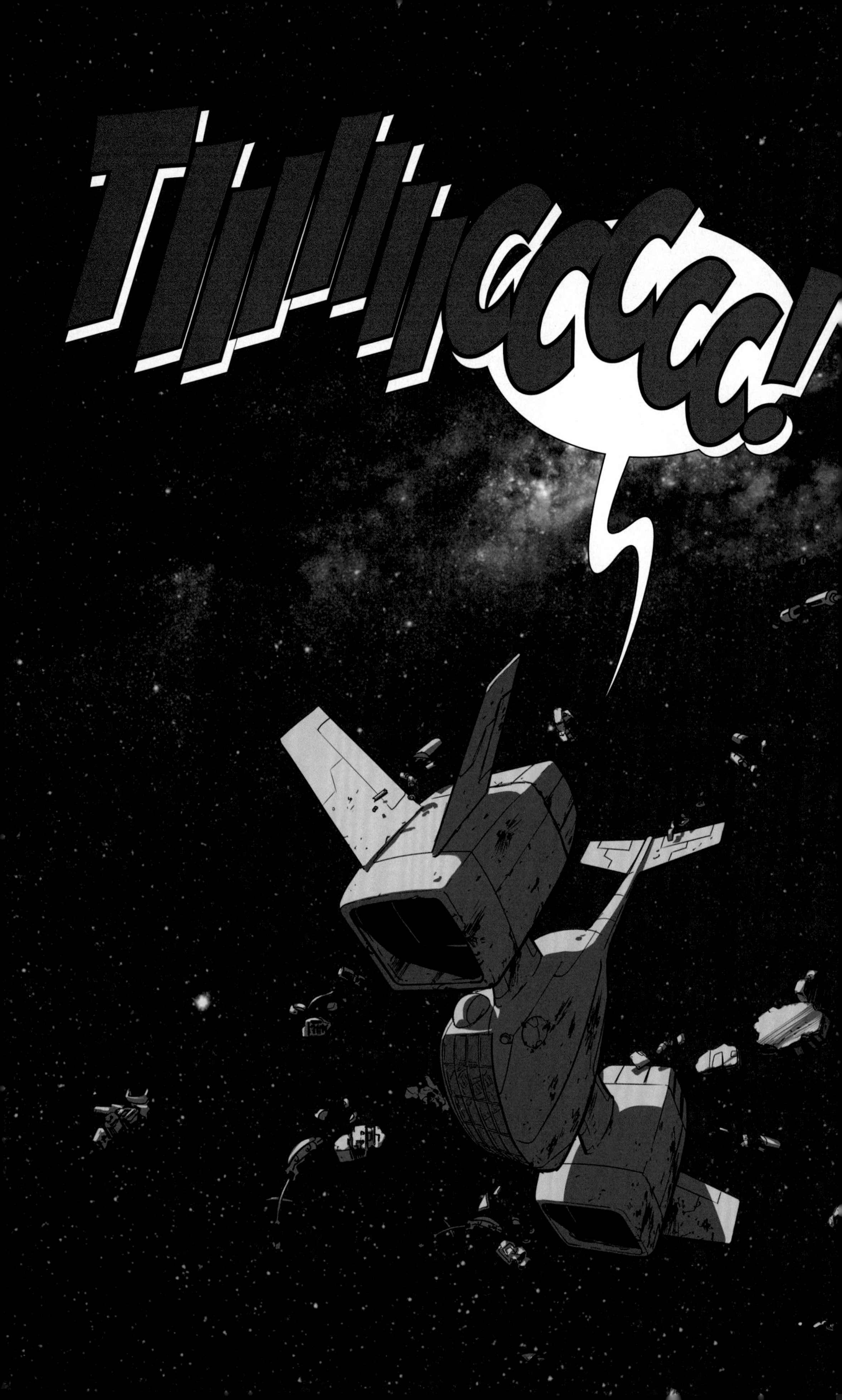
TIIIIIIaaaa!

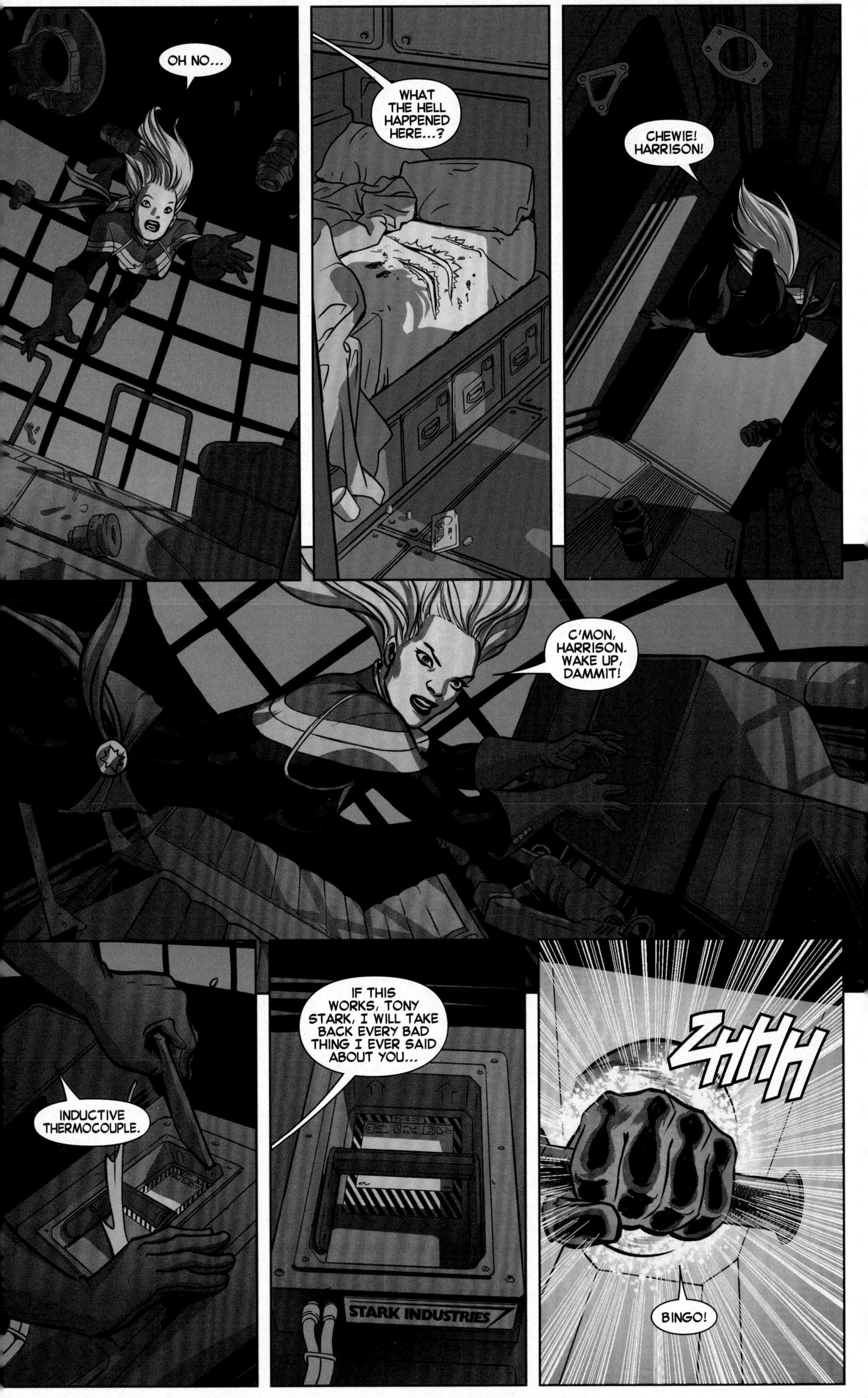
OH NO...
WHAT THE HELL HAPPENED HERE...?
CHEWIE! HARRISON!
C'MON, HARRISON. WAKE UP, DAMMIT!
INDUCTIVE THERMOCOUPLE.
IF THIS WORKS, TONY STARK, I WILL TAKE BACK EVERY BAD THING I EVER SAID ABOUT YOU...
STARK INDUSTRIES
ZHHH
BINGO!

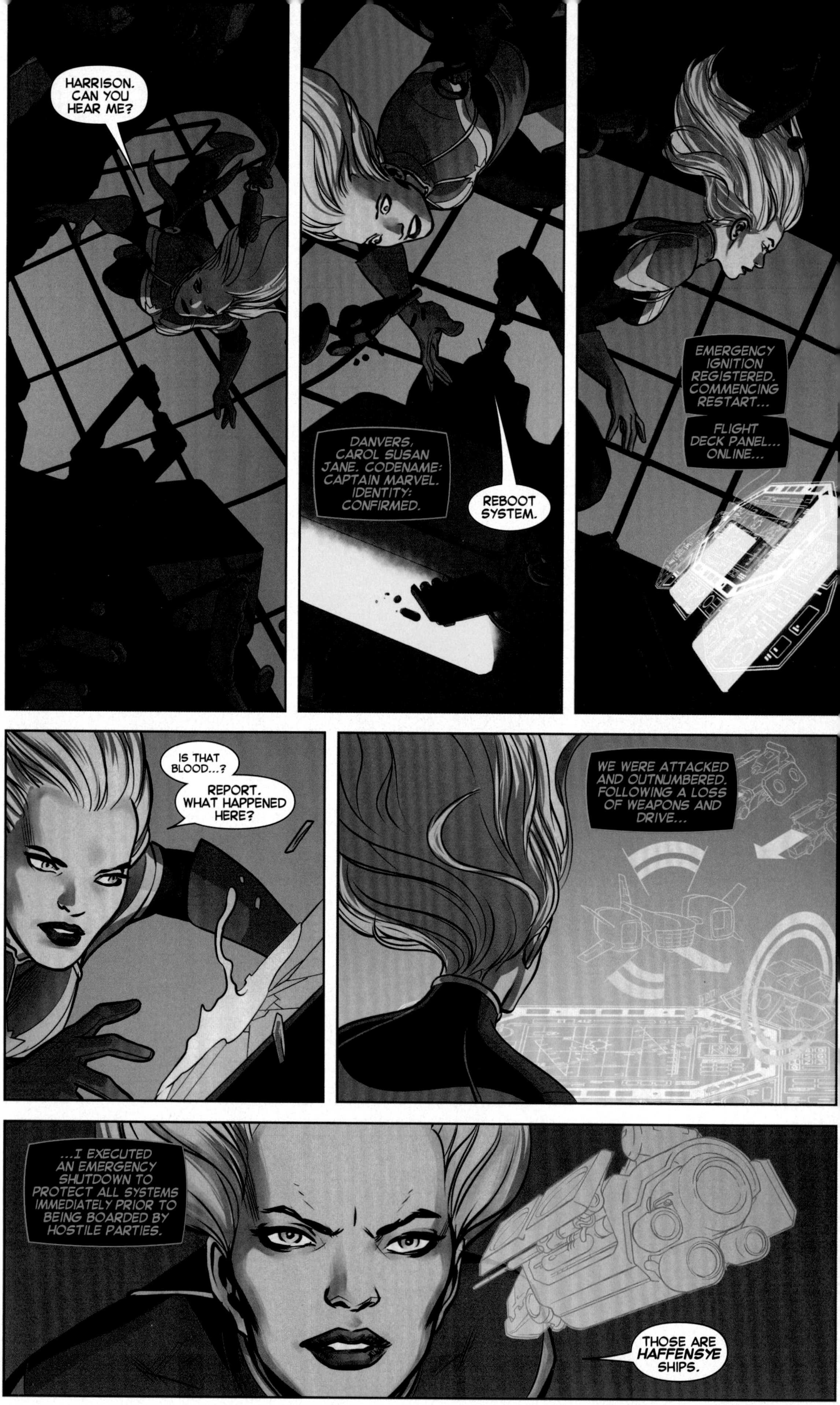
HARRISON. CAN YOU HEAR ME?
DANVERS, CAROL SUSAN JANE. CODENAME: CAPTAIN MARVEL. IDENTITY: CONFIRMED.
REBOOT SYSTEM.
EMERGENCY IGNITION REGISTERED. COMMENCING RESTART...
FLIGHT DECK PANEL... ONLINE...
IS THAT BLOOD...?
REPORT. WHAT HAPPENED HERE?
WE WERE ATTACKED AND OUTNUMBERED. FOLLOWING A LOSS OF WEAPONS AND DRIVE...
...I EXECUTED AN EMERGENCY SHUTDOWN TO PROTECT ALL SYSTEMS IMMEDIATELY PRIOR TO BEING BOARDED BY HOSTILE PARTIES.
THOSE ARE HAFFENSYE SHIPS.

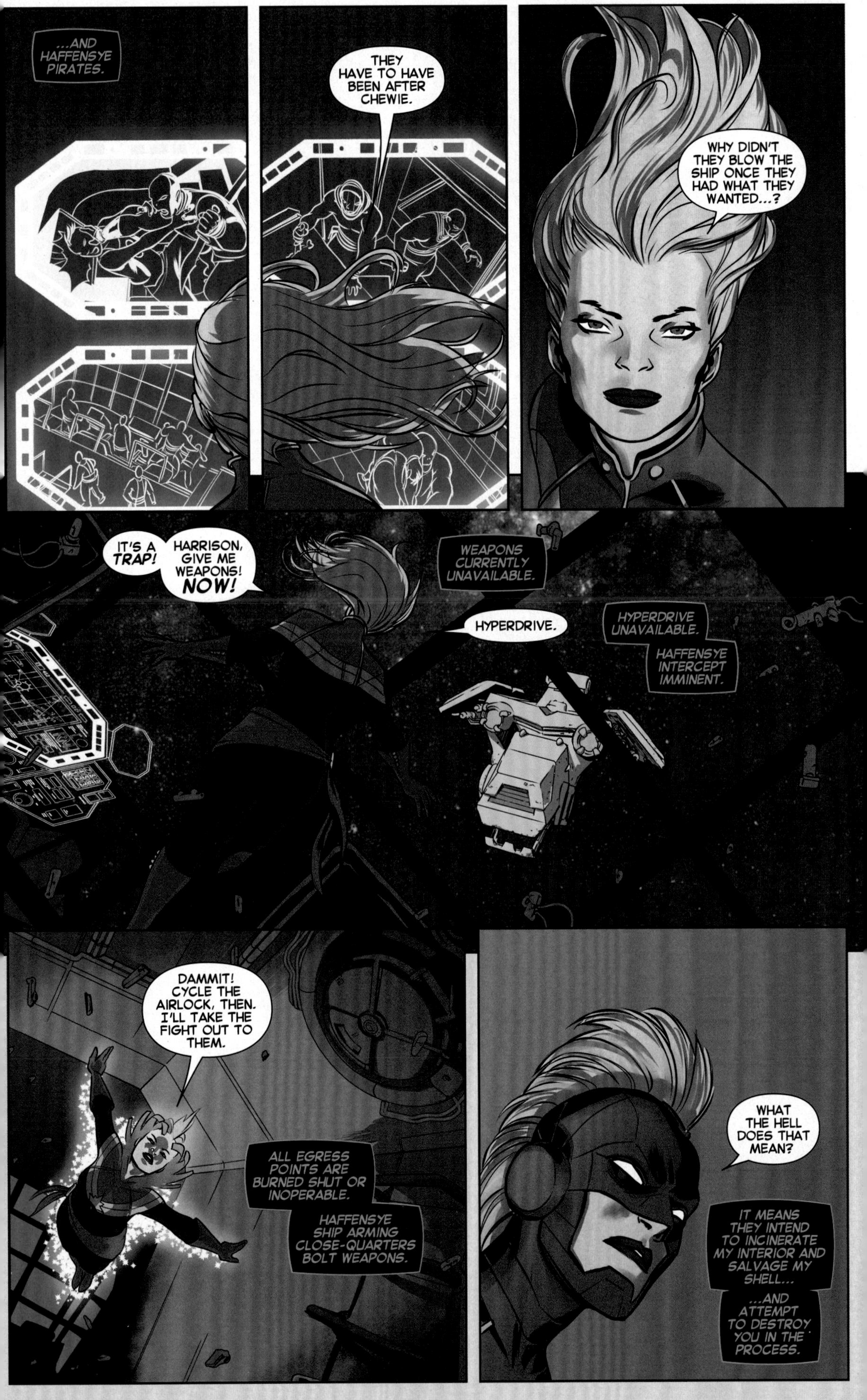

...AND HAFFENSYE PIRATES.
THEY HAVE TO HAVE BEEN AFTER CHEWIE.
WHY DIDN'T THEY BLOW THE SHIP ONCE THEY HAD WHAT THEY WANTED...?
IT'S A TRAP!
HARRISON, GIVE ME WEAPONS! NOW!
WEAPONS CURRENTLY UNAVAILABLE.
HYPERDRIVE.
HYPERDRIVE UNAVAILABLE.
HAFFENSYE INTERCEPT IMMINENT.
DAMMIT! CYCLE THE AIRLOCK, THEN. I'LL TAKE THE FIGHT OUT TO THEM.
ALL EGRESS POINTS ARE BURNED SHUT OR INOPERABLE.
HAFFENSYE SHIP ARMING CLOSE-QUARTERS BOLT WEAPONS.
WHAT THE HELL DOES THAT MEAN?
IT MEANS THEY INTEND TO INCINERATE MY INTERIOR AND SALVAGE MY SHELL...
...AND ATTEMPT TO DESTROY YOU IN THE PROCESS.

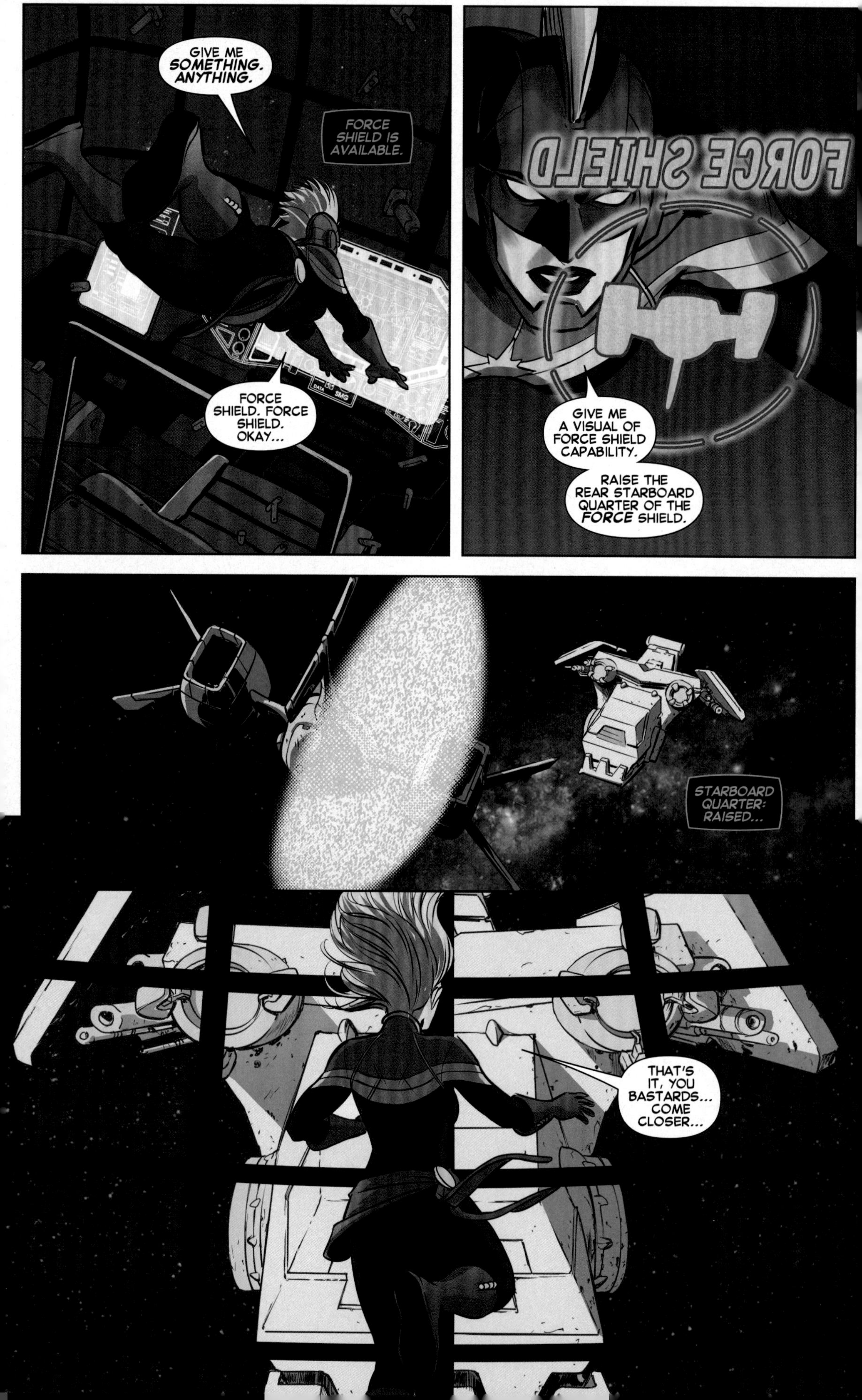

GIVE ME SOMETHING. ANYTHING.
FORCE SHIELD IS AVAILABLE.
FORCE SHIELD. FORCE SHIELD. OKAY...
DATA
SMG
FORCE SHIELD
GIVE ME A VISUAL OF FORCE SHIELD CAPABILITY.
RAISE THE REAR STARBOARD QUARTER OF THE FORCE SHIELD.
STARBOARD QUARTER: RAISED...
THAT'S IT, YOU BASTARDS... COME CLOSER...

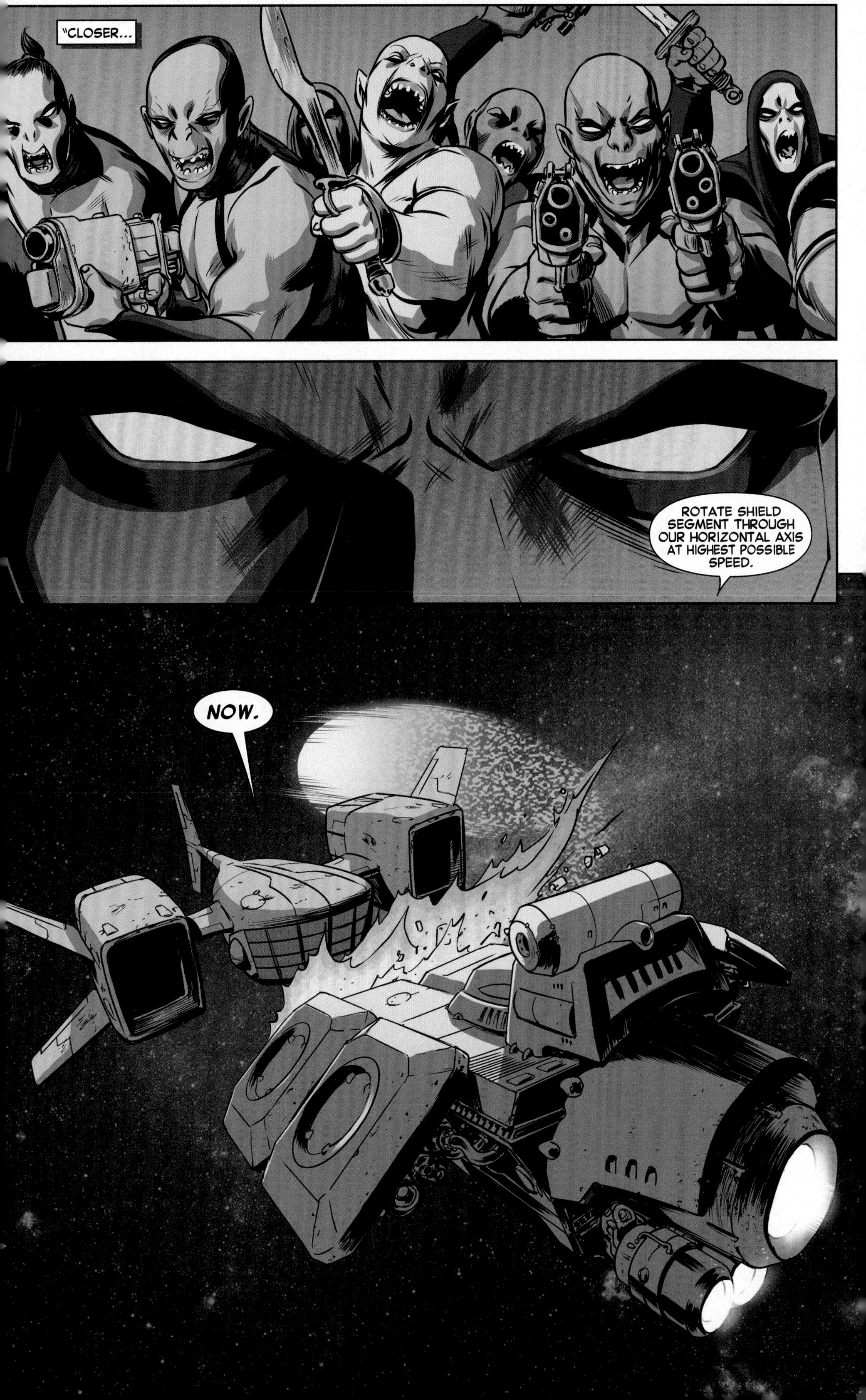
"CLOSER...
ROTATE SHIELD SEGMENT THROUGH OUR HORIZONTAL AXIS AT HIGHEST POSSIBLE SPEED.
NOW.

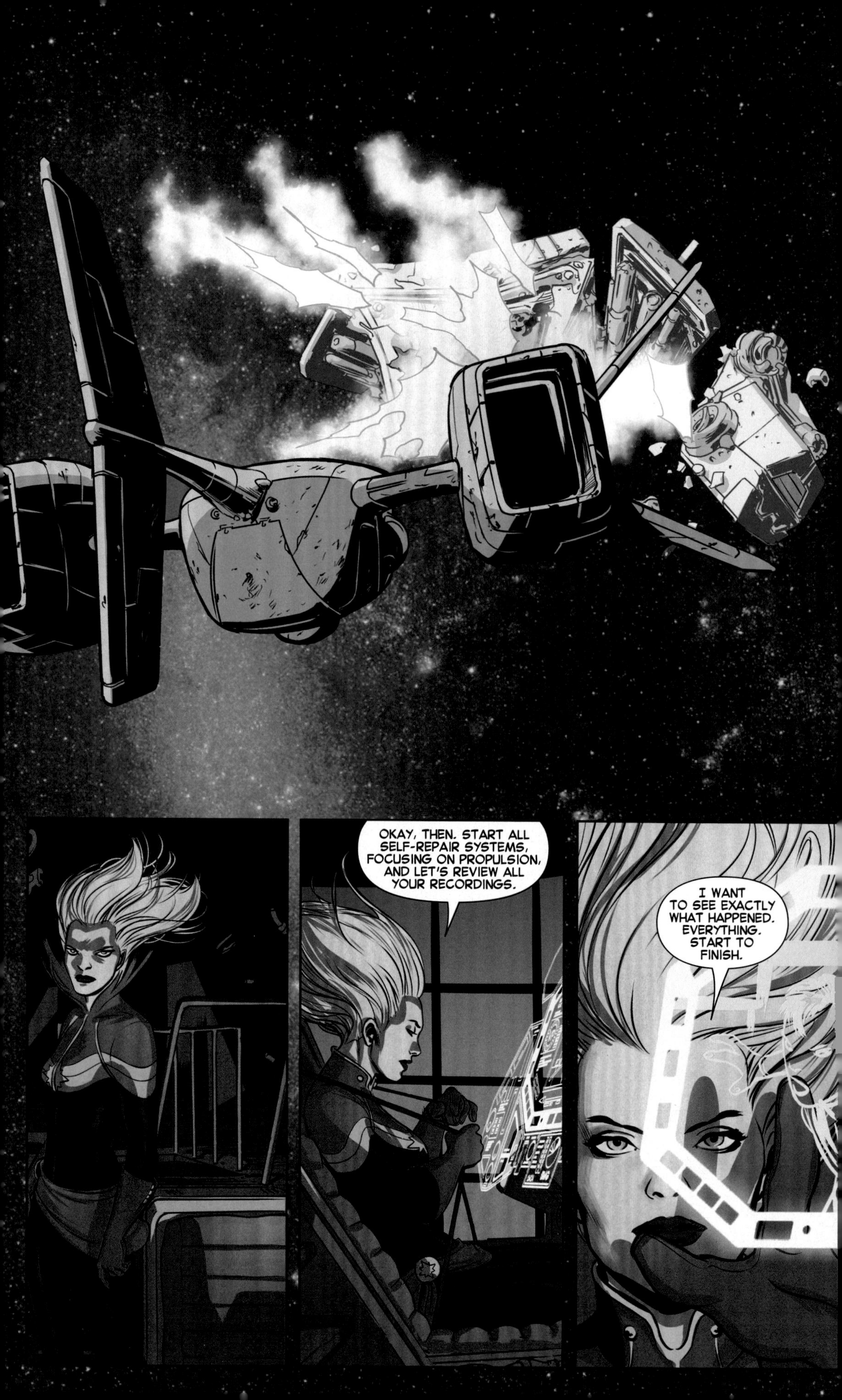
OKAY, THEN. START ALL SELF-REPAIR SYSTEMS, FOCUSING ON PROPULSION, AND LET'S REVIEW ALL YOUR RECORDINGS.
I WANT TO SEE EXACTLY WHAT HAPPENED. EVERYTHING. START TO FINISH.

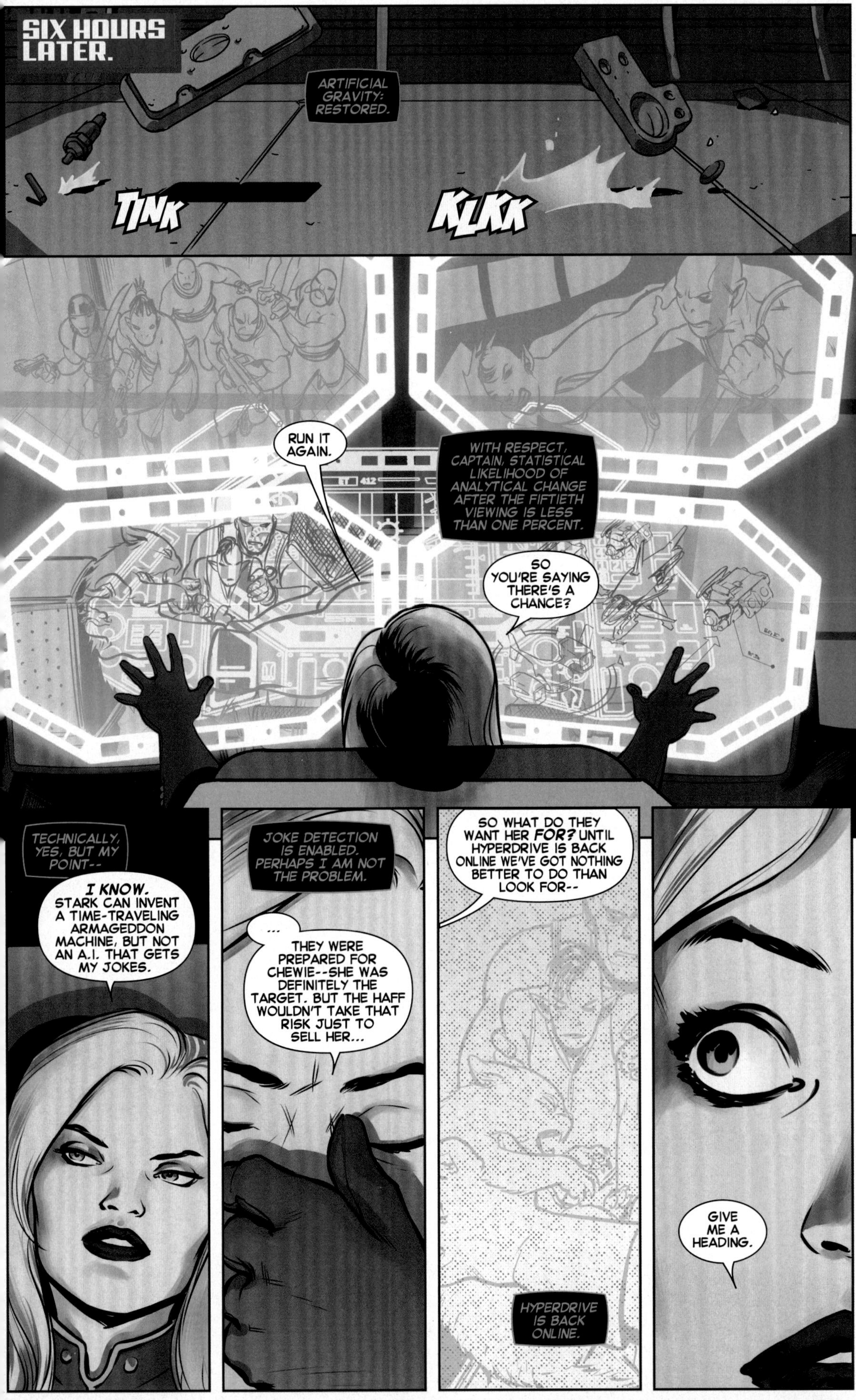
SIX HOURS LATER.
ARTIFICIAL GRAVITY: RESTORED.
TINK
KLKK
RUN IT AGAIN.
WITH RESPECT, CAPTAIN, STATISTICAL LIKELIHOOD OF ANALYTICAL CHANGE AFTER THE FIFTIETH VIEWING IS LESS THAN ONE PERCENT.
SO YOU'RE SAYING THERE'S A CHANCE?
TECHNICALLY, YES, BUT MY POINT--
I KNOW. STARK CAN INVENT A TIME-TRAVELING ARMAGEDDON MACHINE, BUT NOT AN A.I. THAT GETS MY JOKES.
JOKE DETECTION IS ENABLED. PERHAPS I AM NOT THE PROBLEM.
...
THEY WERE PREPARED FOR CHEWIE--SHE WAS DEFINITELY THE TARGET. BUT THE HAFF WOULDN'T TAKE THAT RISK JUST TO SELL HER...
SO WHAT DO THEY WANT HER FOR? UNTIL HYPERDRIVE IS BACK ONLINE WE'VE GOT NOTHING BETTER TO DO THAN LOOK FOR--
HYPERDRIVE IS BACK ONLINE.
GIVE ME A HEADING.

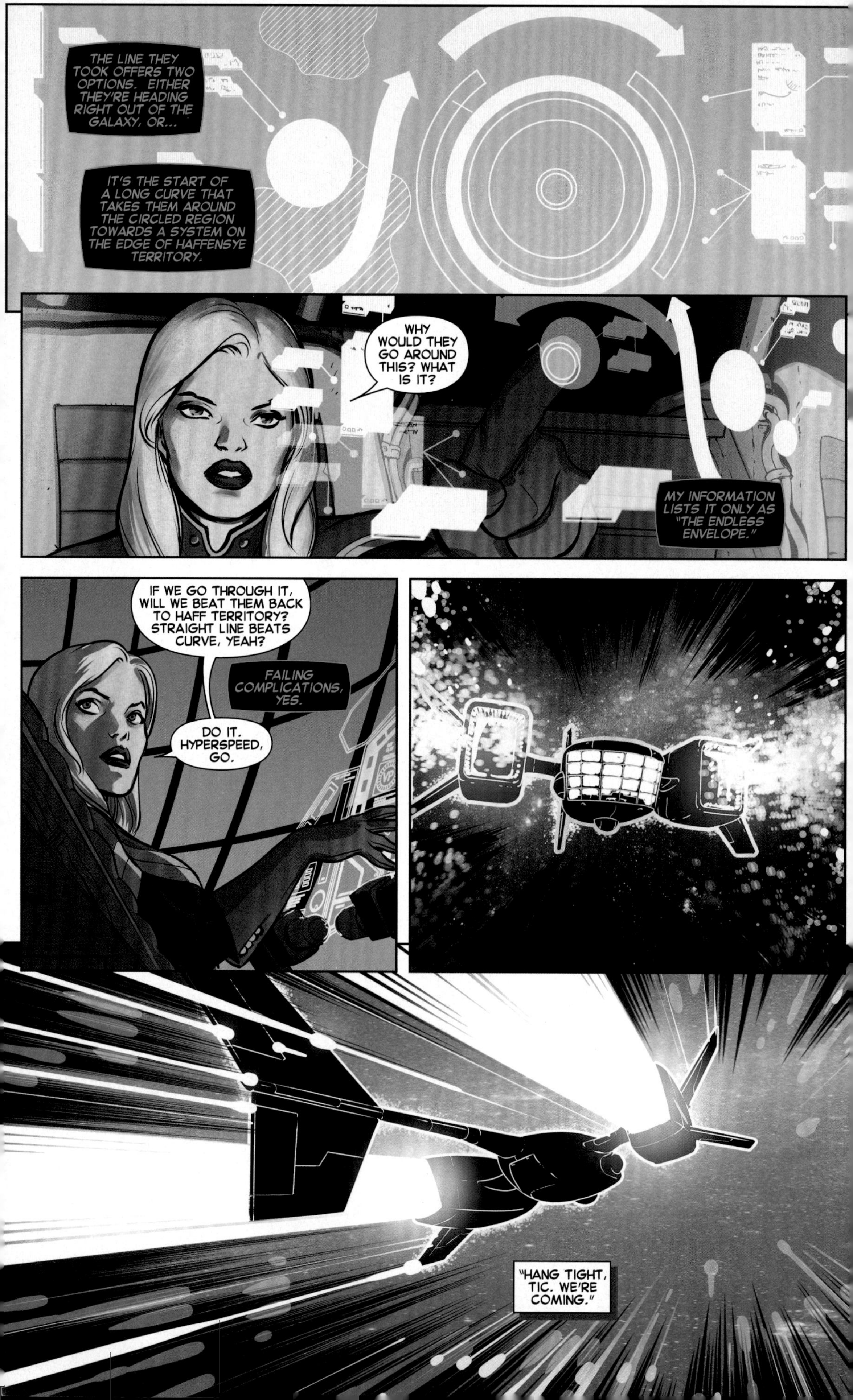
THE LINE THEY TOOK OFFERS TWO OPTIONS. EITHER THEY'RE HEADING RIGHT OUT OF THE GALAXY, OR...
IT'S THE START OF A LONG CURVE THAT TAKES THEM AROUND THE CIRCLED REGION TOWARDS A SYSTEM ON THE EDGE OF HAFFENSYE TERRITORY.
WHY WOULD THEY GO AROUND THIS? WHAT IS IT?
MY INFORMATION LISTS IT ONLY AS "THE ENDLESS ENVELOPE."
IF WE GO THROUGH IT, WILL WE BEAT THEM BACK TO HAFF TERRITORY? STRAIGHT LINE BEATS CURVE, YEAH?
FAILING COMPLICATIONS, YES.
DO IT. HYPERSPEED, GO.
"HANG TIGHT, TIC. WE'RE COMING."

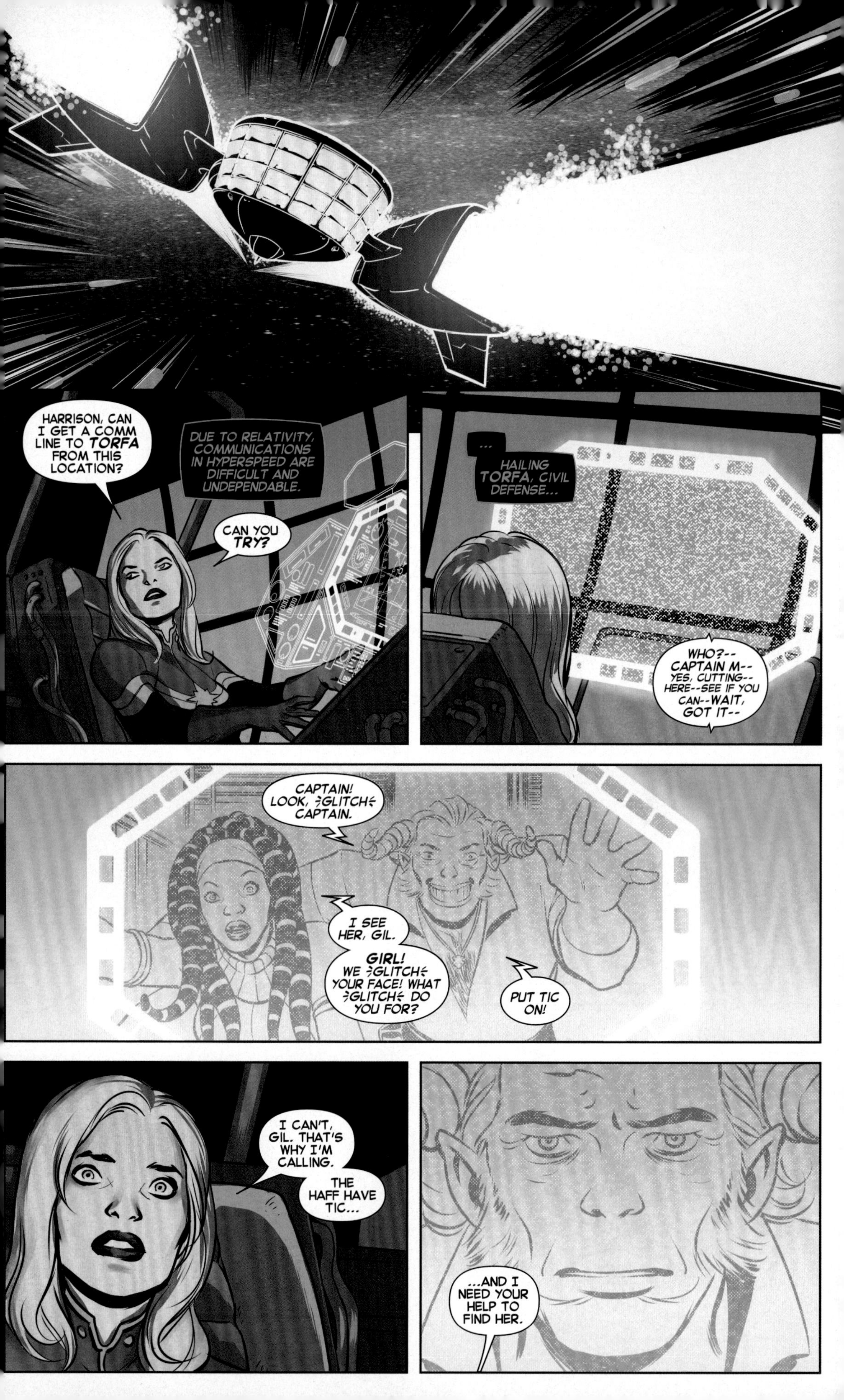

HARRISON, CAN I GET A COMM LINE TO TORFA FROM THIS LOCATION?
DUE TO RELATIVITY, COMMUNICATIONS IN HYPERSPEED ARE DIFFICULT AND UNDEPENDABLE.
CAN YOU TRY?
...
HAILING TORFA, CIVIL DEFENSE...
WHO?--CAPTAIN M--YES, CUTTING--HERE--SEE IF YOU CAN--WAIT, GOT IT--
CAPTAIN! LOOK, ⸗GLITCH⸗ CAPTAIN.
I SEE HER, GIL.
GIRL! WE ⸗GLITCH⸗ YOUR FACE! WHAT ⸗GLITCH⸗ DO YOU FOR?
PUT TIC ON!
I CAN'T, GIL. THAT'S WHY I'M CALLING.
THE HAFF HAVE TIC...
...AND I NEED YOUR HELP TO FIND HER.

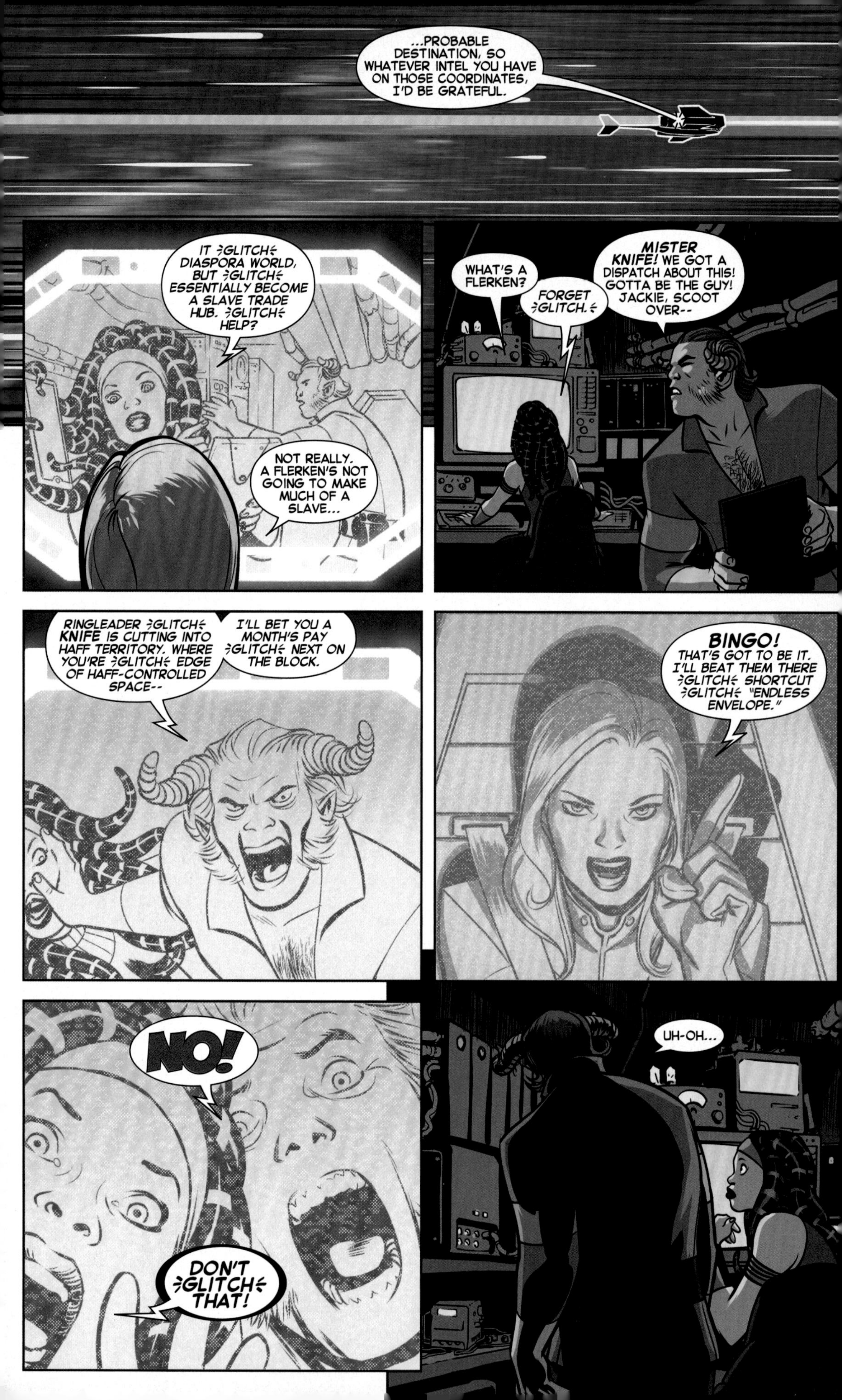
...PROBABLE DESTINATION, SO WHATEVER INTEL YOU HAVE ON THOSE COORDINATES, I'D BE GRATEFUL.
IT ⇛GLITCH⇚ DIASPORA WORLD, BUT ⇛GLITCH⇚ ESSENTIALLY BECOME A SLAVE TRADE HUB. ⇛GLITCH⇚ HELP?
NOT REALLY. A FLERKEN'S NOT GOING TO MAKE MUCH OF A SLAVE...
WHAT'S A FLERKEN?
FORGET ⇛GLITCH.⇚
MISTER KNIFE! WE GOT A DISPATCH ABOUT THIS! GOTTA BE THE GUY! JACKIE, SCOOT OVER--
RINGLEADER ⇛GLITCH⇚ KNIFE IS CUTTING INTO HAFF TERRITORY. WHERE YOU'RE ⇛GLITCH⇚ EDGE OF HAFF-CONTROLLED SPACE--
I'LL BET YOU A MONTH'S PAY ⇛GLITCH⇚ NEXT ON THE BLOCK.
BINGO! THAT'S GOT TO BE IT. I'LL BEAT THEM THERE ⇛GLITCH⇚ SHORTCUT ⇛GLITCH⇚ "ENDLESS ENVELOPE."
NO!
DON'T ⇛GLITCH⇚ THAT!
UH-OH...

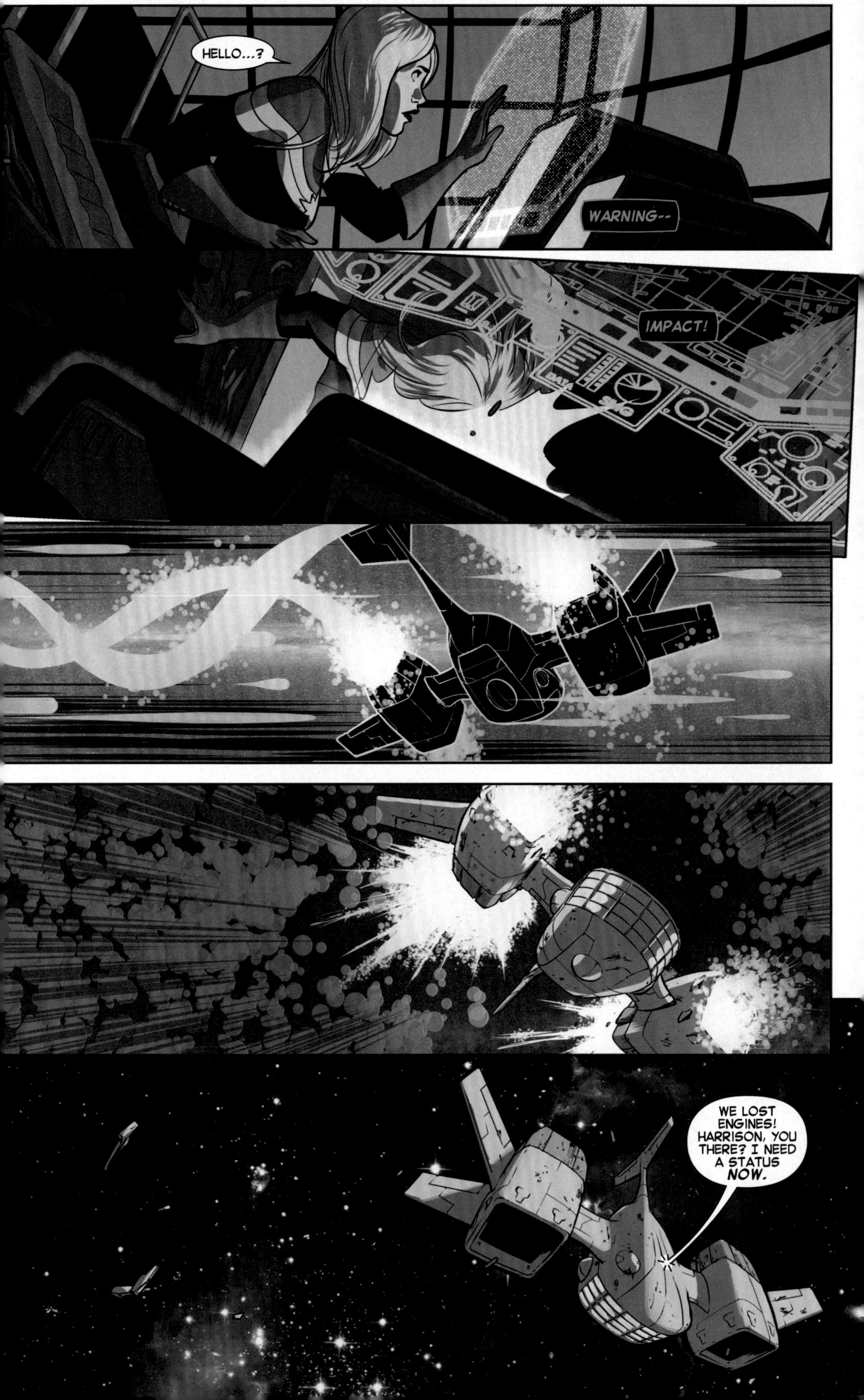
HELLO...?
WARNING--
IMPACT!
DATA
WE LOST ENGINES! HARRISON, YOU THERE? I NEED A STATUS NOW.

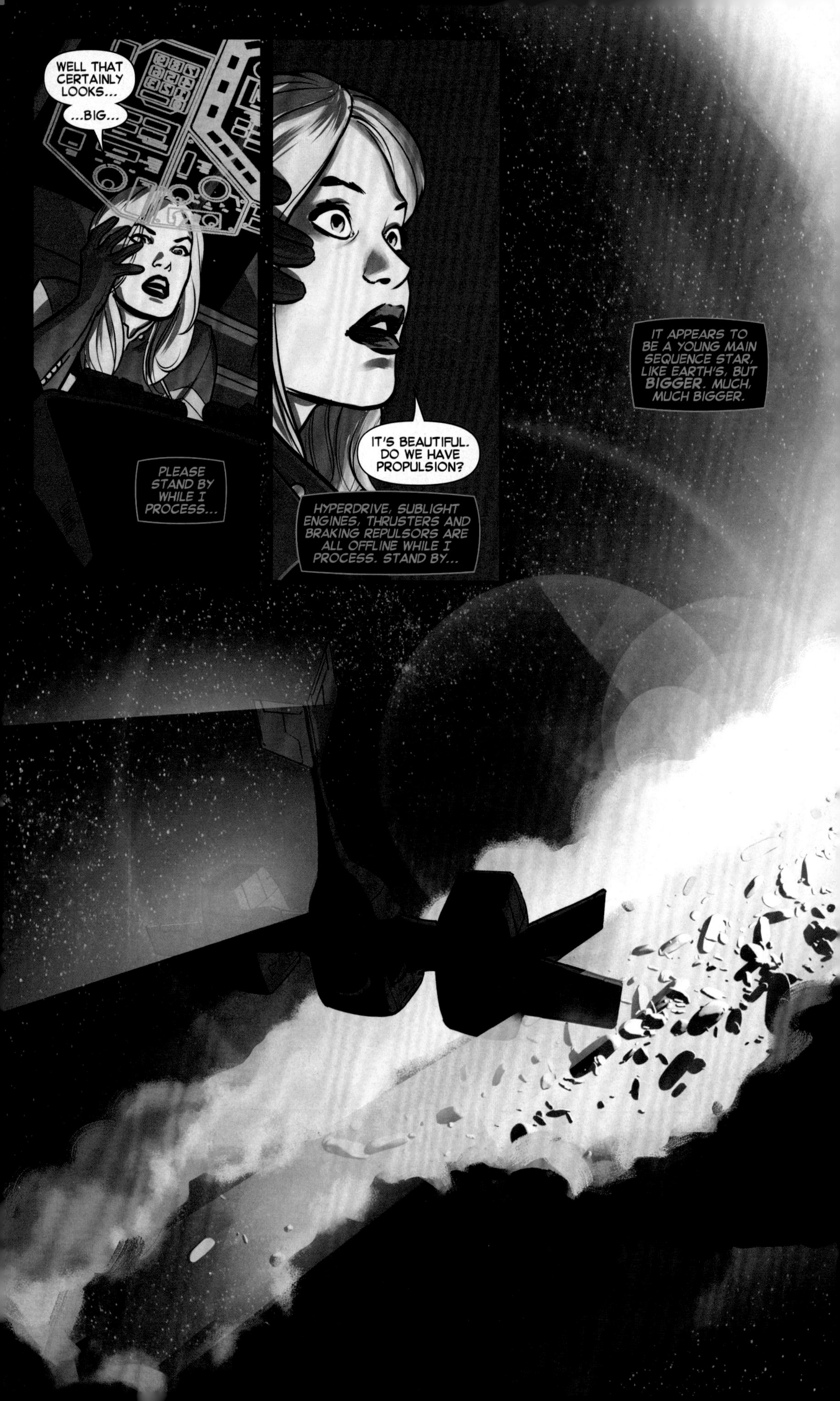
WELL THAT CERTAINLY LOOKS...
...BIG...
PLEASE STAND BY WHILE I PROCESS...
IT'S BEAUTIFUL. DO WE HAVE PROPULSION?
HYPERDRIVE, SUBLIGHT ENGINES, THRUSTERS AND BRAKING REPULSORS ARE ALL OFFLINE WHILE I PROCESS. STAND BY...
IT APPEARS TO BE A YOUNG MAIN SEQUENCE STAR, LIKE EARTH'S, BUT BIGGER. MUCH, MUCH BIGGER.

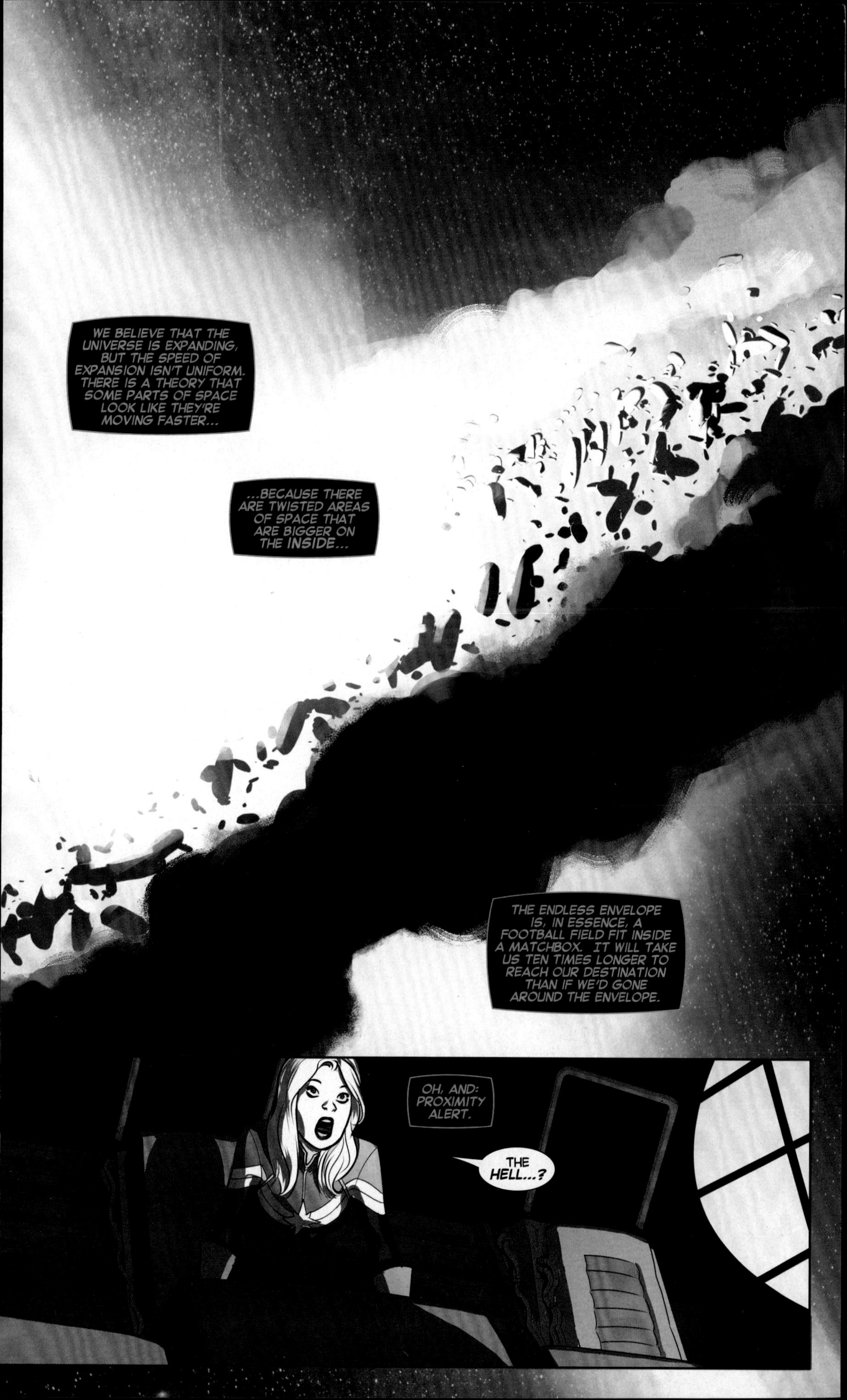
WE BELIEVE THAT THE UNIVERSE IS EXPANDING, BUT THE SPEED OF EXPANSION ISN'T UNIFORM. THERE IS A THEORY THAT SOME PARTS OF SPACE LOOK LIKE THEY'RE MOVING FASTER...
...BECAUSE THERE ARE TWISTED AREAS OF SPACE THAT ARE BIGGER ON THE INSIDE...
THE ENDLESS ENVELOPE IS, IN ESSENCE, A FOOTBALL FIELD FIT INSIDE A MATCHBOX. IT WILL TAKE US TEN TIMES LONGER TO REACH OUR DESTINATION THAN IF WE'D GONE AROUND THE ENVELOPE.
OH, AND: PROXIMITY ALERT.
THE HELL...?

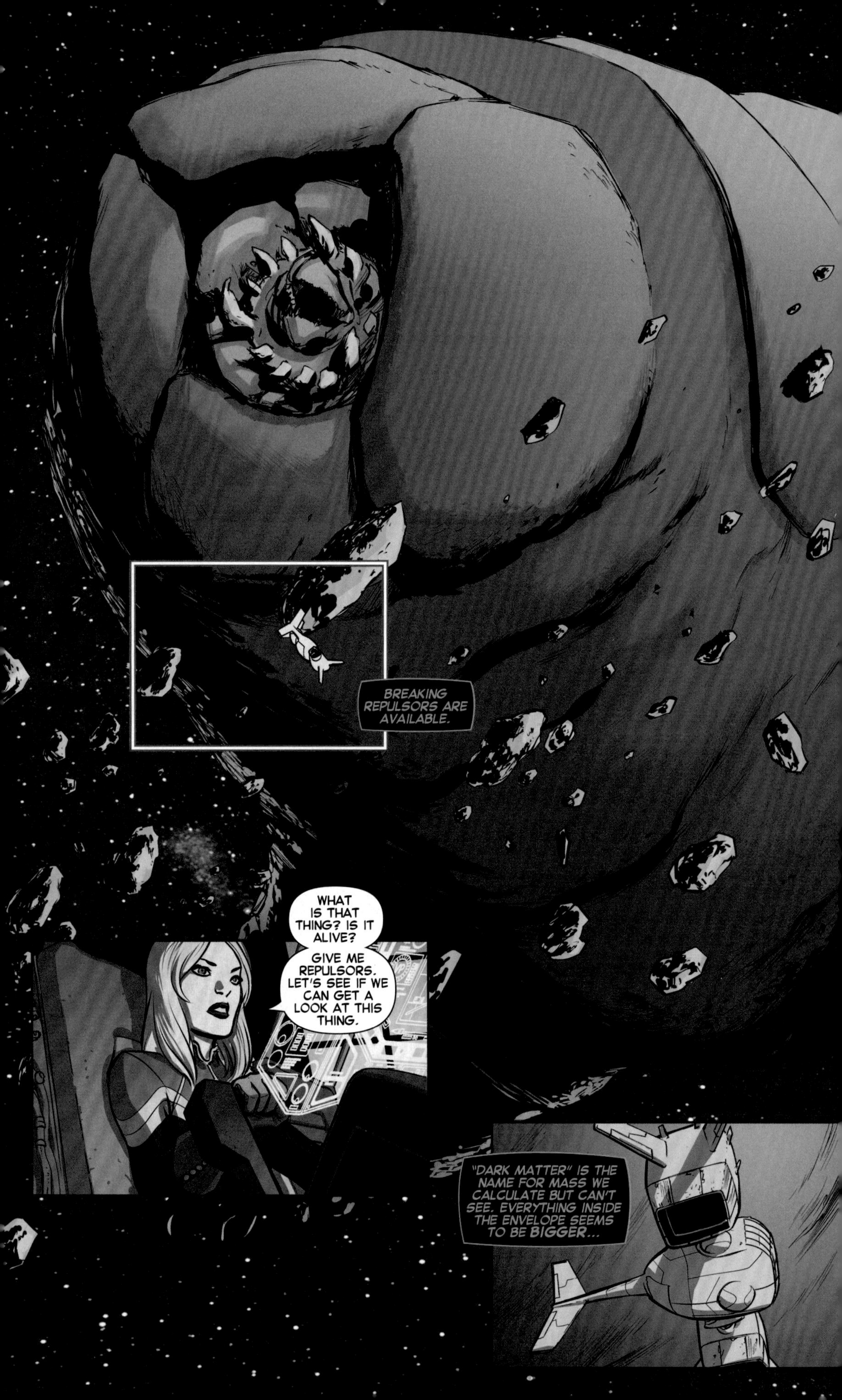
BREAKING REPULSORS ARE AVAILABLE.
WHAT IS THAT THING? IS IT ALIVE?
GIVE ME REPULSORS. LET'S SEE IF WE CAN GET A LOOK AT THIS THING.
"DARK MATTER" IS THE NAME FOR MASS WE CALCULATE BUT CAN'T SEE. EVERYTHING INSIDE THE ENVELOPE SEEMS TO BE BIGGER...

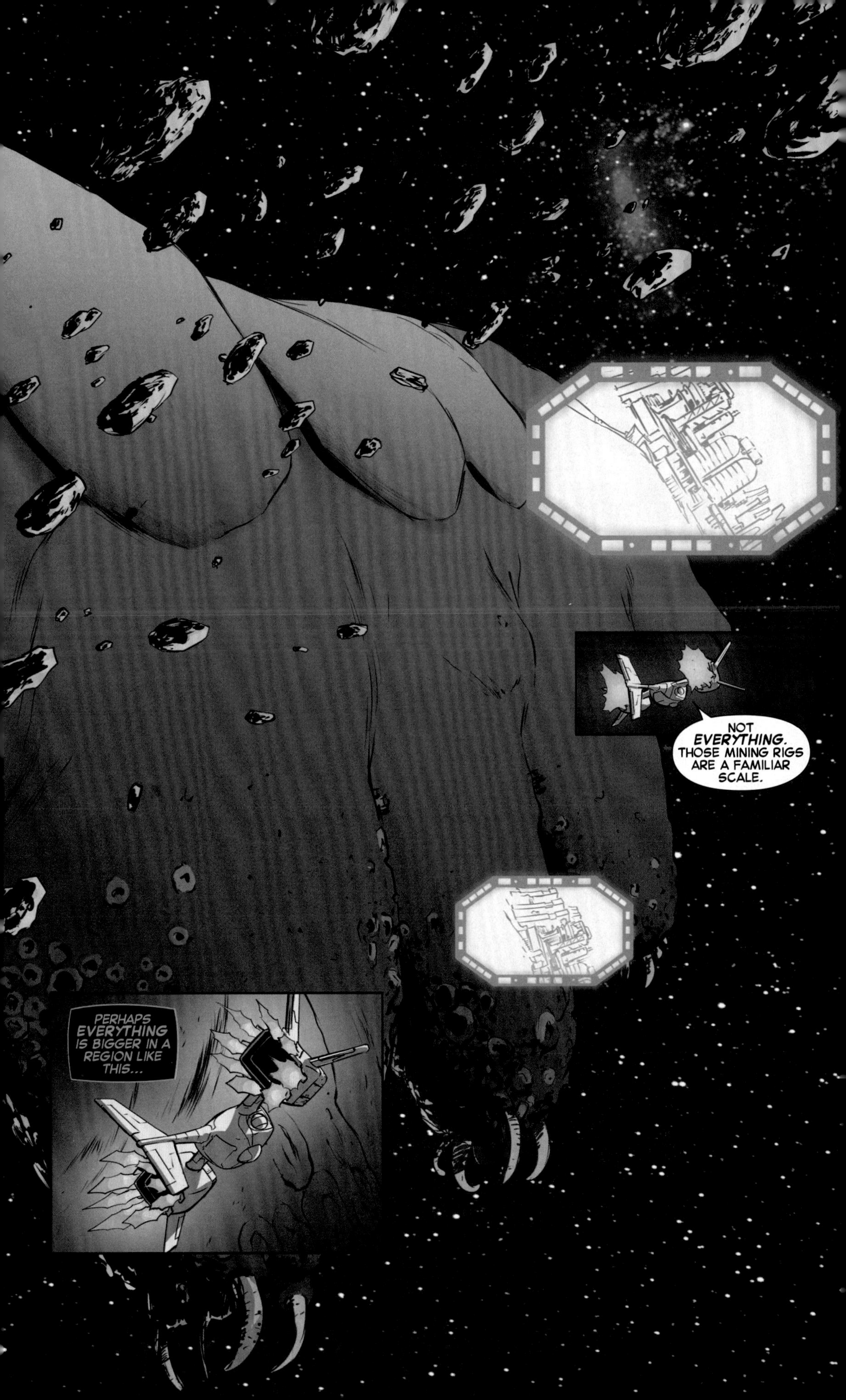
NOT EVERYTHING. THOSE MINING RIGS ARE A FAMILIAR SCALE.
PERHAPS EVERYTHING IS BIGGER IN A REGION LIKE THIS...

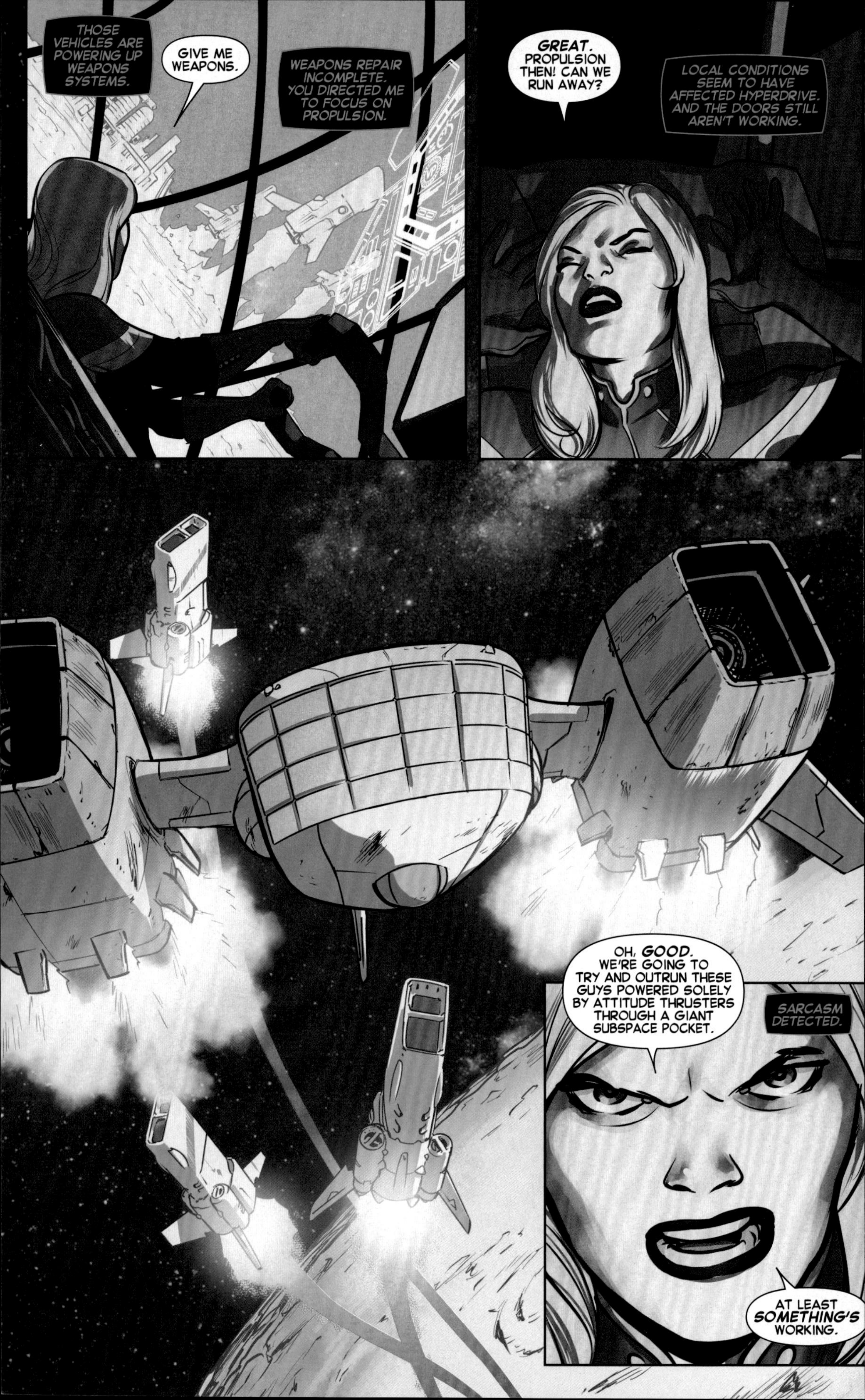
THOSE VEHICLES ARE POWERING UP WEAPONS SYSTEMS.
GIVE ME WEAPONS.
WEAPONS REPAIR INCOMPLETE. YOU DIRECTED ME TO FOCUS ON PROPULSION.
GREAT. PROPULSION THEN! CAN WE RUN AWAY?
LOCAL CONDITIONS SEEM TO HAVE AFFECTED HYPERDRIVE. AND THE DOORS STILL AREN'T WORKING.
OH, GOOD. WE'RE GOING TO TRY AND OUTRUN THESE GUYS POWERED SOLELY BY ATTITUDE THRUSTERS THROUGH A GIANT SUBSPACE POCKET.
SARCASM DETECTED.
AT LEAST SOMETHING'S WORKING.

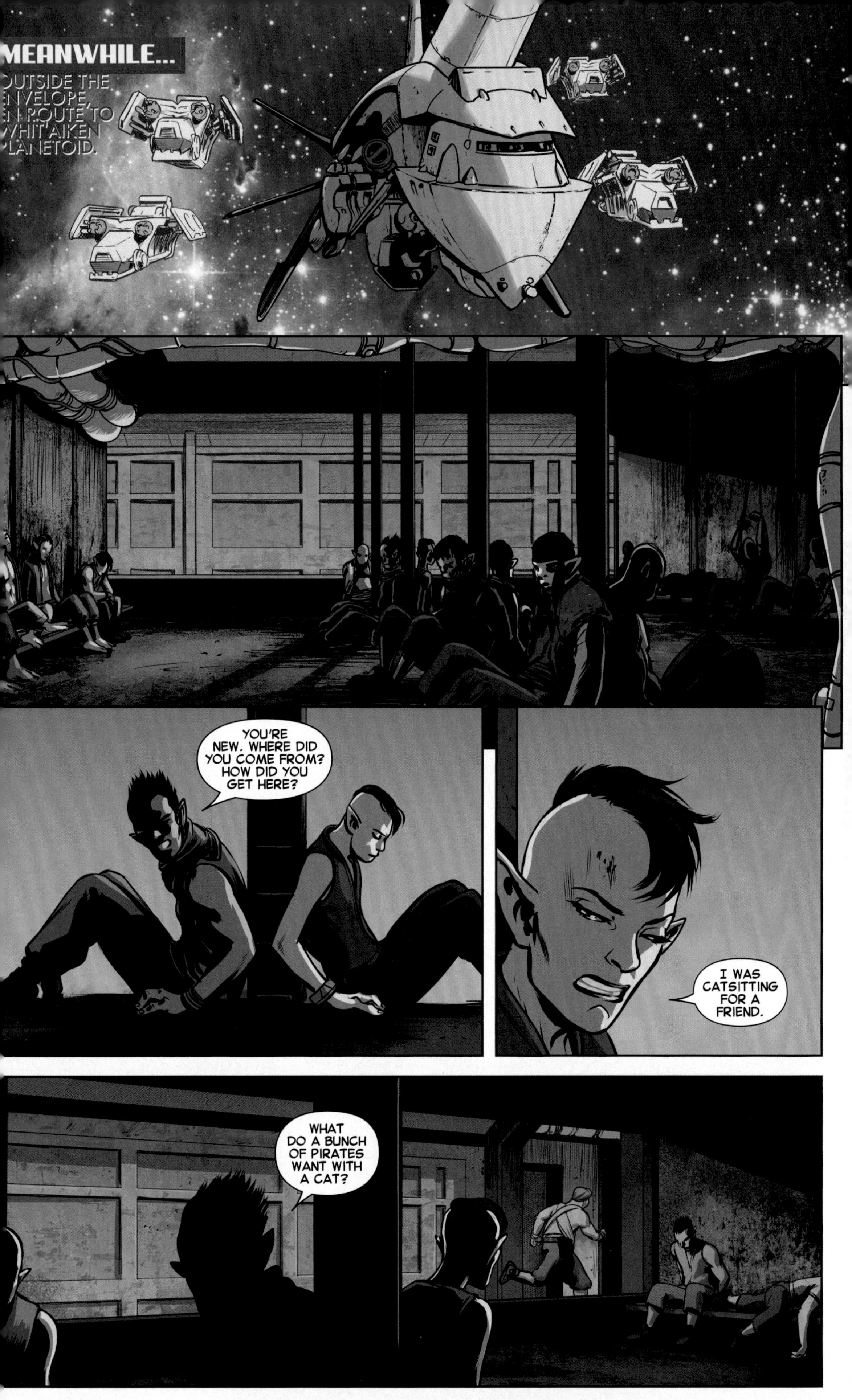
MEANWHILE...
OUTSIDE THE ENVELOPE, EN ROUTE TO WHIT'AIKEN PLANETOID.
YOU'RE NEW. WHERE DID YOU COME FROM? HOW DID YOU GET HERE?
I WAS CATSITTING FOR A FRIEND.
WHAT DO A BUNCH OF PIRATES WANT WITH A CAT?

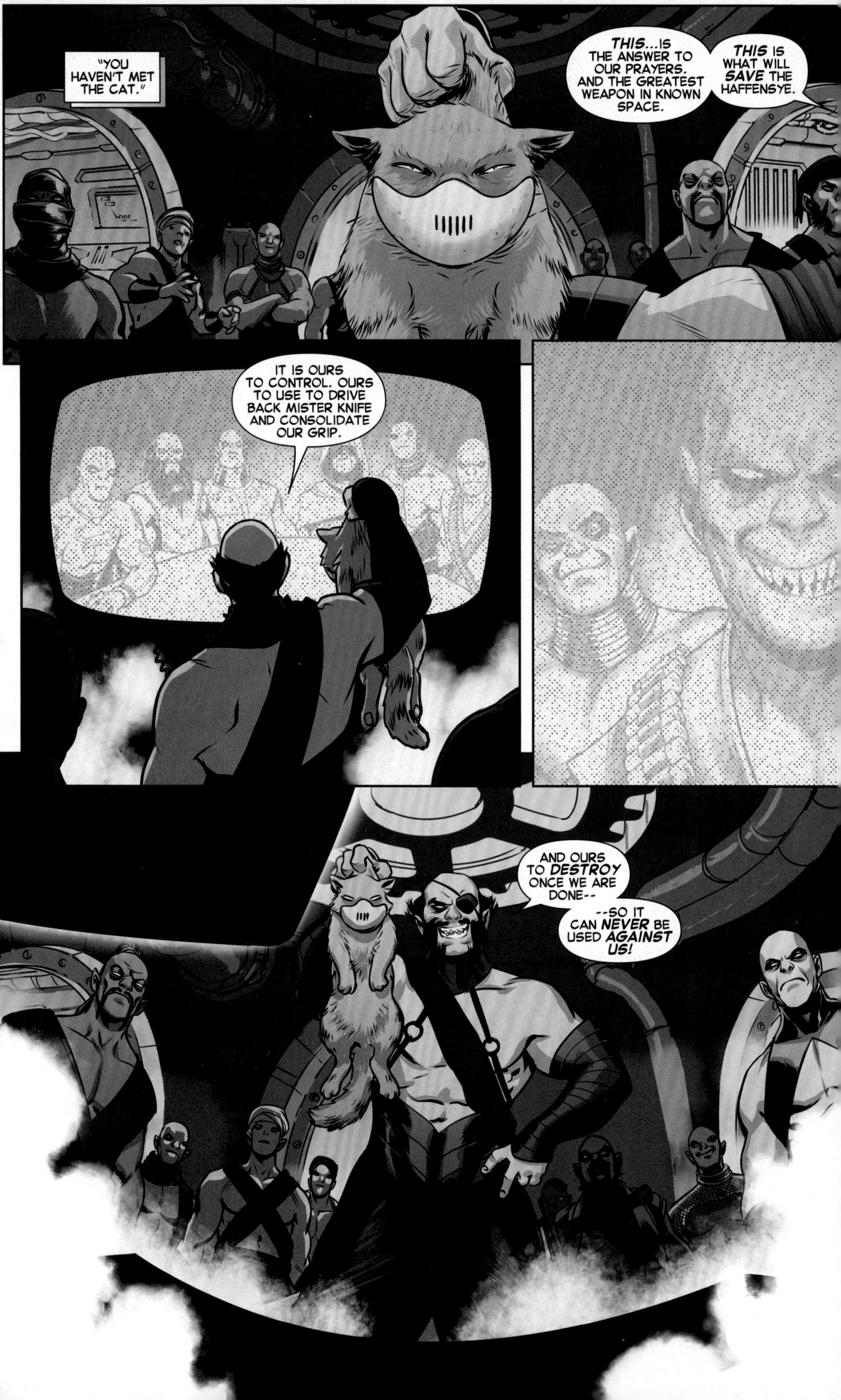
"YOU HAVEN'T MET THE CAT."
THIS...IS THE ANSWER TO OUR PRAYERS. AND THE GREATEST WEAPON IN KNOWN SPACE.
THIS IS WHAT WILL SAVE THE HAFFENSYE.
IT IS OURS TO CONTROL. OURS TO USE TO DRIVE BACK MISTER KNIFE AND CONSOLIDATE OUR GRIP.
AND OURS TO DESTROY ONCE WE ARE DONE--
--SO IT CAN NEVER BE USED AGAINST US!

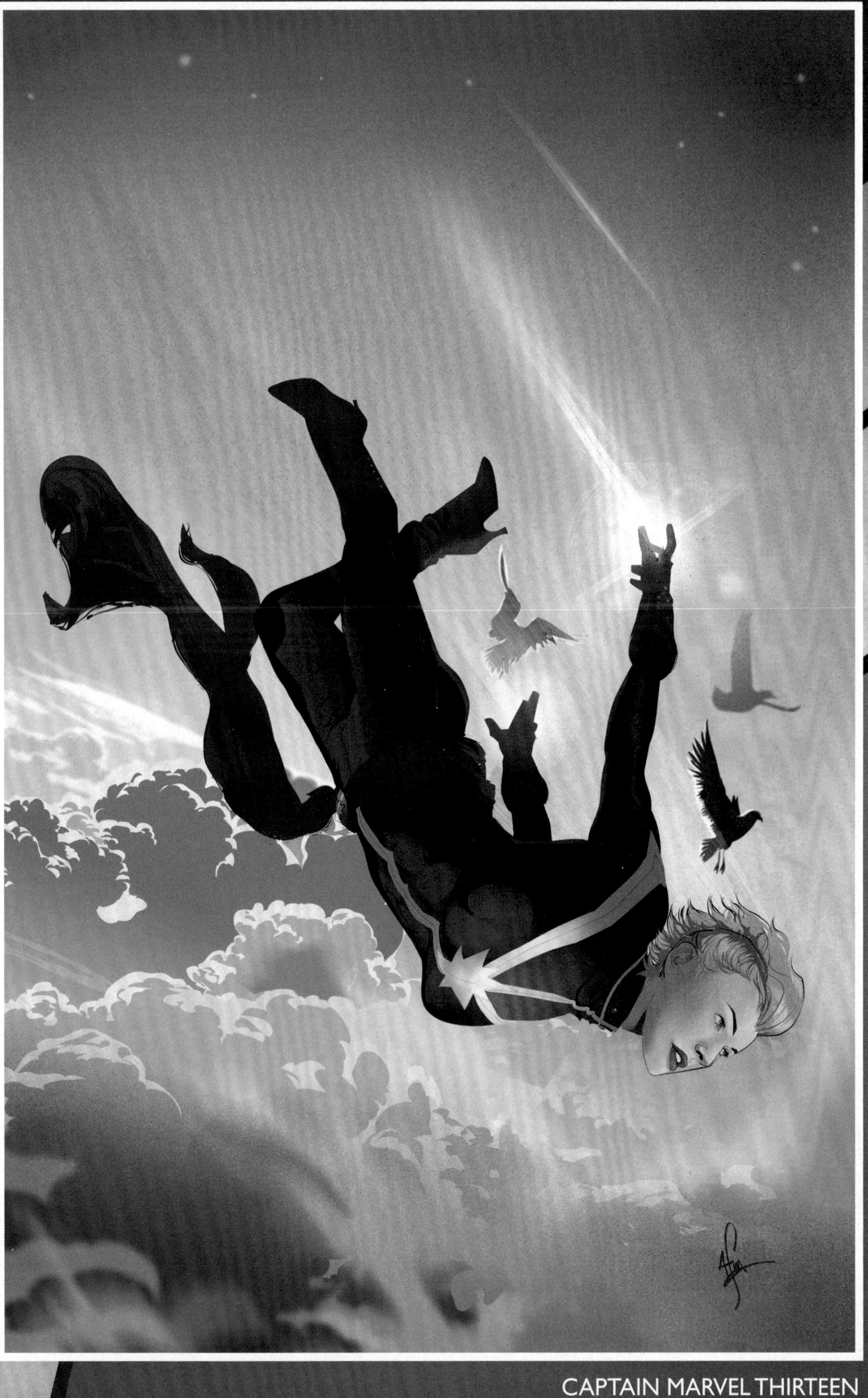

CAPTAIN MARVEL THIRTEEN
WOMEN OF MARVEL VARIANT BY AFUA RICHARDSON

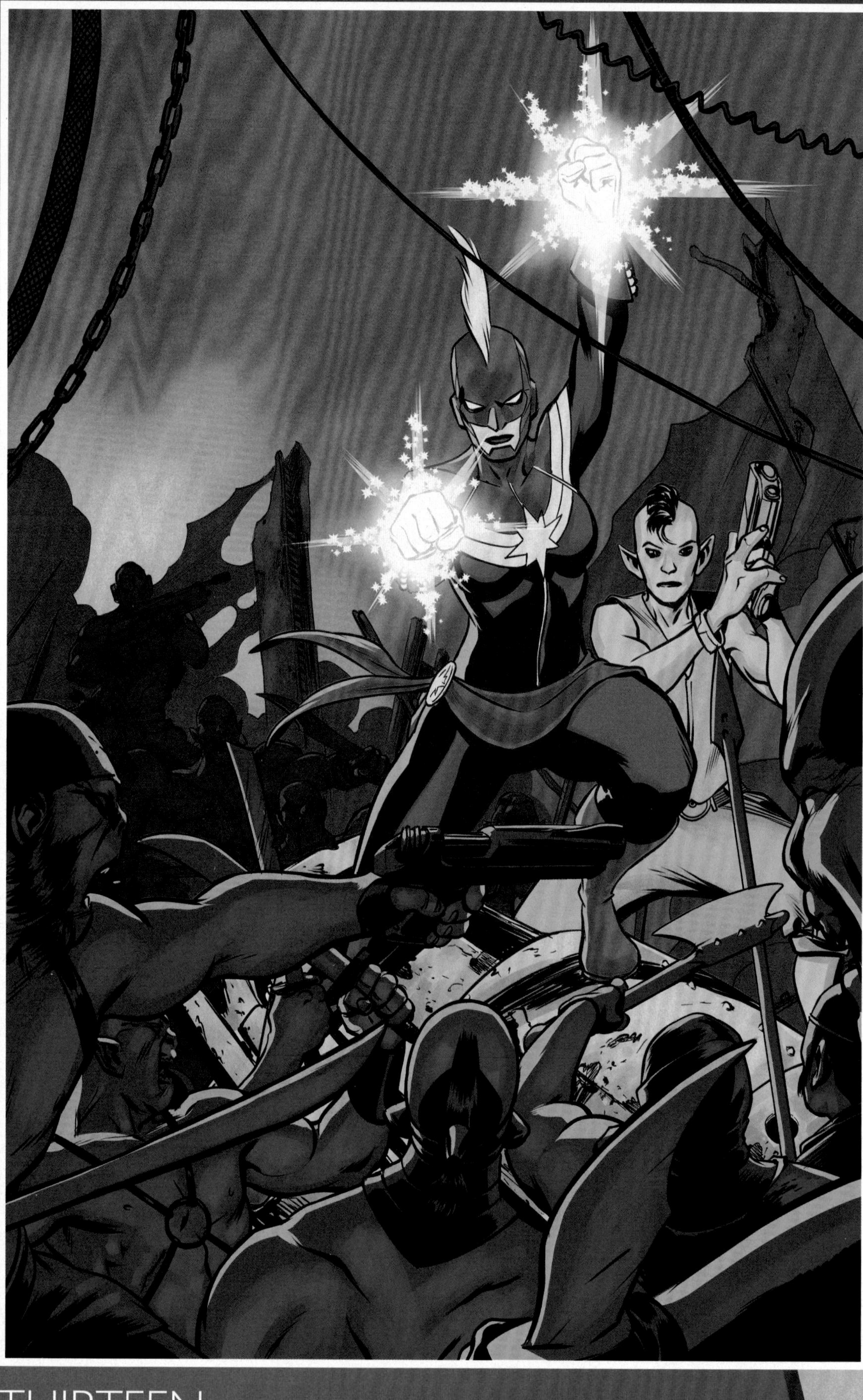

THIRTEEN THE 7 SECONDS BEFORE YOU DIE PART 2

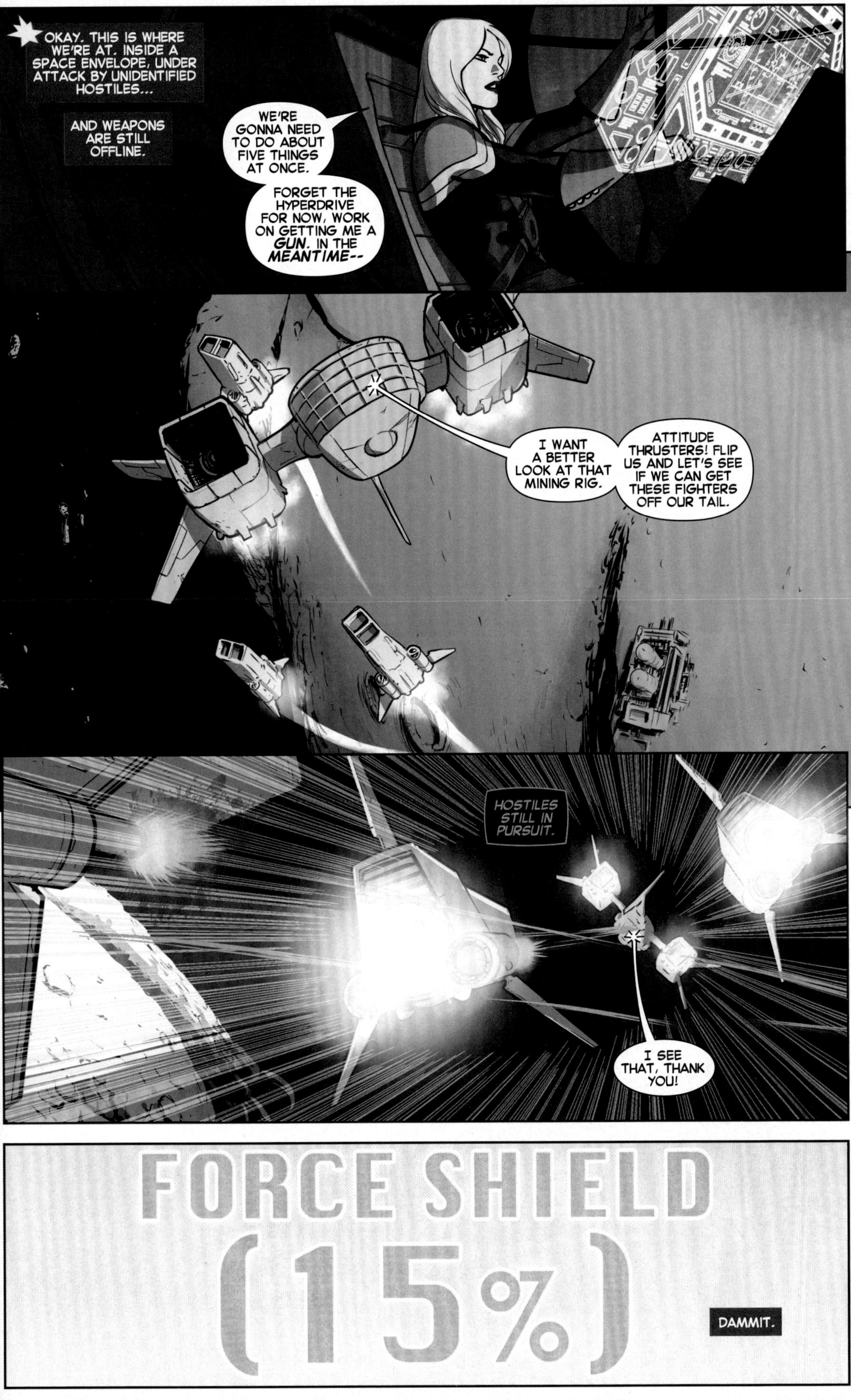
OKAY. THIS IS WHERE WE'RE AT. INSIDE A SPACE ENVELOPE, UNDER ATTACK BY UNIDENTIFIED HOSTILES...
AND WEAPONS ARE STILL OFFLINE.
WE'RE GONNA NEED TO DO ABOUT FIVE THINGS AT ONCE.
FORGET THE HYPERDRIVE FOR NOW, WORK ON GETTING ME A *GUN*. IN THE *MEANTIME--*
I WANT A BETTER LOOK AT THAT MINING RIG.
ATTITUDE THRUSTERS! FLIP US AND LET'S SEE IF WE CAN GET THESE FIGHTERS OFF OUR TAIL.
HOSTILES STILL IN PURSUIT.
I SEE THAT, THANK YOU!
FORCE SHIELD (15%)
DAMMIT.

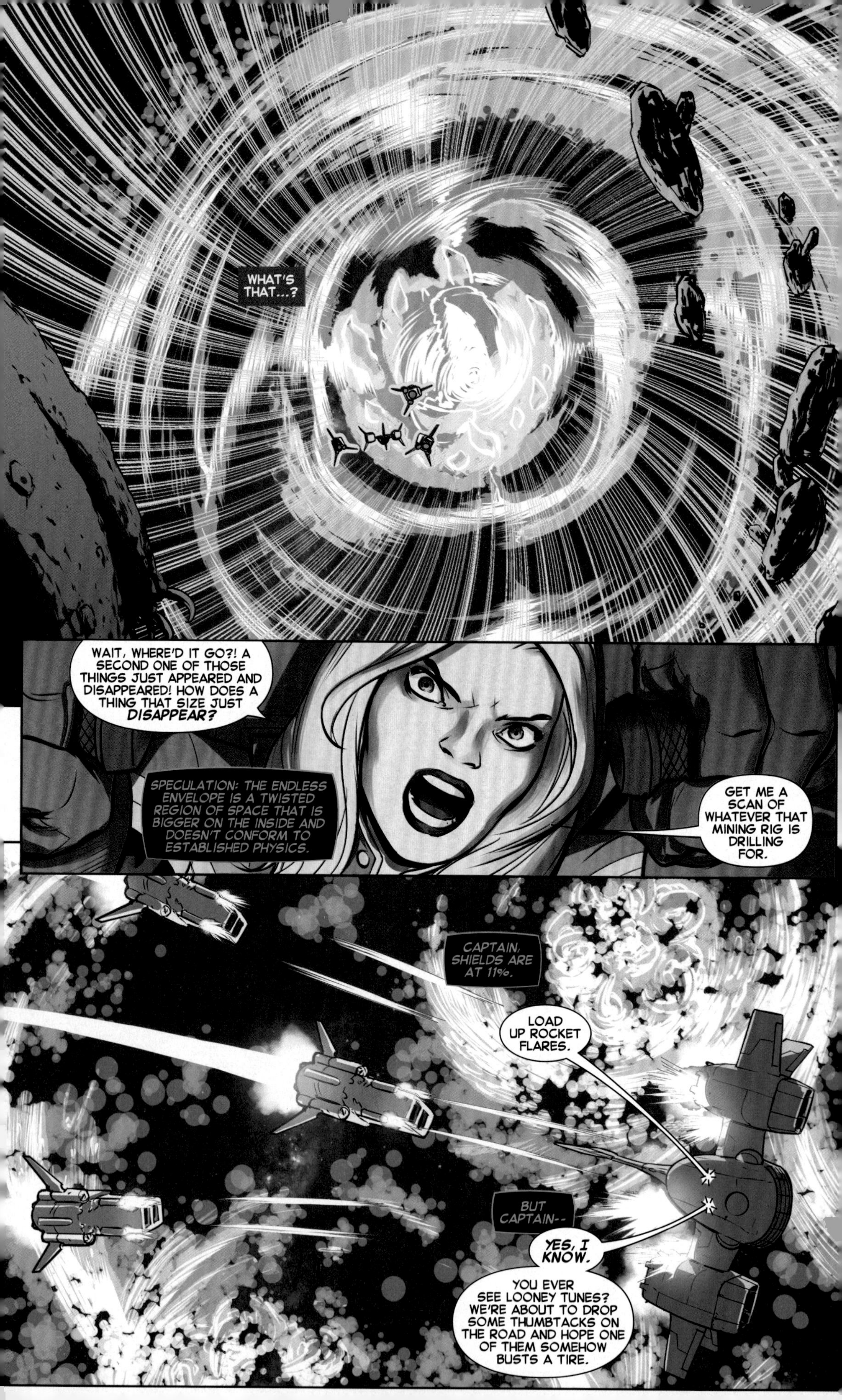
WHAT'S THAT...?
WAIT, WHERE'D IT GO?! A SECOND ONE OF THOSE THINGS JUST APPEARED AND DISAPPEARED! HOW DOES A THING THAT SIZE JUST *DISAPPEAR?*
SPECULATION: THE ENDLESS ENVELOPE IS A TWISTED REGION OF SPACE THAT IS BIGGER ON THE INSIDE AND DOESN'T CONFORM TO ESTABLISHED PHYSICS.
GET ME A SCAN OF WHATEVER THAT MINING RIG IS DRILLING FOR.
CAPTAIN, SHIELDS ARE AT 11%.
LOAD UP ROCKET FLARES.
BUT CAPTAIN--
YES, I KNOW.
YOU EVER SEE LOONEY TUNES? WE'RE ABOUT TO DROP SOME THUMBTACKS ON THE ROAD AND HOPE ONE OF THEM SOMEHOW BUSTS A TIRE.

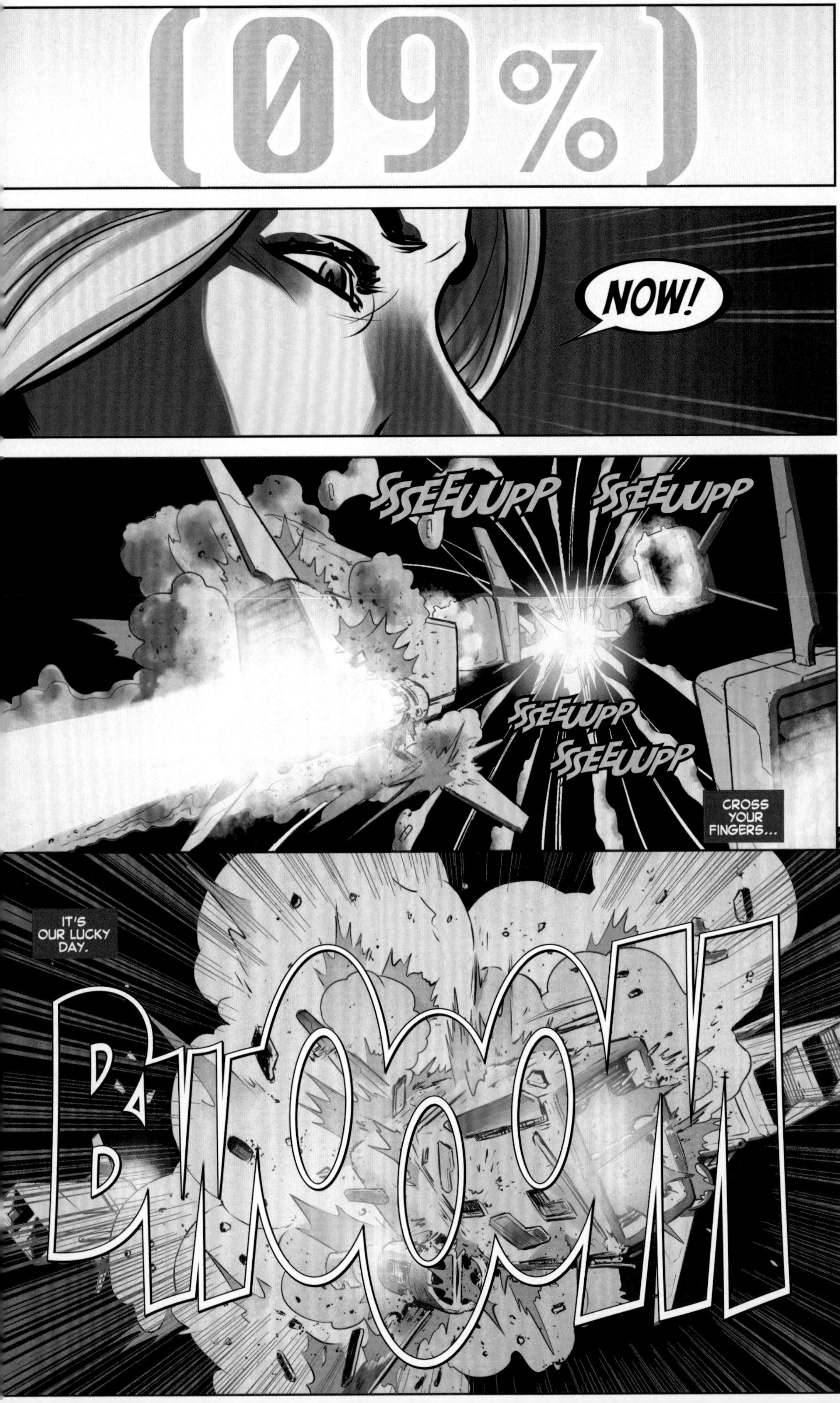
(09%)
NOW!
SSEEWUPP
SSEEWUPP
SSEEWUPP
SSEEWUPP
CROSS YOUR FINGERS...
IT'S OUR LUCKY DAY.
BWOOOOM

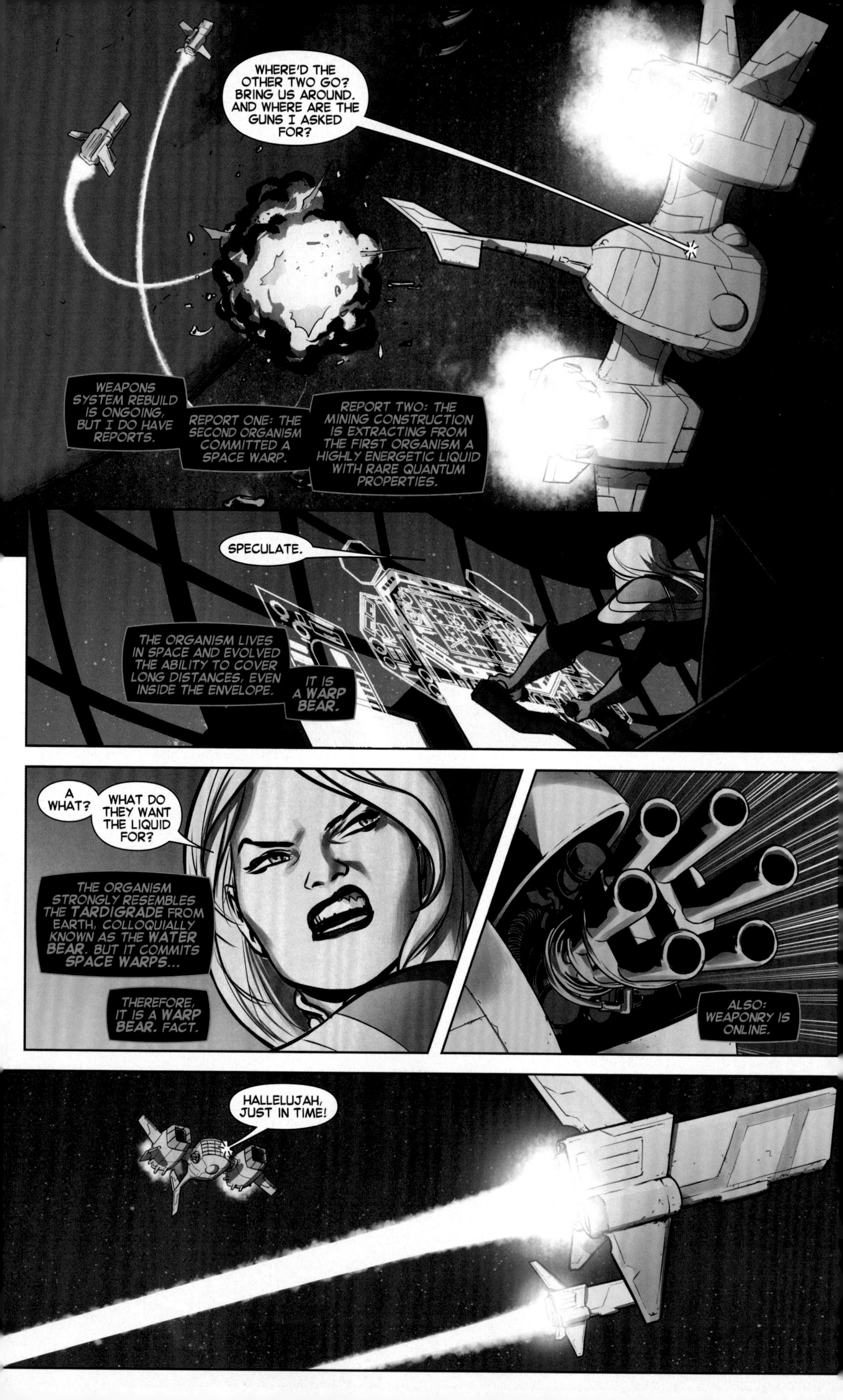
WHERE'D THE OTHER TWO GO? BRING US AROUND. AND WHERE ARE THE GUNS I ASKED FOR?
WEAPONS SYSTEM REBUILD IS ONGOING, BUT I DO HAVE REPORTS.
REPORT ONE: THE SECOND ORGANISM COMMITTED A SPACE WARP.
REPORT TWO: THE MINING CONSTRUCTION IS EXTRACTING FROM THE FIRST ORGANISM A HIGHLY ENERGETIC LIQUID WITH RARE QUANTUM PROPERTIES.
SPECULATE.
THE ORGANISM LIVES IN SPACE AND EVOLVED THE ABILITY TO COVER LONG DISTANCES, EVEN INSIDE THE ENVELOPE.
IT IS A WARP BEAR.
A WHAT?
WHAT DO THEY WANT THE LIQUID FOR?
THE ORGANISM STRONGLY RESEMBLES THE TARDIGRADE FROM EARTH, COLLOQUIALLY KNOWN AS THE WATER BEAR. BUT IT COMMITS SPACE WARPS...
THEREFORE, IT IS A WARP BEAR. FACT.
ALSO: WEAPONRY IS ONLINE.
HALLELUJAH, JUST IN TIME!

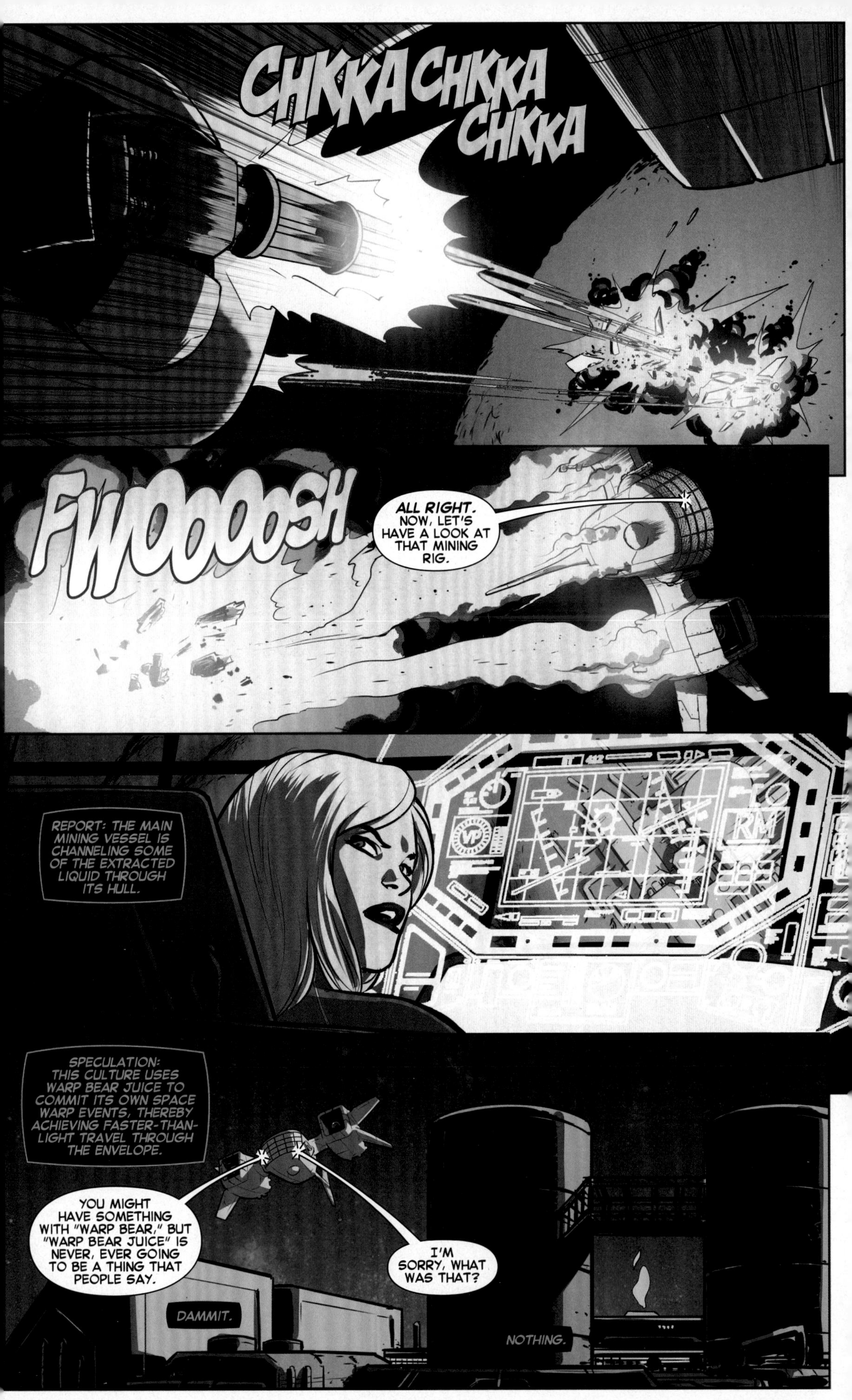
CHKKA CHKKA CHKKA
FWOOOOSH
ALL RIGHT. NOW, LET'S HAVE A LOOK AT THAT MINING RIG.
REPORT: THE MAIN MINING VESSEL IS CHANNELING SOME OF THE EXTRACTED LIQUID THROUGH ITS HULL.
SPECULATION: THIS CULTURE USES WARP BEAR JUICE TO COMMIT ITS OWN SPACE WARP EVENTS, THEREBY ACHIEVING FASTER-THAN-LIGHT TRAVEL THROUGH THE ENVELOPE.
YOU MIGHT HAVE SOMETHING WITH "WARP BEAR," BUT "WARP BEAR JUICE" IS NEVER, EVER GOING TO BE A THING THAT PEOPLE SAY.
I'M SORRY, WHAT WAS THAT?
DAMMIT.
NOTHING.

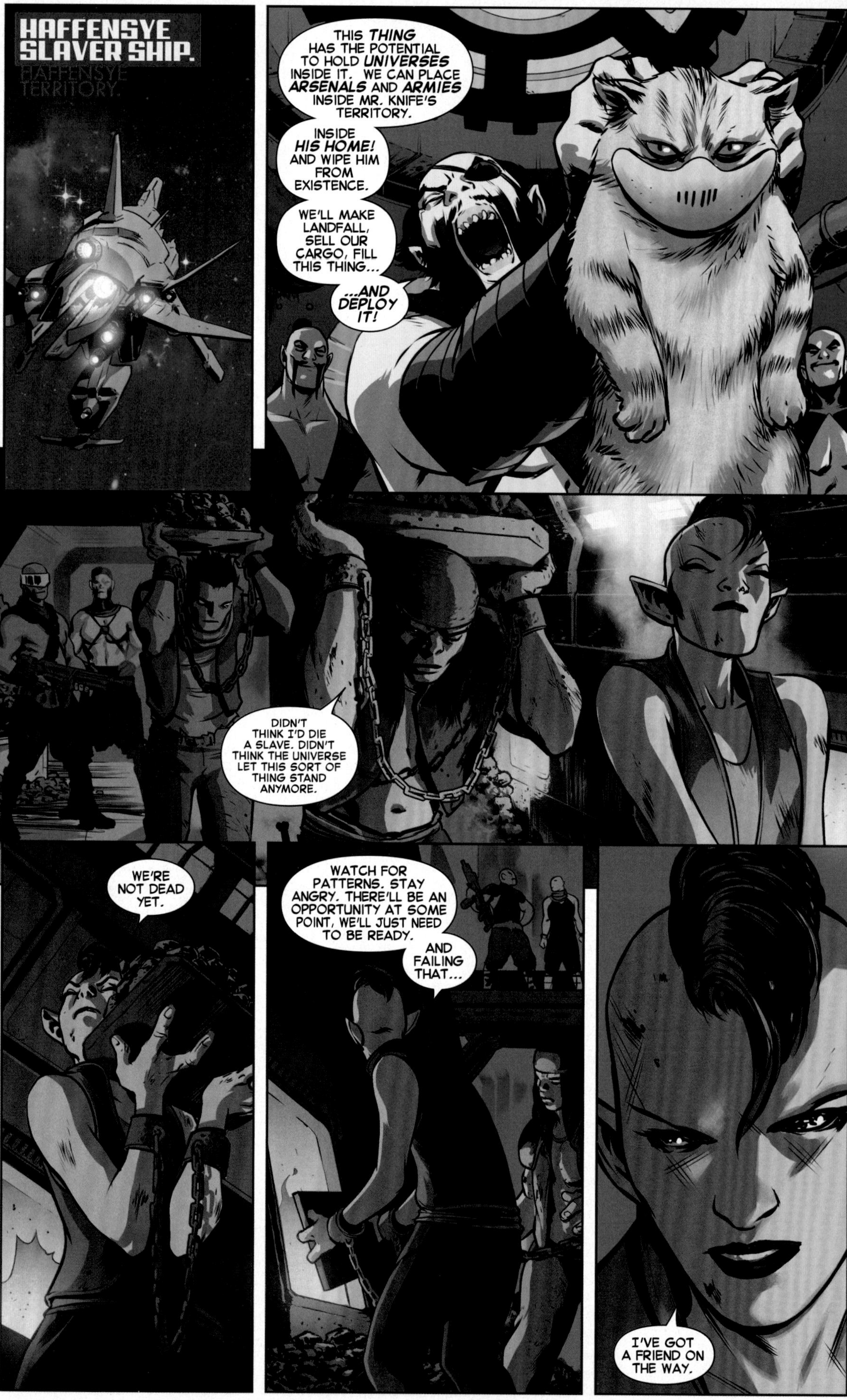

HAFFENSYE SLAVER SHIP.
HAFFENSYE TERRITORY.
THIS THING HAS THE POTENTIAL TO HOLD UNIVERSES INSIDE IT. WE CAN PLACE ARSENALS AND ARMIES INSIDE MR. KNIFE'S TERRITORY.
INSIDE HIS HOME! AND WIPE HIM FROM EXISTENCE.
WE'LL MAKE LANDFALL, SELL OUR CARGO, FILL THIS THING...
...AND DEPLOY IT!
DIDN'T THINK I'D DIE A SLAVE. DIDN'T THINK THE UNIVERSE LET THIS SORT OF THING STAND ANYMORE.
WE'RE NOT DEAD YET.
WATCH FOR PATTERNS. STAY ANGRY. THERE'LL BE AN OPPORTUNITY AT SOME POINT, WE'LL JUST NEED TO BE READY.
AND FAILING THAT...
I'VE GOT A FRIEND ON THE WAY.

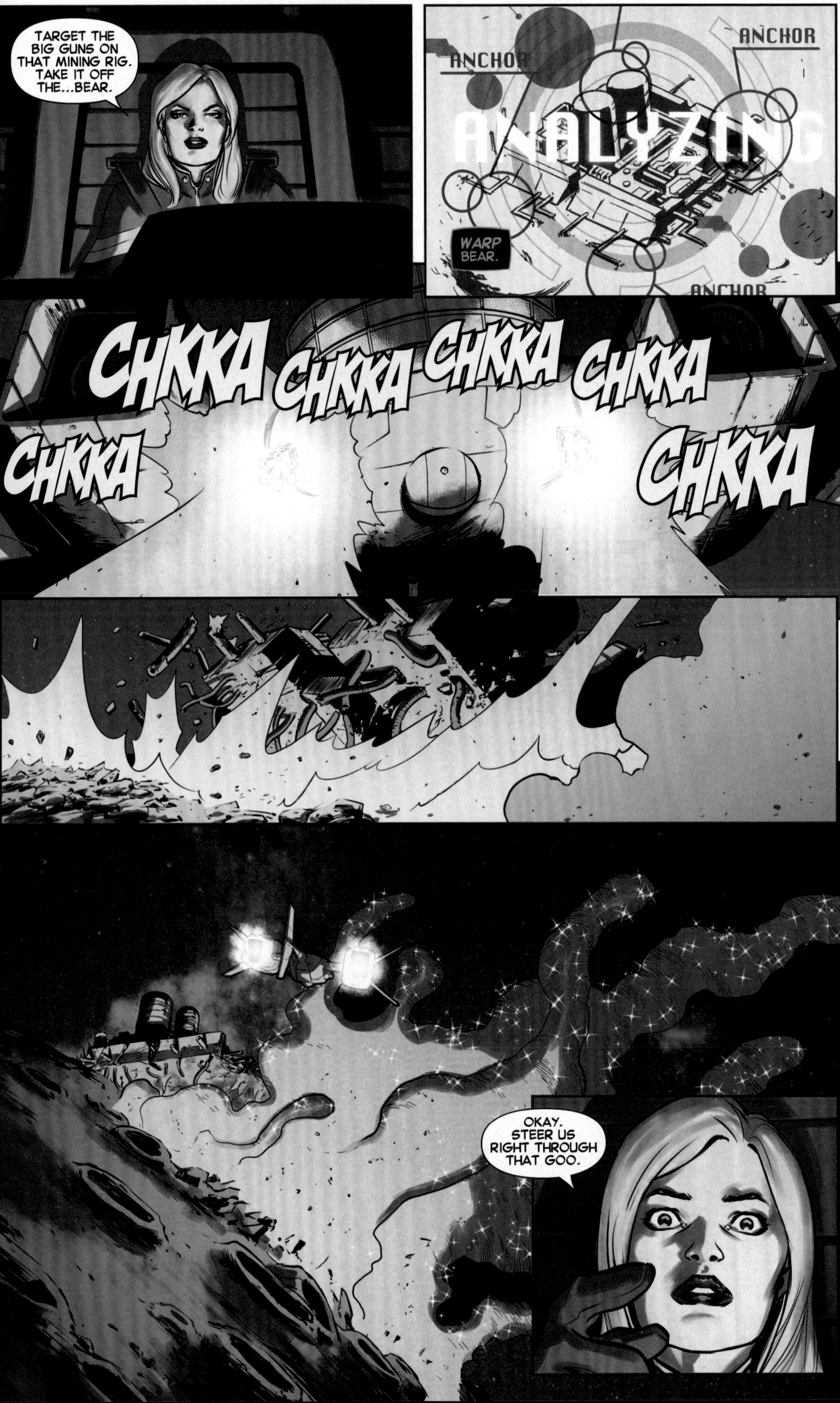
TARGET THE BIG GUNS ON THAT MINING RIG. TAKE IT OFF THE...BEAR.
ANCHOR
ANCHOR
ANALYZING
WARP BEAR.
ANCHOR
CHKKA
CHKKA
CHKKA
CHKKA
CHKKA
CHKKA
OKAY. STEER US RIGHT THROUGH THAT GOO.

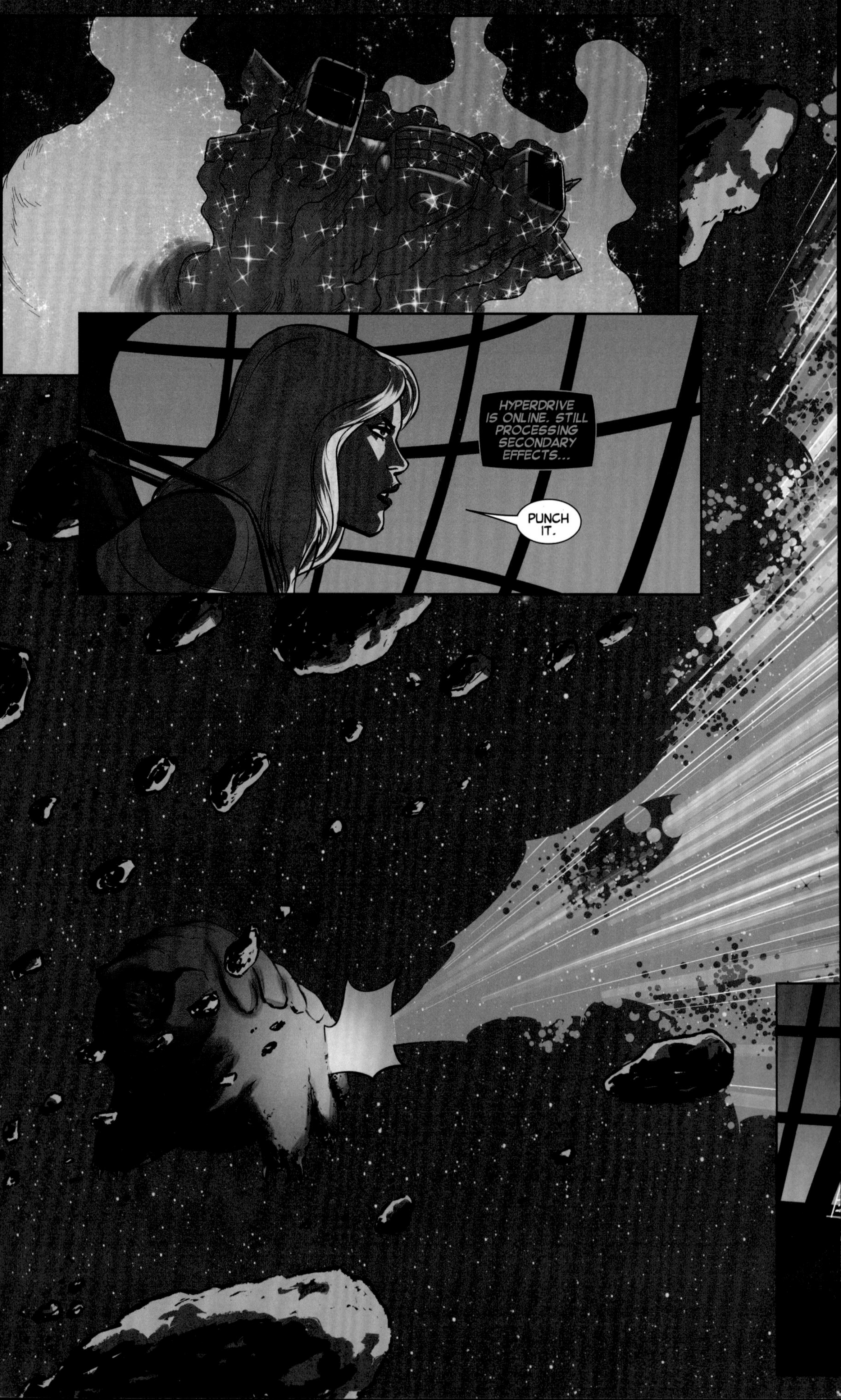
HYPERDRIVE IS ONLINE. STILL PROCESSING SECONDARY EFFECTS...
PUNCH IT.

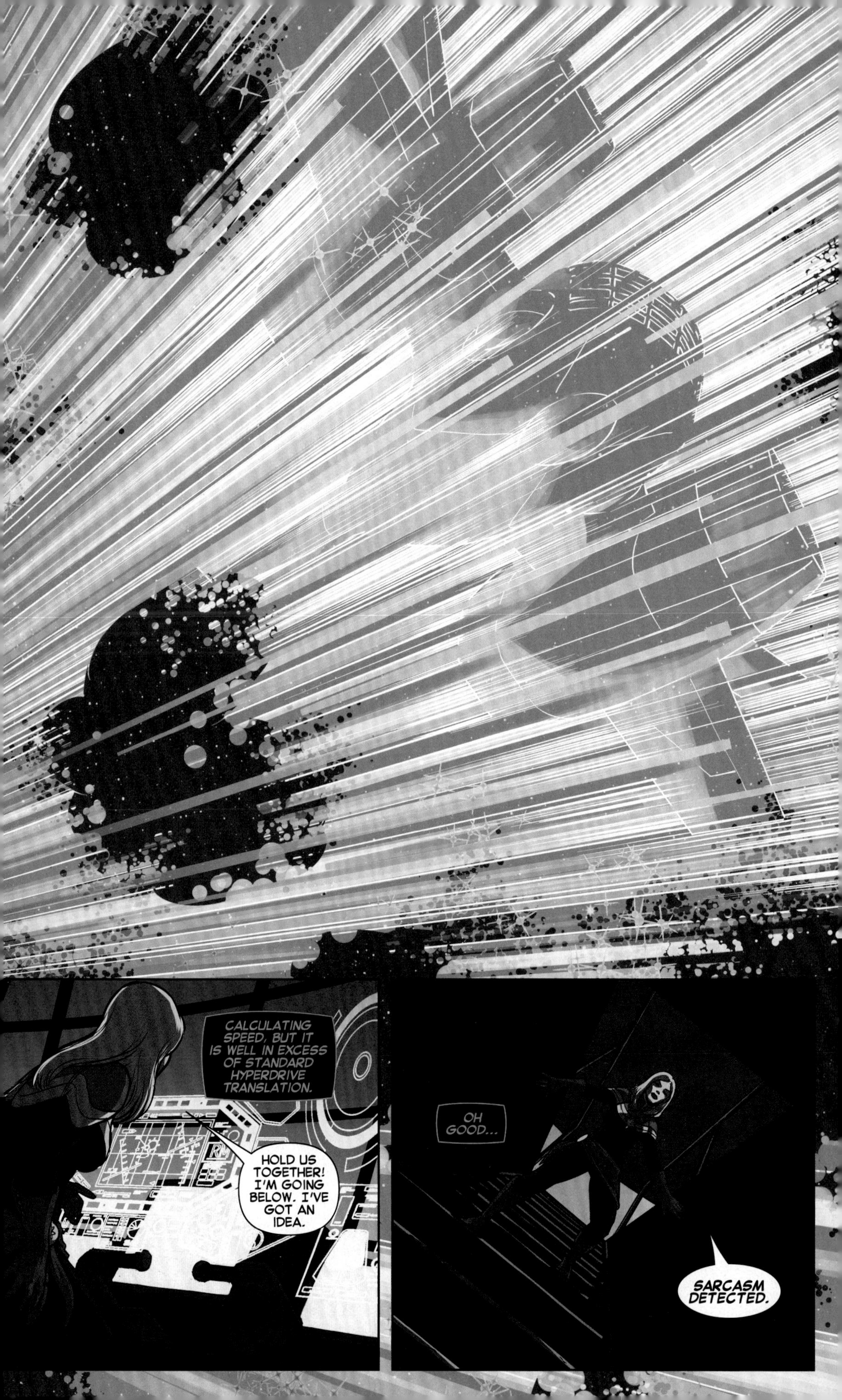

CALCULATING SPEED, BUT IT IS WELL IN EXCESS OF STANDARD HYPERDRIVE TRANSLATION.
HOLD US TOGETHER! I'M GOING BELOW. I'VE GOT AN IDEA.
OH GOOD...
SARCASM DETECTED.

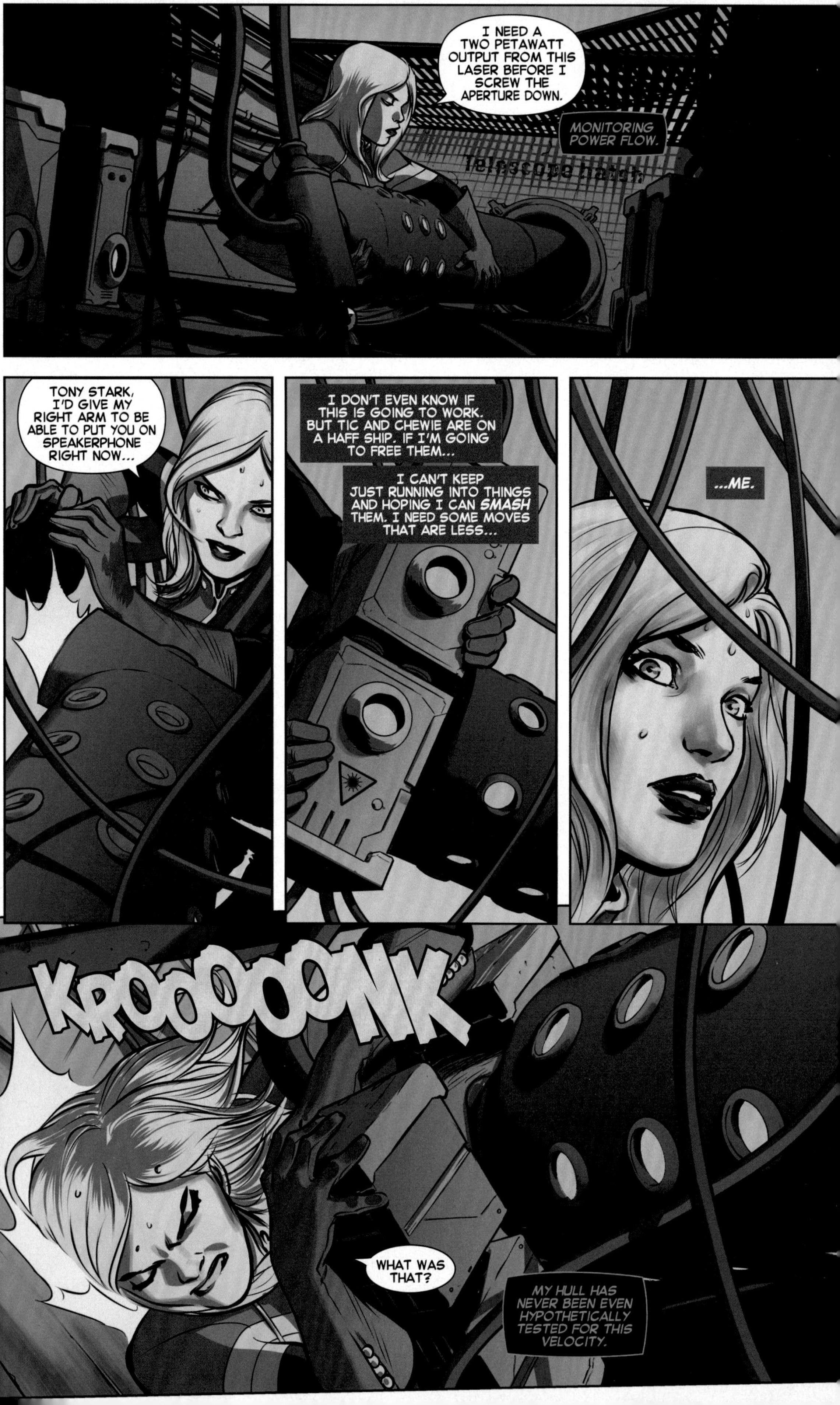

I NEED A TWO PETAWATT OUTPUT FROM THIS LASER BEFORE I SCREW THE APERTURE DOWN.
MONITORING POWER FLOW.
Telescope hatch
TONY STARK, I'D GIVE MY RIGHT ARM TO BE ABLE TO PUT YOU ON SPEAKERPHONE RIGHT NOW...
I DON'T EVEN KNOW IF THIS IS GOING TO WORK. BUT TIC AND CHEWIE ARE ON A HAFF SHIP. IF I'M GOING TO FREE THEM...
I CAN'T KEEP JUST RUNNING INTO THINGS AND HOPING I CAN SMASH THEM. I NEED SOME MOVES THAT ARE LESS...
...ME.
KROOOOONK
WHAT WAS THAT?
MY HULL HAS NEVER BEEN EVEN HYPOTHETICALLY TESTED FOR THIS VELOCITY.

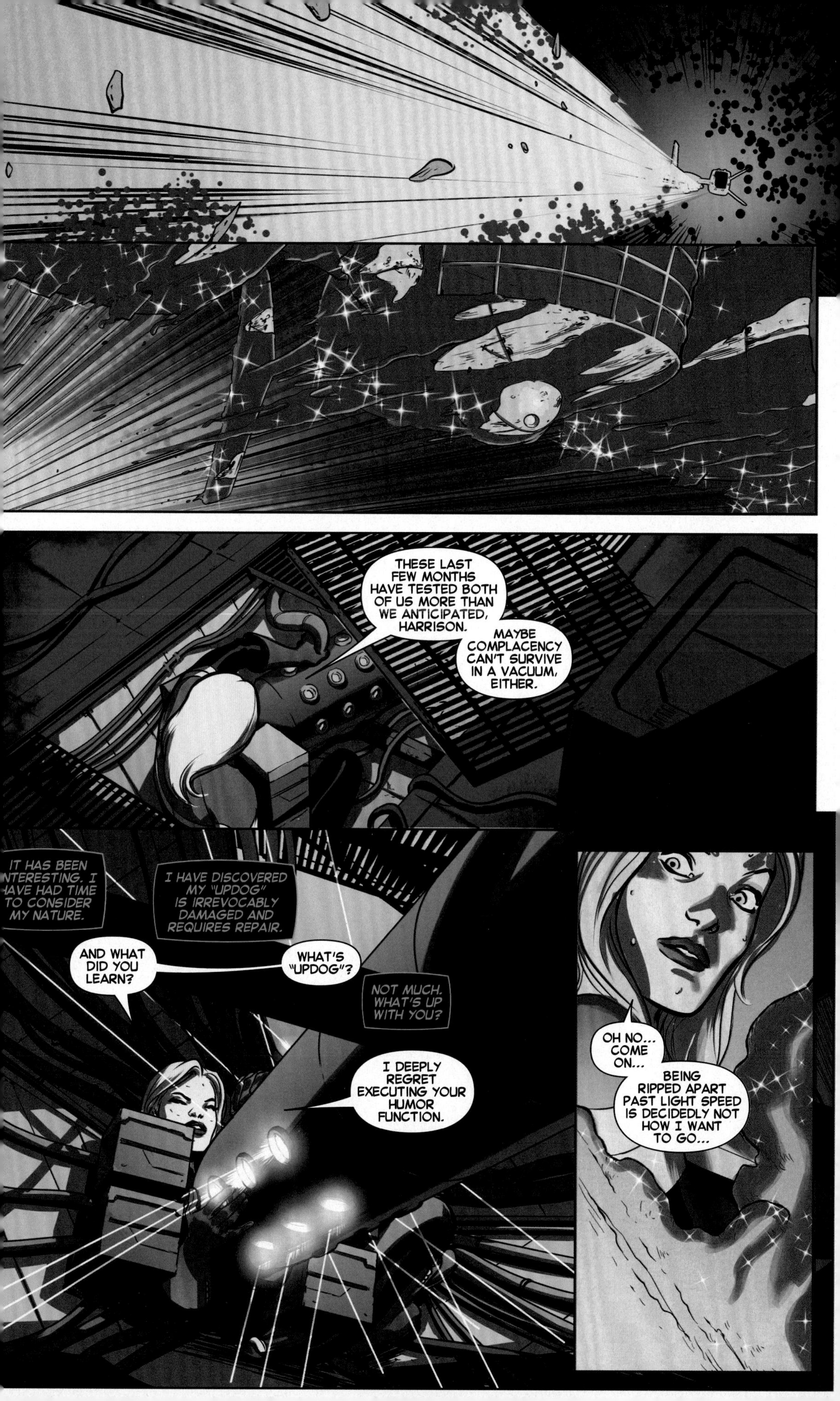
THESE LAST FEW MONTHS HAVE TESTED BOTH OF US MORE THAN WE ANTICIPATED, HARRISON.
MAYBE COMPLACENCY CAN'T SURVIVE IN A VACUUM, EITHER.
IT HAS BEEN INTERESTING. I HAVE HAD TIME TO CONSIDER MY NATURE.
AND WHAT DID YOU LEARN?
I HAVE DISCOVERED MY "UPDOG" IS IRREVOCABLY DAMAGED AND REQUIRES REPAIR.
WHAT'S "UPDOG"?
NOT MUCH. WHAT'S UP WITH YOU?
I DEEPLY REGRET EXECUTING YOUR HUMOR FUNCTION.
OH NO... COME ON...
BEING RIPPED APART PAST LIGHT SPEED IS DECIDEDLY NOT HOW I WANT TO GO...

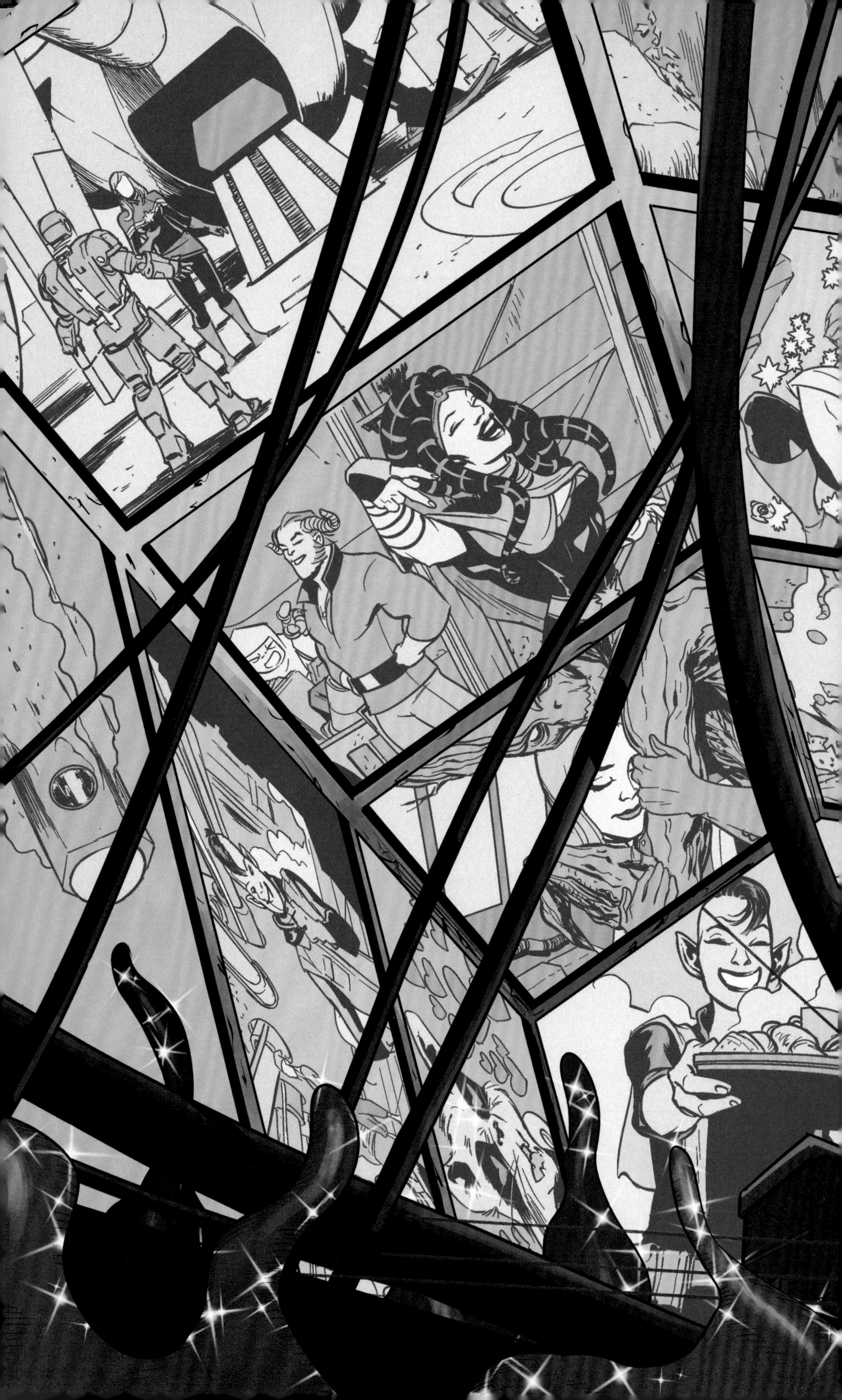

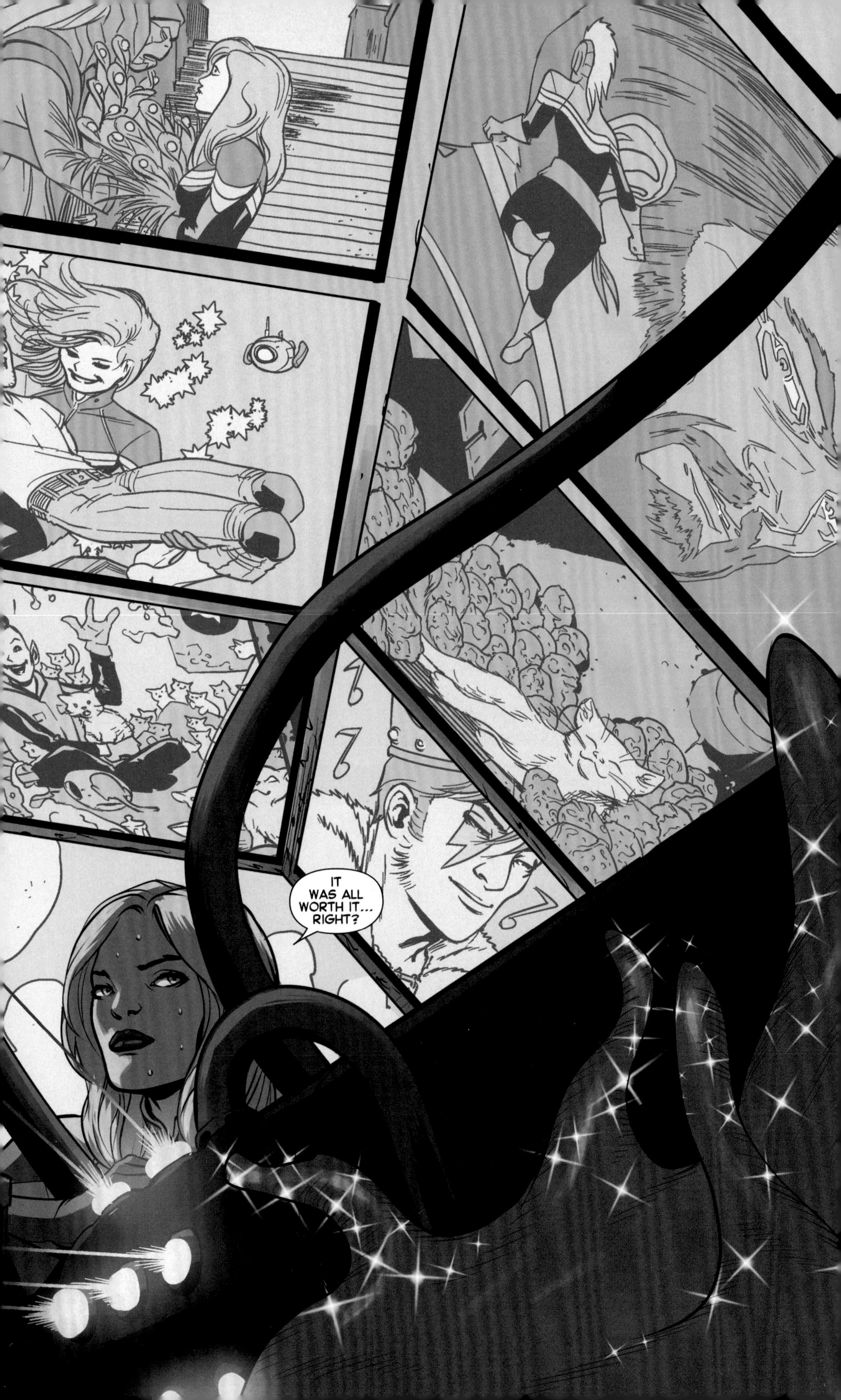
IT WAS ALL WORTH IT... RIGHT?

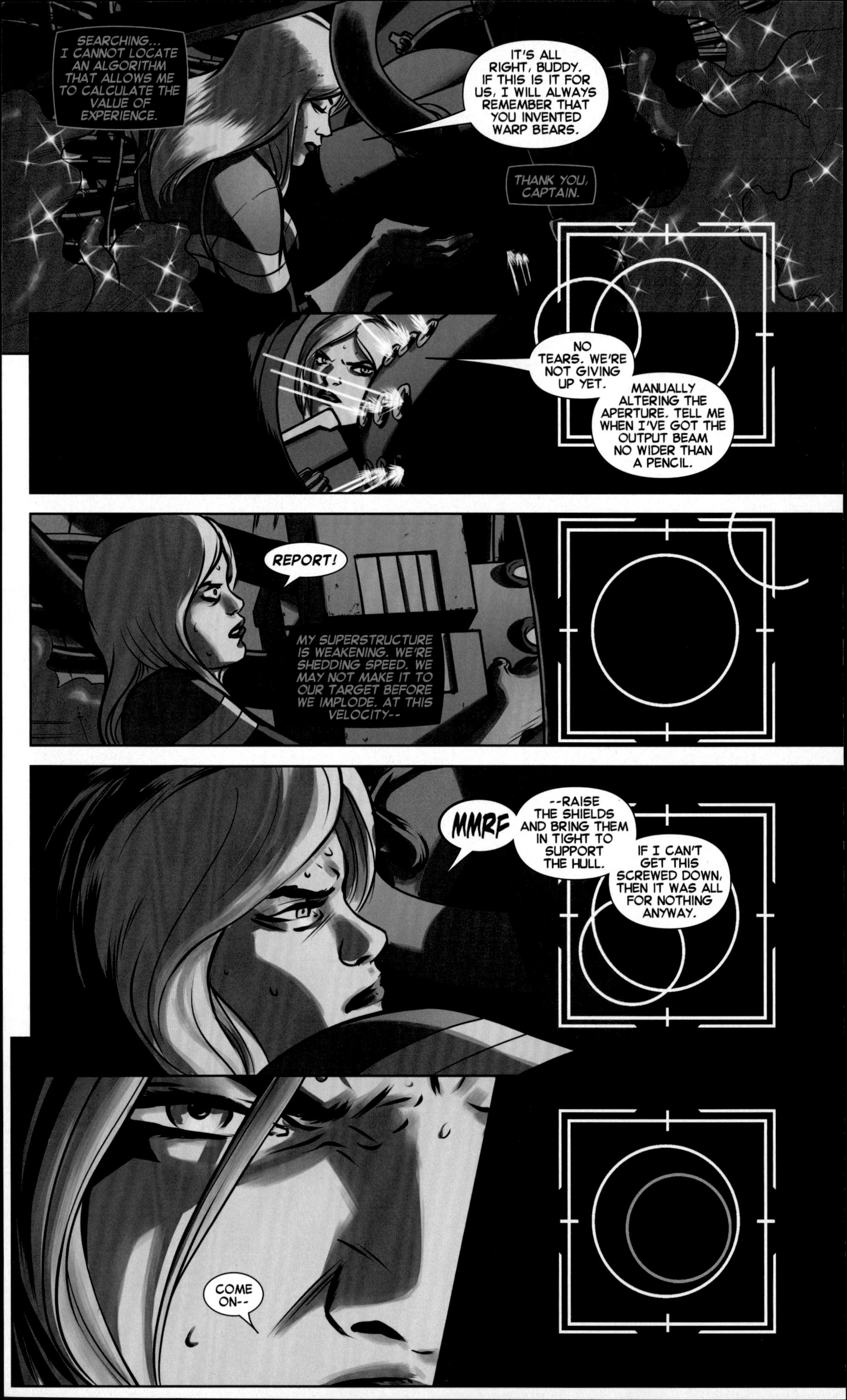
SEARCHING... I CANNOT LOCATE AN ALGORITHM THAT ALLOWS ME TO CALCULATE THE VALUE OF EXPERIENCE.
IT'S ALL RIGHT, BUDDY. IF THIS IS IT FOR US, I WILL ALWAYS REMEMBER THAT YOU INVENTED WARP BEARS.
THANK YOU, CAPTAIN.
NO TEARS. WE'RE NOT GIVING UP YET.
MANUALLY ALTERING THE APERTURE. TELL ME WHEN I'VE GOT THE OUTPUT BEAM NO WIDER THAN A PENCIL.
REPORT!
MY SUPERSTRUCTURE IS WEAKENING. WE'RE SHEDDING SPEED. WE MAY NOT MAKE IT TO OUR TARGET BEFORE WE IMPLODE. AT THIS VELOCITY--
MMRF
--RAISE THE SHIELDS AND BRING THEM IN TIGHT TO SUPPORT THE HULL.
IF I CAN'T GET THIS SCREWED DOWN, THEN IT WAS ALL FOR NOTHING ANYWAY.
COME ON--

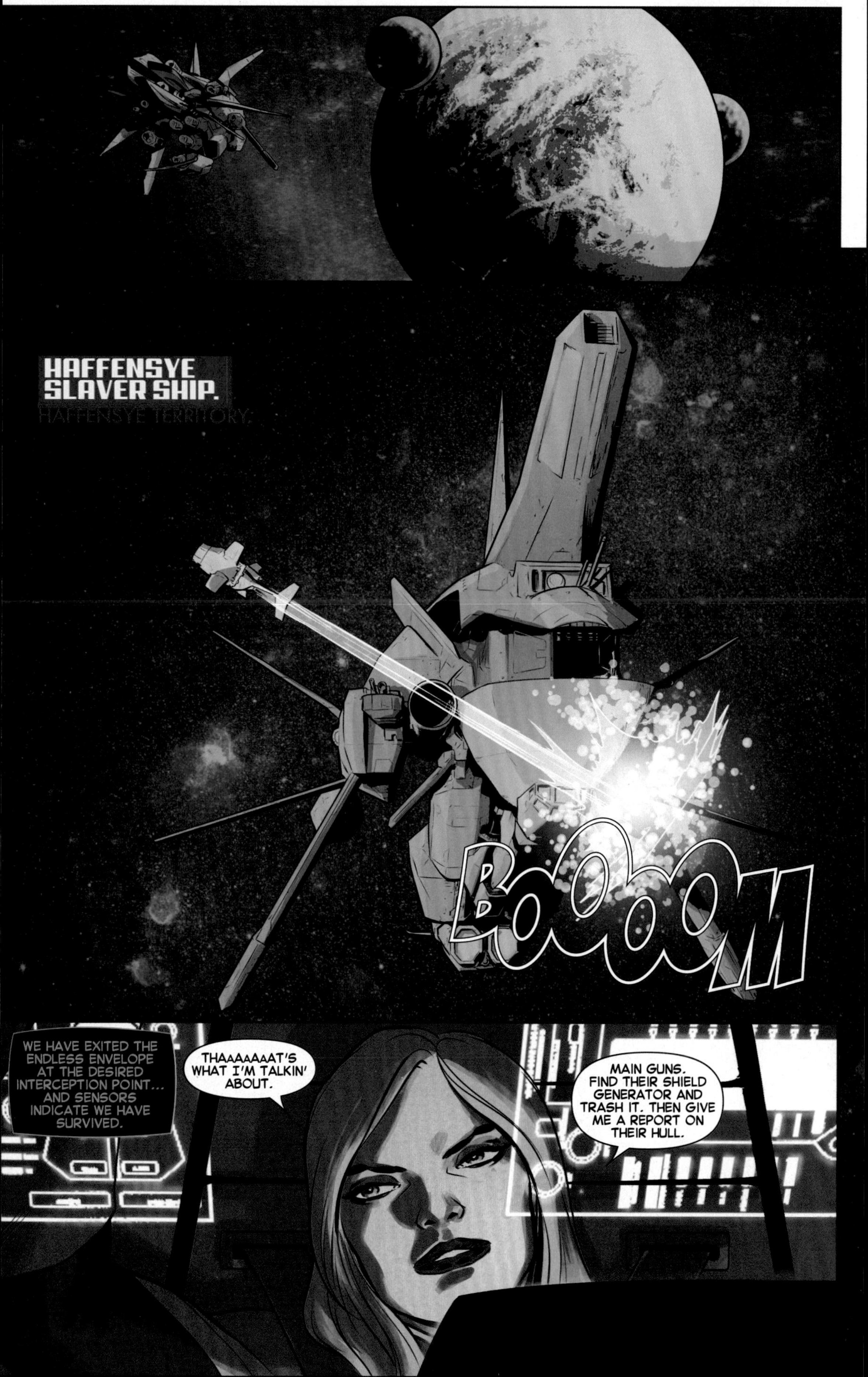
HAFFENSYE SLAVER SHIP.
HAFFENSYE TERRITORY.
BOOOOM
WE HAVE EXITED THE ENDLESS ENVELOPE AT THE DESIRED INTERCEPTION POINT... AND SENSORS INDICATE WE HAVE SURVIVED.
THAAAAAAAT'S WHAT I'M TALKIN' ABOUT.
MAIN GUNS. FIND THEIR SHIELD GENERATOR AND TRASH IT. THEN GIVE ME A REPORT ON THEIR HULL.

THEIR HULL HAS STANDARD SELF-SEALING DEFENSES DESIGNED FOR METEORITE STRIKES.

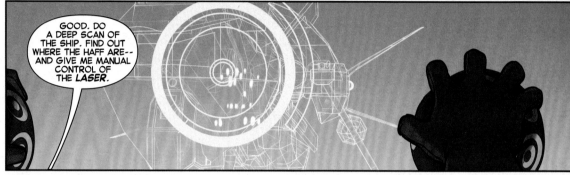

GOOD. DO A DEEP SCAN OF THE SHIP. FIND OUT WHERE THE HAFF ARE-- AND GIVE ME MANUAL CONTROL OF THE *LASER.*

SHE WON'T FIRE ON A SHIP WITH A HOLD FULL OF SENTIENT COLLATERAL. TARGET WEAPONS.

OPEN SHIP-TO-SHIP.

HAFFENSYE, THIS IS *CAPTAIN MARVEL* OF EARTH. ABANDON YOUR SHIP NOW. LEAVE THE CAPTIVES.

BURN HER OUT OF MY SKY.

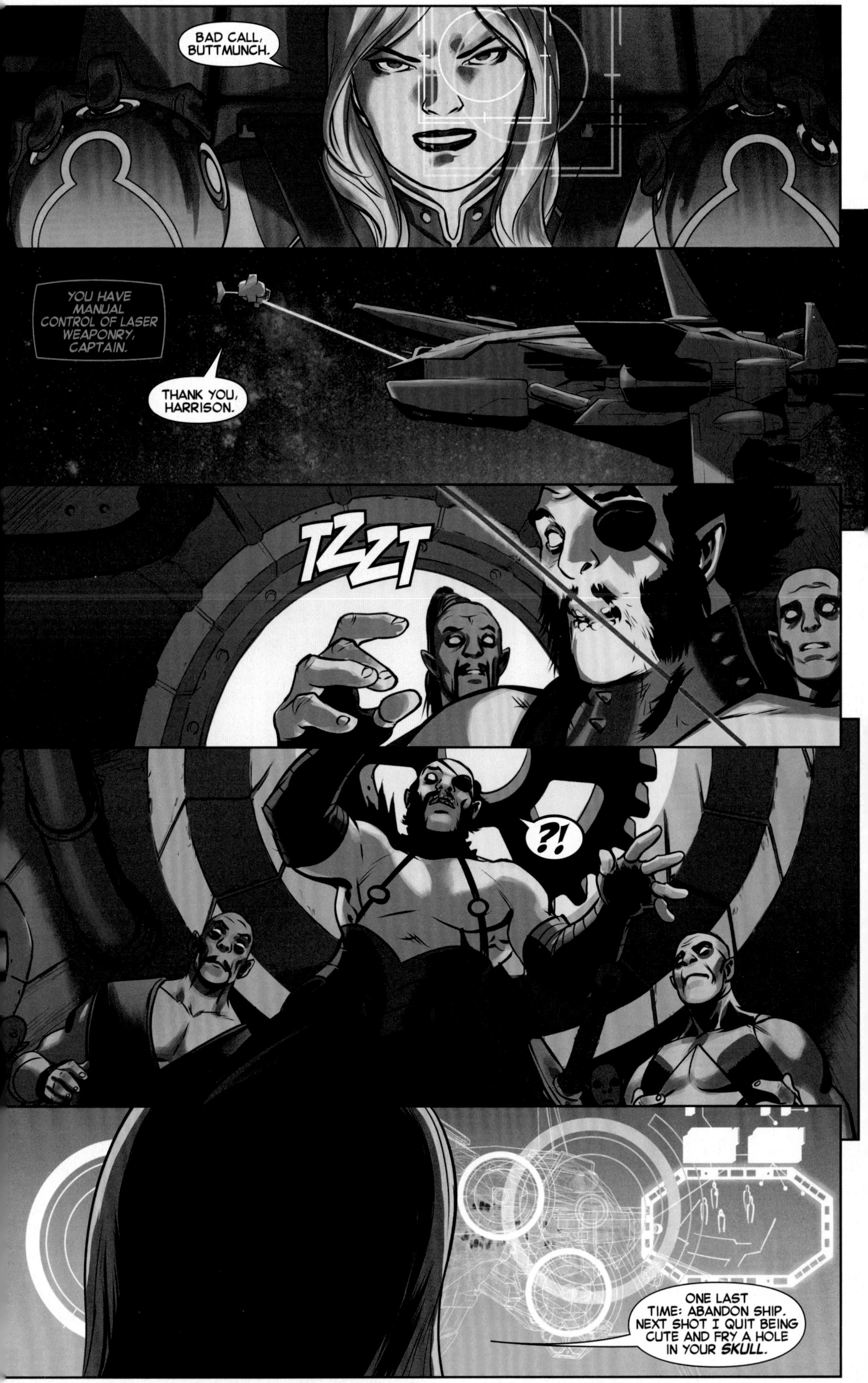
BAD CALL, BUTTMUNCH.
YOU HAVE MANUAL CONTROL OF LASER WEAPONRY, CAPTAIN.
THANK YOU, HARRISON.
TZZT
?!
ONE LAST TIME: ABANDON SHIP. NEXT SHOT I QUIT BEING CUTE AND FRY A HOLE IN YOUR SKULL.

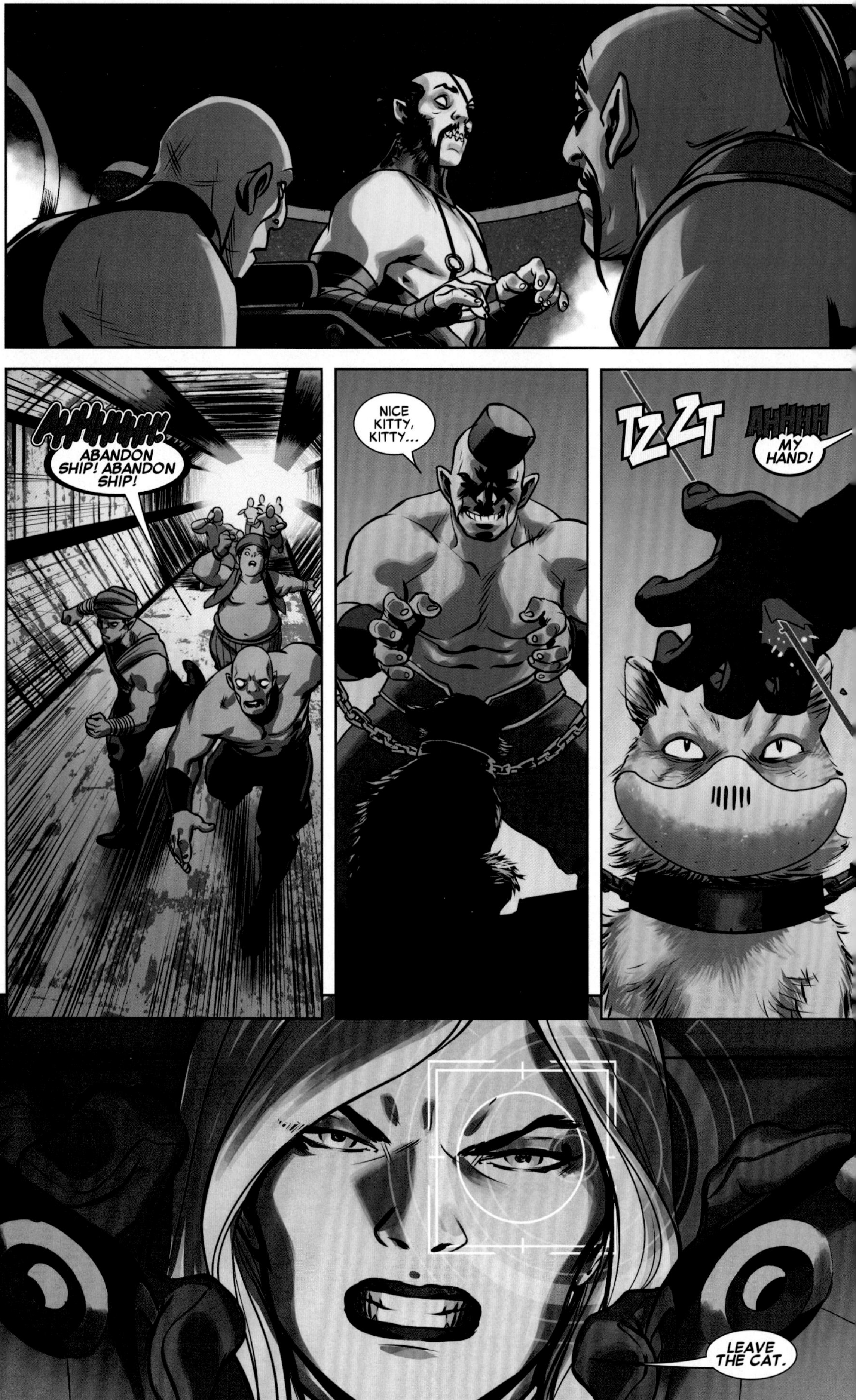
AHHHHHH!
ABANDON SHIP! ABANDON SHIP!
NICE KITTY, KITTY...
TZZT
AHHHH
MY HAND!
LEAVE THE CAT.

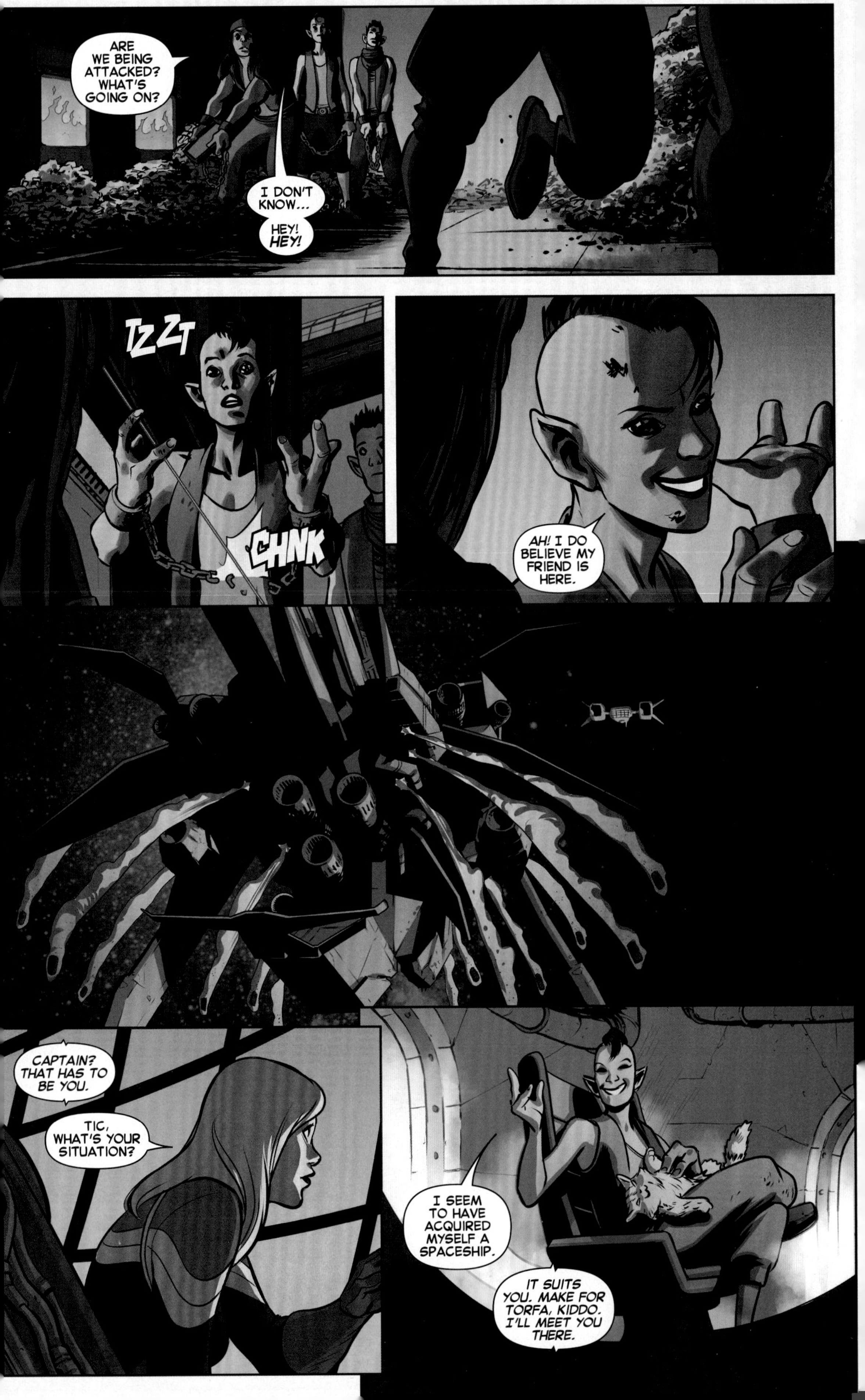
ARE WE BEING ATTACKED? WHAT'S GOING ON?
I DON'T KNOW...
HEY! HEY!
TZZT
CHNK
AH! I DO BELIEVE MY FRIEND IS HERE.
CAPTAIN? THAT HAS TO BE YOU.
TIC, WHAT'S YOUR SITUATION?
I SEEM TO HAVE ACQUIRED MYSELF A SPACESHIP.
IT SUITS YOU. MAKE FOR TORFA, KIDDO. I'LL MEET YOU THERE.

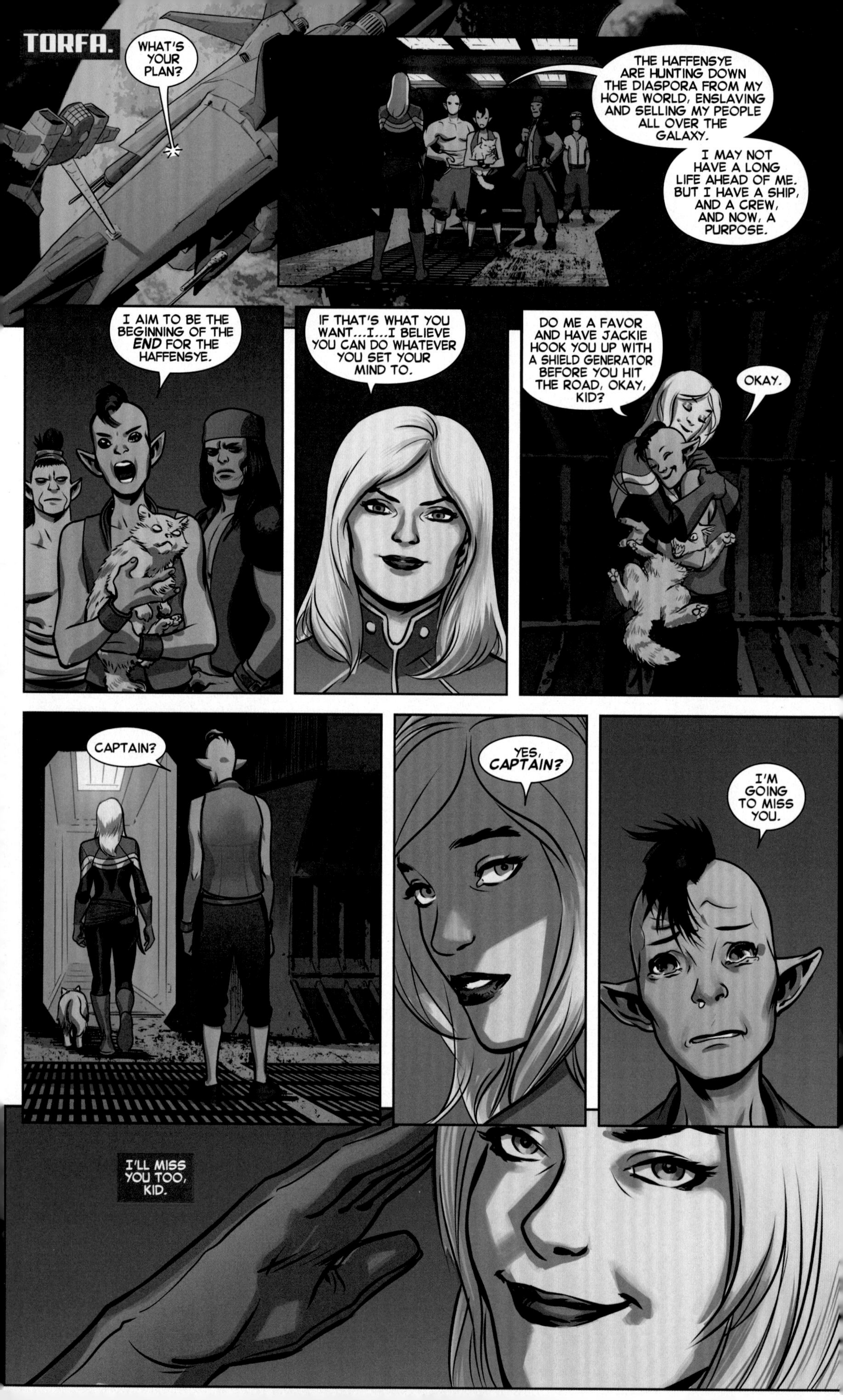
TORFA.
WHAT'S YOUR PLAN?
THE HAFFENSYE ARE HUNTING DOWN THE DIASPORA FROM MY HOME WORLD, ENSLAVING AND SELLING MY PEOPLE ALL OVER THE GALAXY.
I MAY NOT HAVE A LONG LIFE AHEAD OF ME. BUT I HAVE A SHIP, AND A CREW, AND NOW, A PURPOSE.
I AIM TO BE THE BEGINNING OF THE END FOR THE HAFFENSYE.
IF THAT'S WHAT YOU WANT...I...I BELIEVE YOU CAN DO WHATEVER YOU SET YOUR MIND TO.
DO ME A FAVOR AND HAVE JACKIE HOOK YOU UP WITH A SHIELD GENERATOR BEFORE YOU HIT THE ROAD, OKAY, KID?
OKAY.
CAPTAIN?
YES, CAPTAIN?
I'M GOING TO MISS YOU.
I'LL MISS YOU TOO, KID.

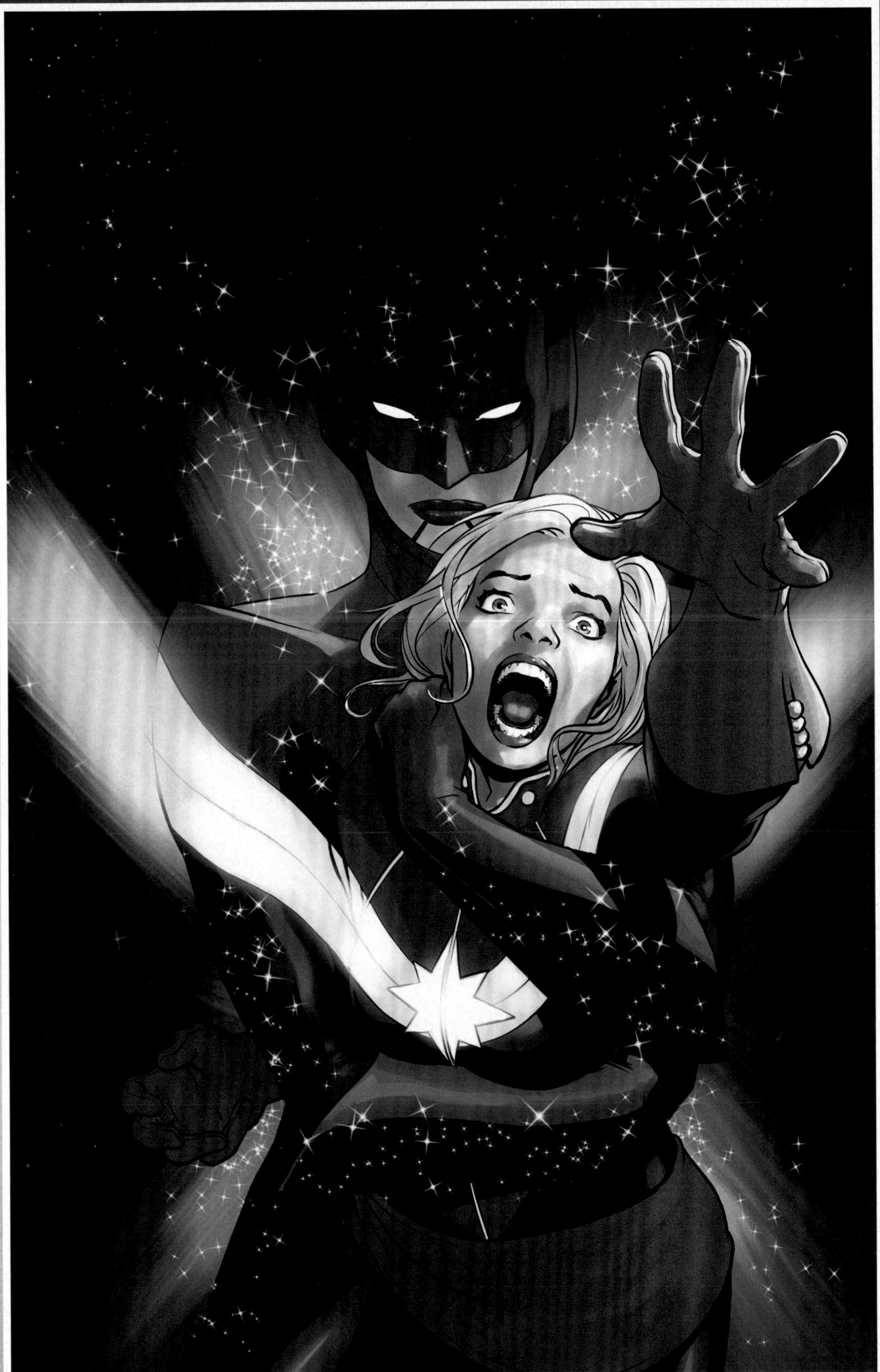

THE BLACK VORTEX FOURTEEN

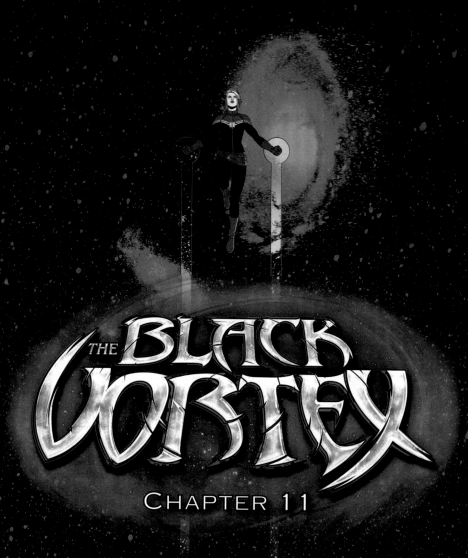

THE BLACK VORTEX

CHAPTER 11

PREVIOUSLY IN THE BLACK VORTEX...

The Black Vortex, an ancient artifact that unlocks the cosmic potential of its viewers, recently fell into the hands of the menacing Mr. Knife.

The unseen Ebony Maw convinced Thane, son of Thanos, to gaze into the vortex and join Knife and the Slaughter Squad.
With his new cosmic abilities, Thane encased the inhabitants of Planet Spartax in amber.

In a last-ditch effort to save the planet, Captain Marvel, the Avengers' interstellar emissary, swooped into Knife's fortress and intercepted the mirror.
Now, she has the fate of a planet in her hands...and every heavy hitter in the galaxy on her trail.

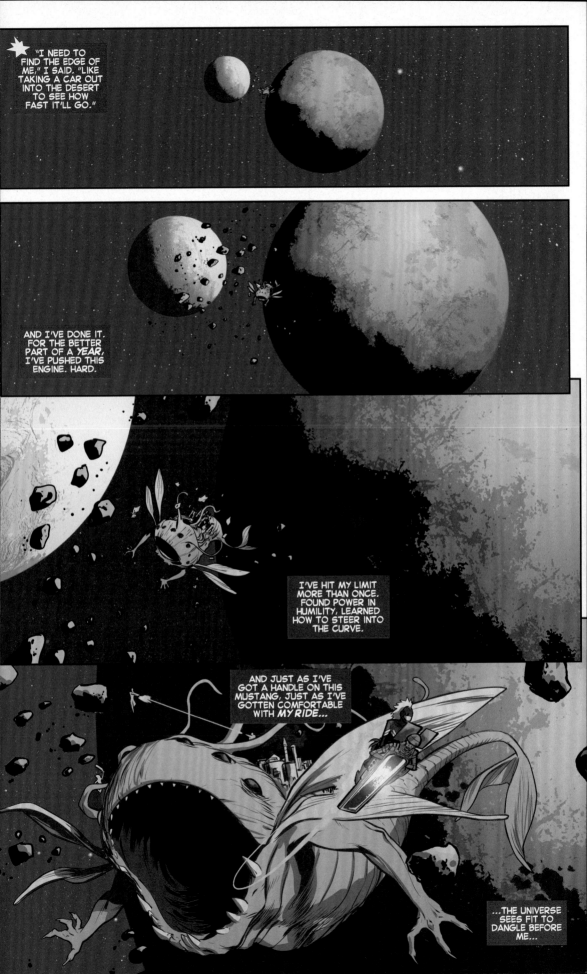

"I NEED TO FIND THE EDGE OF ME," I SAID. "LIKE TAKING A CAR OUT INTO THE DESERT TO SEE HOW FAST IT'LL GO."

AND I'VE DONE IT. FOR THE BETTER PART OF A *YEAR*, I'VE PUSHED THIS ENGINE. HARD.

I'VE HIT MY LIMIT MORE THAN ONCE. FOUND POWER IN HUMILITY, LEARNED HOW TO STEER INTO THE CURVE.

AND JUST AS I'VE GOT A HANDLE ON THIS MUSTANG, JUST AS I'VE GOTTEN COMFORTABLE WITH *MY RIDE*...

...THE UNIVERSE SEES FIT TO DANGLE BEFORE ME...

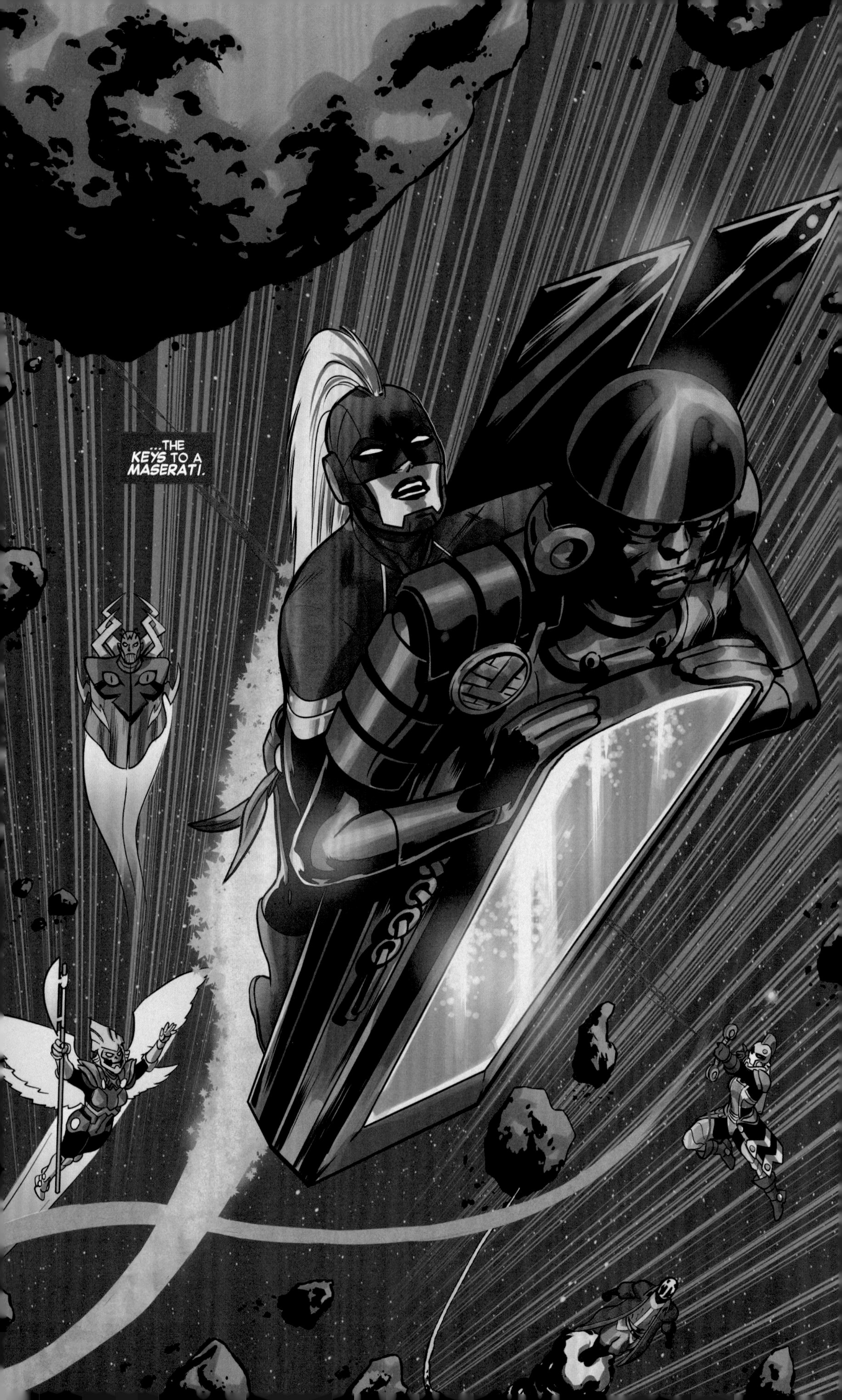
...THE KEYS TO A MASERATI.

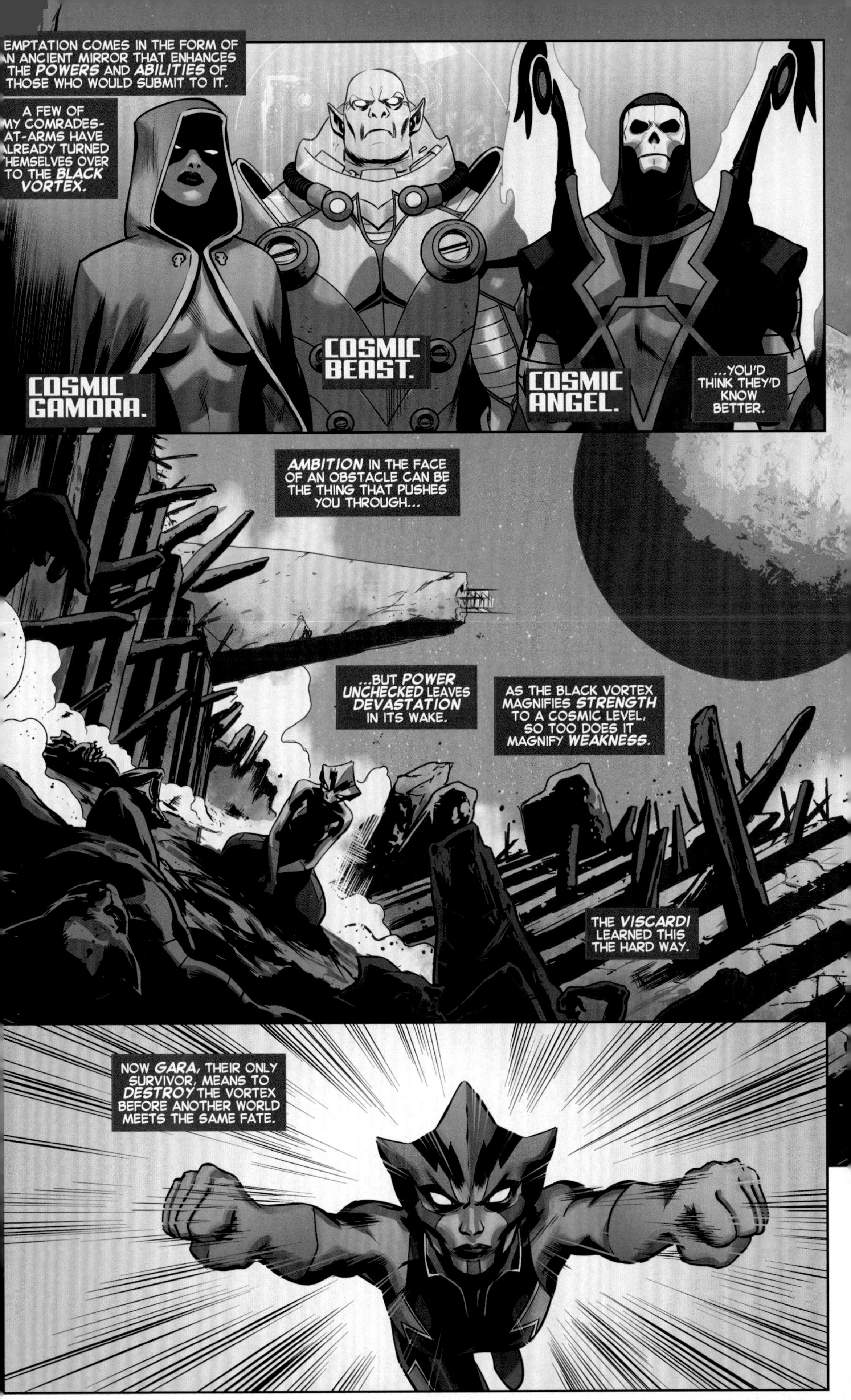

EMPTATION COMES IN THE FORM OF AN ANCIENT MIRROR THAT ENHANCES THE POWERS AND ABILITIES OF THOSE WHO WOULD SUBMIT TO IT.
A FEW OF MY COMRADES-AT-ARMS HAVE ALREADY TURNED HEMSELVES OVER TO THE BLACK VORTEX.
COSMIC GAMORA.
COSMIC BEAST.
COSMIC ANGEL.
...YOU'D THINK THEY'D KNOW BETTER.
AMBITION IN THE FACE OF AN OBSTACLE CAN BE THE THING THAT PUSHES YOU THROUGH...
...BUT POWER UNCHECKED LEAVES DEVASTATION IN ITS WAKE.
AS THE BLACK VORTEX MAGNIFIES STRENGTH TO A COSMIC LEVEL, SO TOO DOES IT MAGNIFY WEAKNESS.
THE VISCARDI LEARNED THIS THE HARD WAY.
NOW GARA, THEIR ONLY SURVIVOR, MEANS TO DESTROY THE VORTEX BEFORE ANOTHER WORLD MEETS THE SAME FATE.

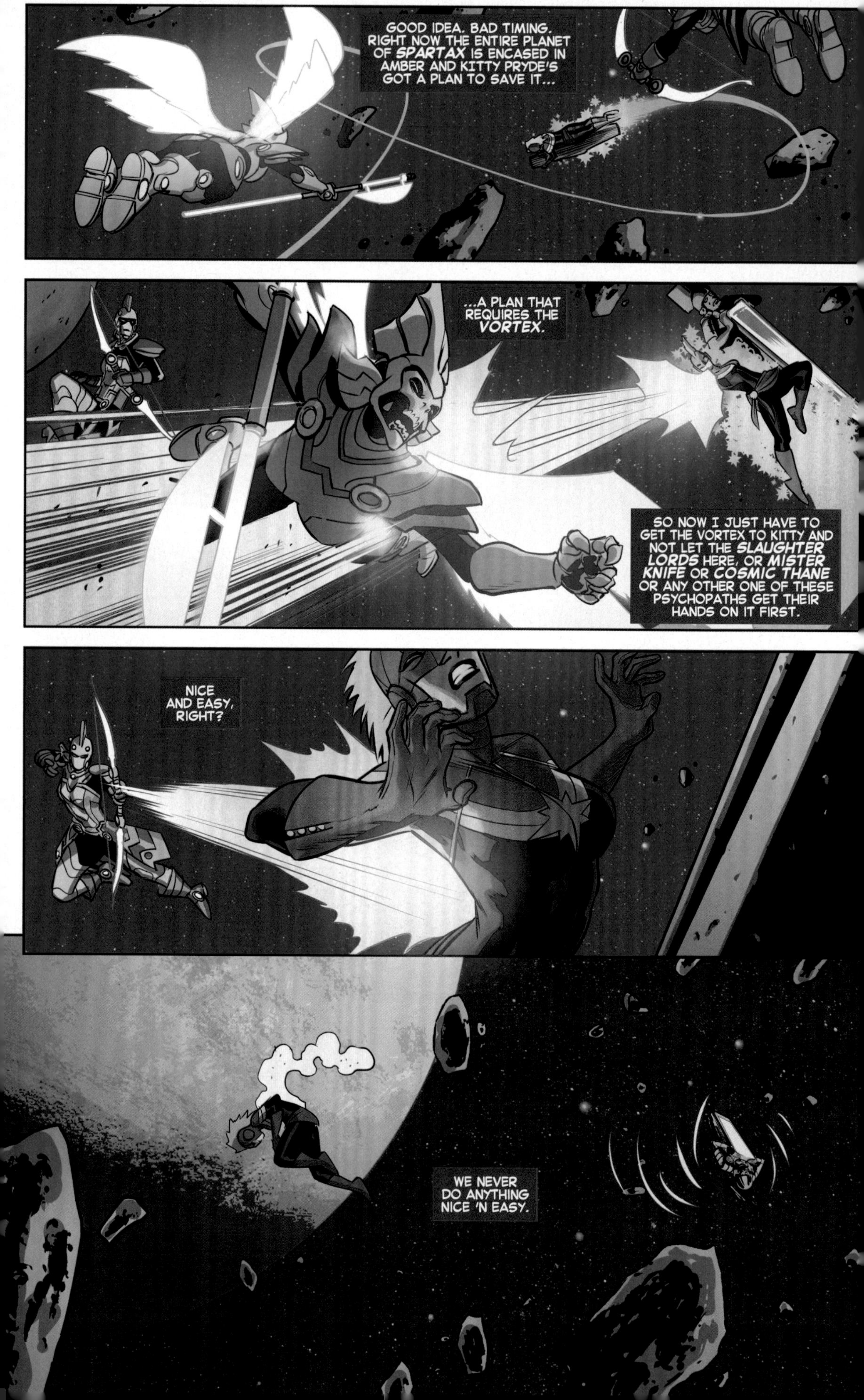
GOOD IDEA. BAD TIMING. RIGHT NOW THE ENTIRE PLANET OF SPARTAX IS ENCASED IN AMBER AND KITTY PRYDE'S GOT A PLAN TO SAVE IT...
...A PLAN THAT REQUIRES THE VORTEX.
SO NOW I JUST HAVE TO GET THE VORTEX TO KITTY AND NOT LET THE SLAUGHTER LORDS HERE, OR MISTER KNIFE OR COSMIC THANE OR ANY OTHER ONE OF THESE PSYCHOPATHS GET THEIR HANDS ON IT FIRST.
NICE AND EASY, RIGHT?
WE NEVER DO ANYTHING NICE 'N EASY.

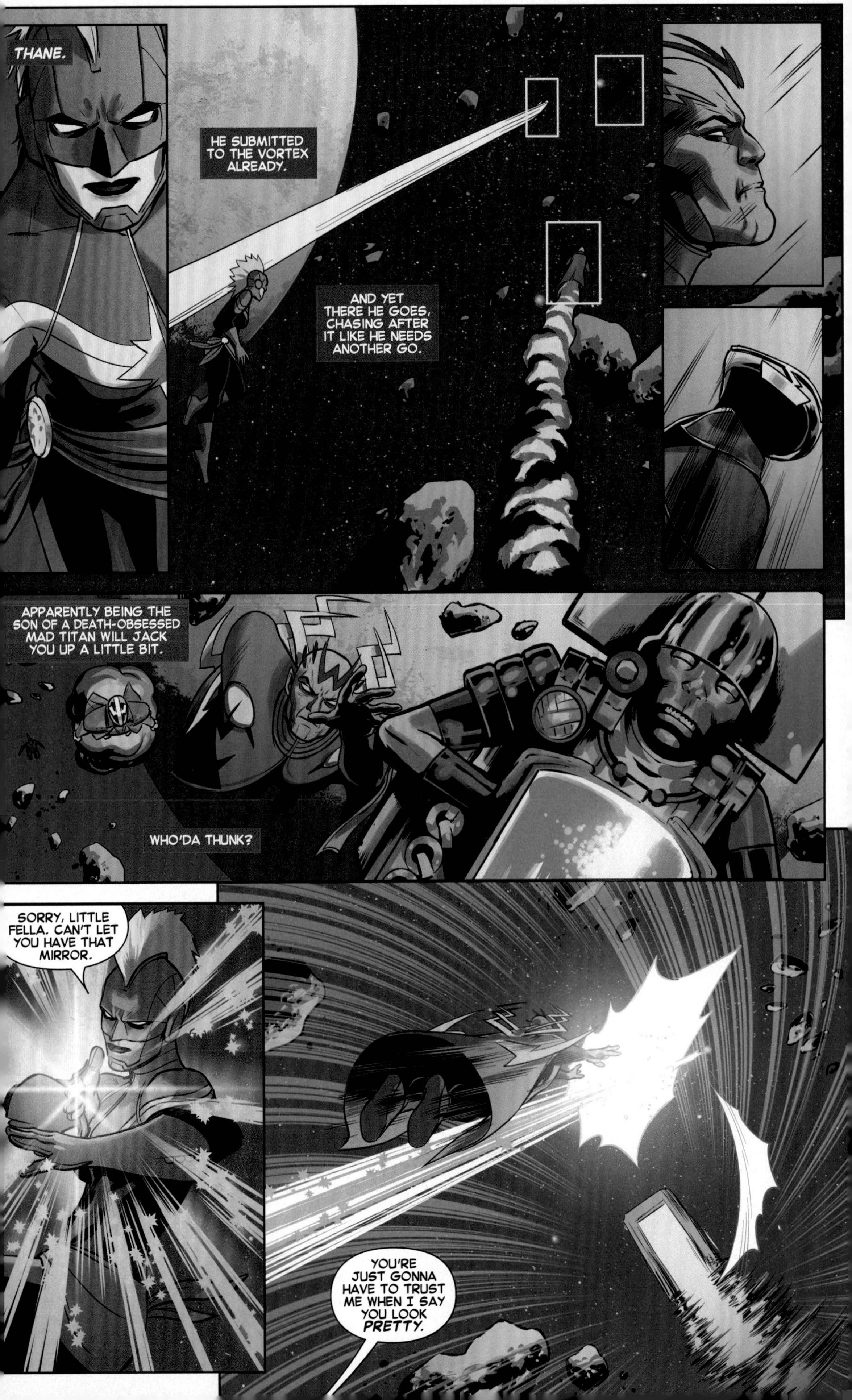
THANE.
HE SUBMITTED TO THE VORTEX ALREADY.
AND YET THERE HE GOES, CHASING AFTER IT LIKE HE NEEDS ANOTHER GO.
APPARENTLY BEING THE SON OF A DEATH-OBSESSED MAD TITAN WILL JACK YOU UP A LITTLE BIT.
WHO'DA THUNK?
SORRY, LITTLE FELLA. CAN'T LET YOU HAVE THAT MIRROR.
YOU'RE JUST GONNA HAVE TO TRUST ME WHEN I SAY YOU LOOK PRETTY.

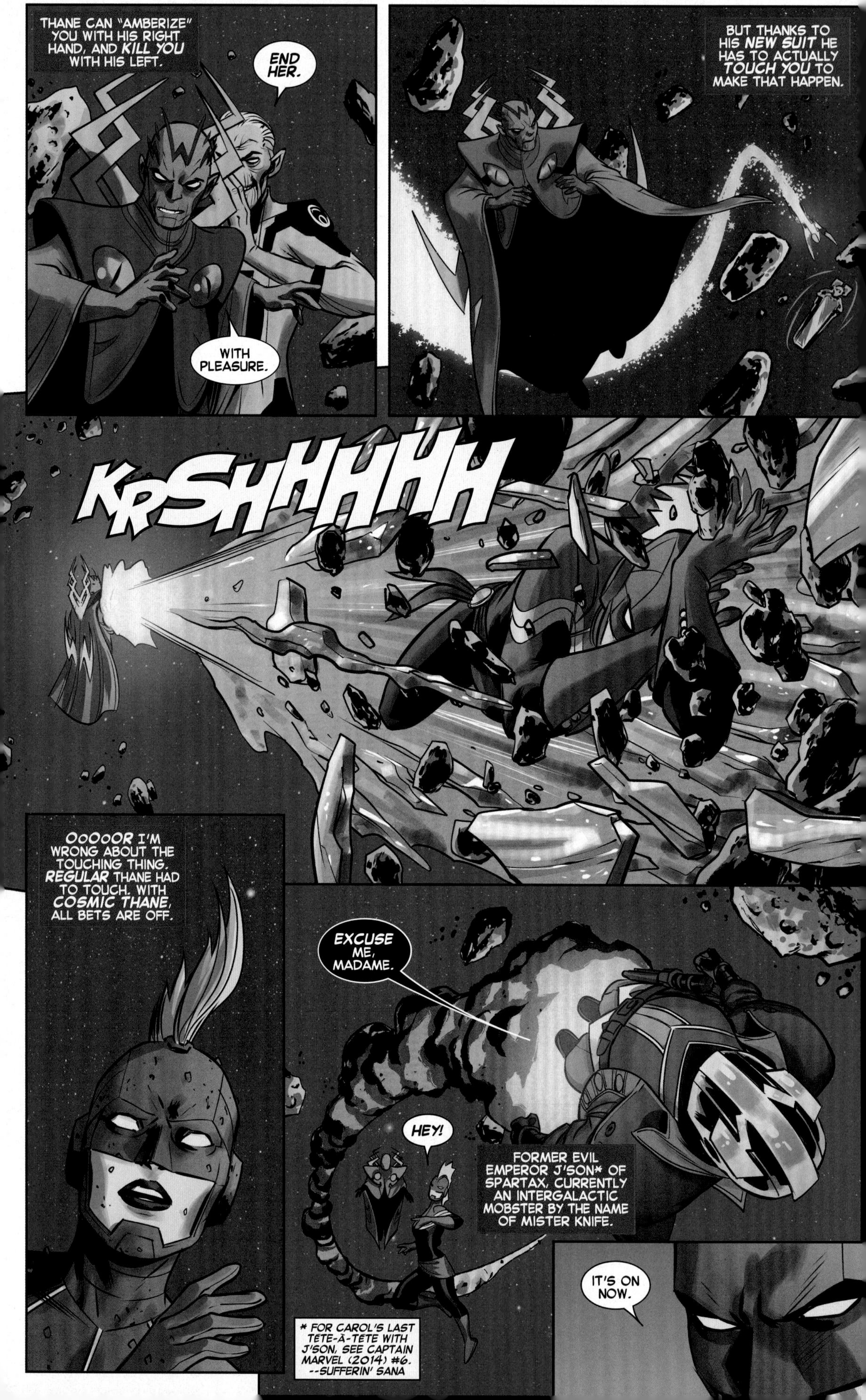
THANE CAN "AMBERIZE" YOU WITH HIS RIGHT HAND, AND KILL YOU WITH HIS LEFT.
END HER.
WITH PLEASURE.
BUT THANKS TO HIS NEW SUIT HE HAS TO ACTUALLY TOUCH YOU TO MAKE THAT HAPPEN.
KRSHHHHHH
OOOOOR I'M WRONG ABOUT THE TOUCHING THING. REGULAR THANE HAD TO TOUCH. WITH COSMIC THANE, ALL BETS ARE OFF.
EXCUSE ME, MADAME.
HEY!
FORMER EVIL EMPEROR J'SON* OF SPARTAX, CURRENTLY AN INTERGALACTIC MOBSTER BY THE NAME OF MISTER KNIFE.
* FOR CAROL'S LAST TÊTE-À-TÊTE WITH J'SON, SEE CAPTAIN MARVEL (2014) #6. --SUFFERIN' SANA
IT'S ON NOW.

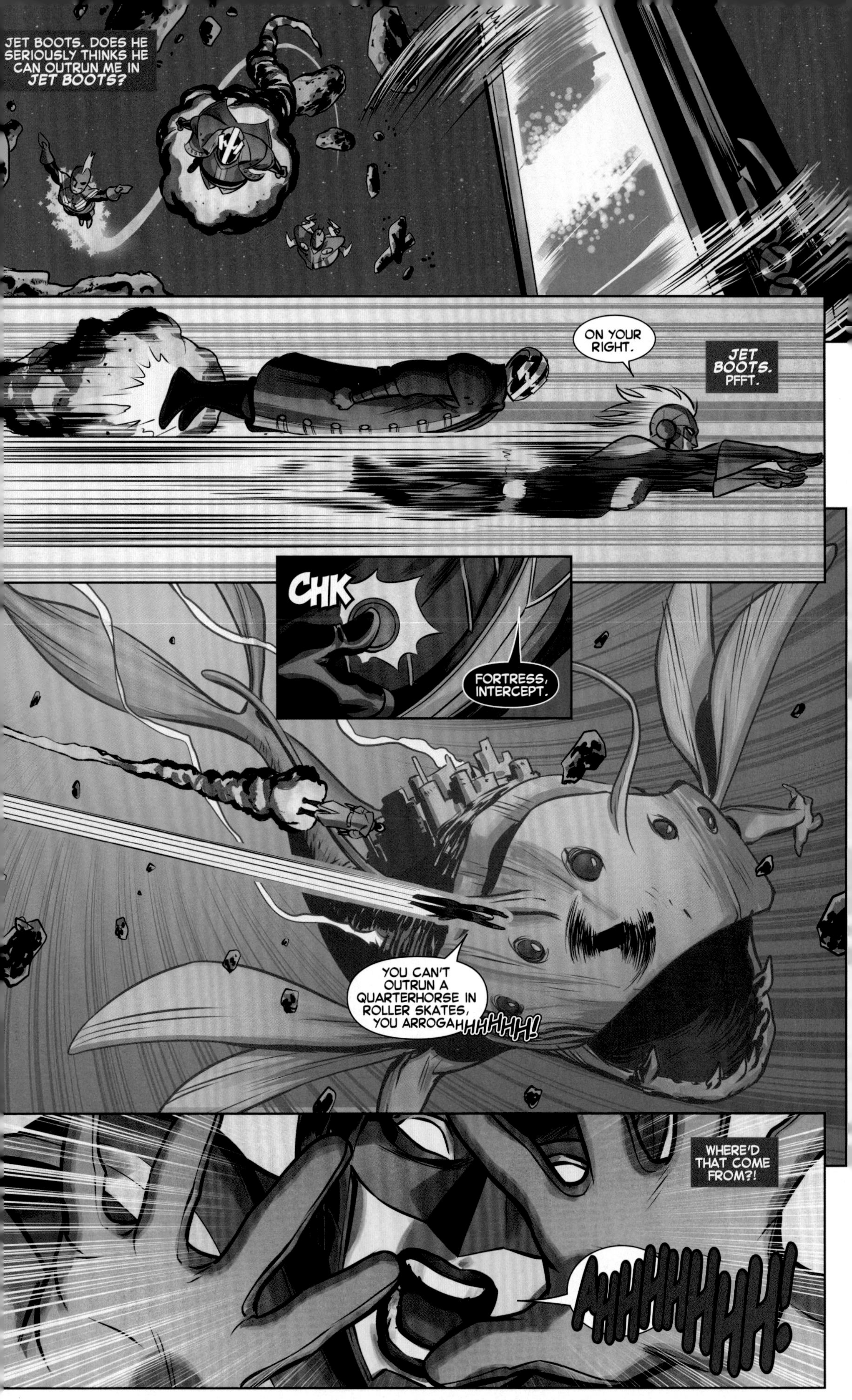
JET BOOTS. DOES HE SERIOUSLY THINKS HE CAN OUTRUN ME IN *JET BOOTS?*
ON YOUR RIGHT.
JET BOOTS. PFFT.
CHK
FORTRESS, INTERCEPT.
YOU CAN'T OUTRUN A QUARTERHORSE IN ROLLER SKATES, YOU ARROGAHHHHHH!
WHERE'D THAT COME FROM?!
AHHHHHHHH!

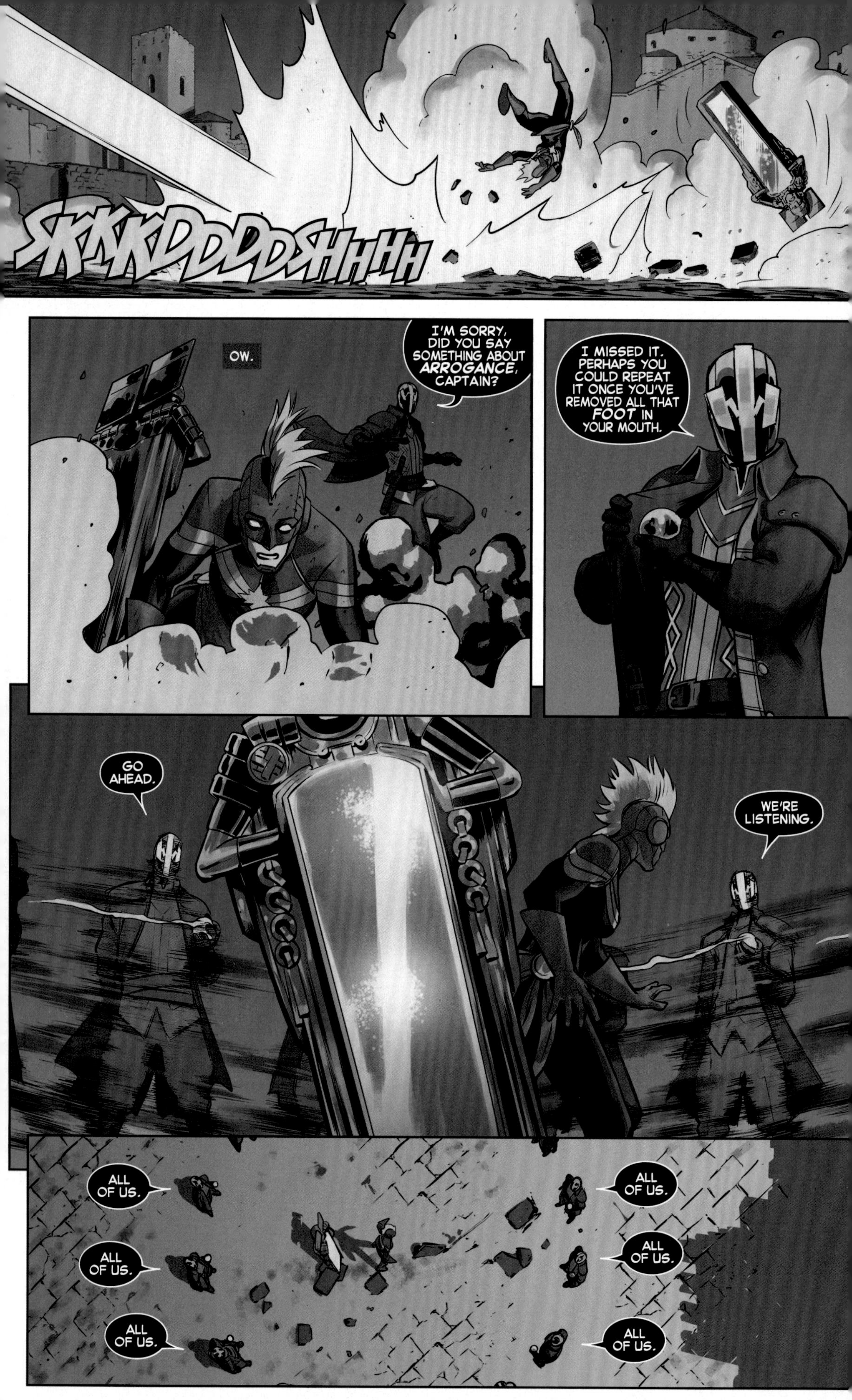
SKKKDDDDSHHHH
OW.
I'M SORRY, DID YOU SAY SOMETHING ABOUT ARROGANCE, CAPTAIN?
I MISSED IT. PERHAPS YOU COULD REPEAT IT ONCE YOU'VE REMOVED ALL THAT FOOT IN YOUR MOUTH.
GO AHEAD.
WE'RE LISTENING.
ALL OF US.
ALL OF US.
ALL OF US.
ALL OF US.
ALL OF US.
ALL OF US.

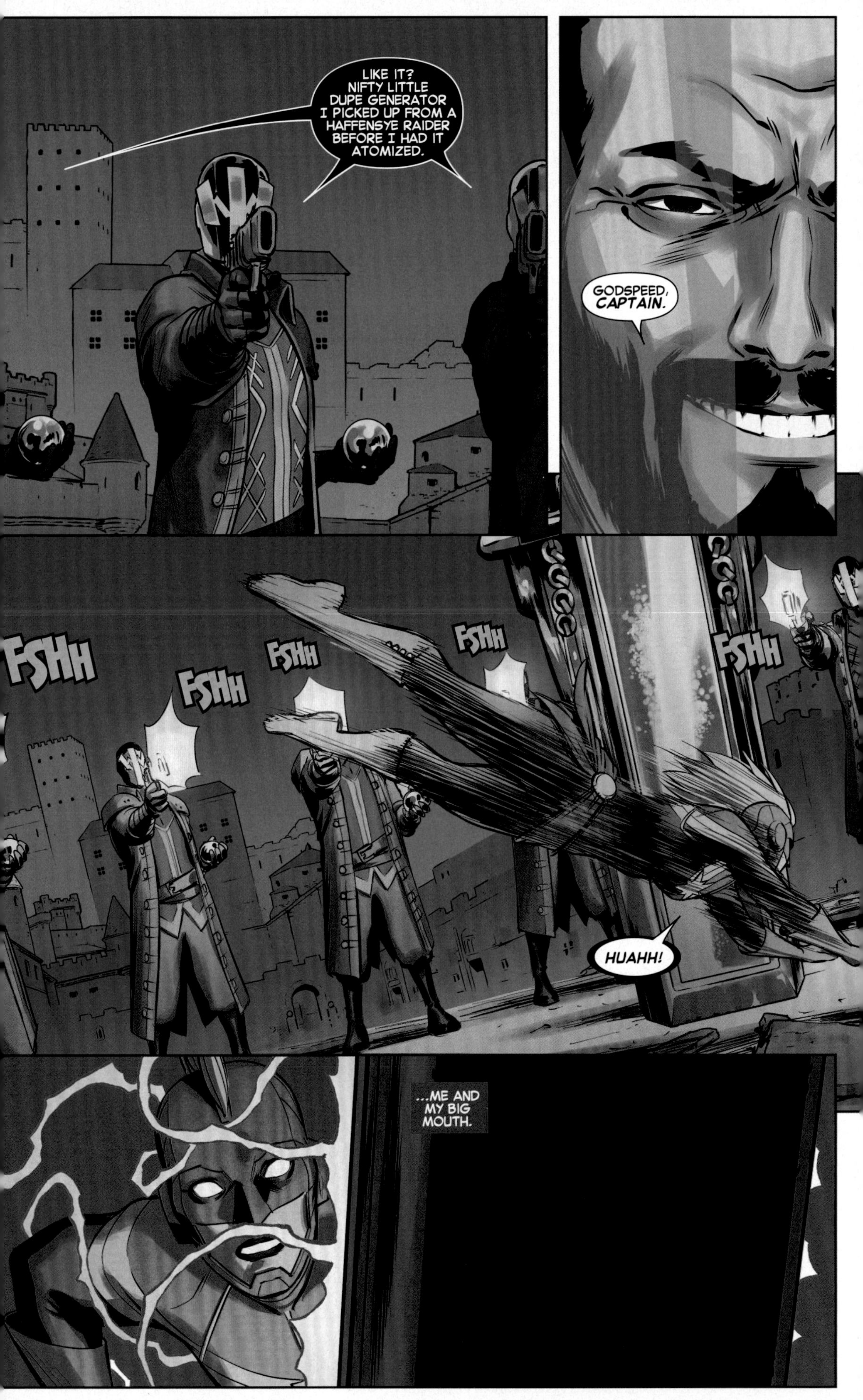

LIKE IT? NIFTY LITTLE DUPE GENERATOR I PICKED UP FROM A HAFFENSYE RAIDER BEFORE I HAD IT ATOMIZED.
GODSPEED, CAPTAIN.
FSHH
FSHH
FSHH
FSHH
FSHH
HUAHH!
...ME AND MY BIG MOUTH.

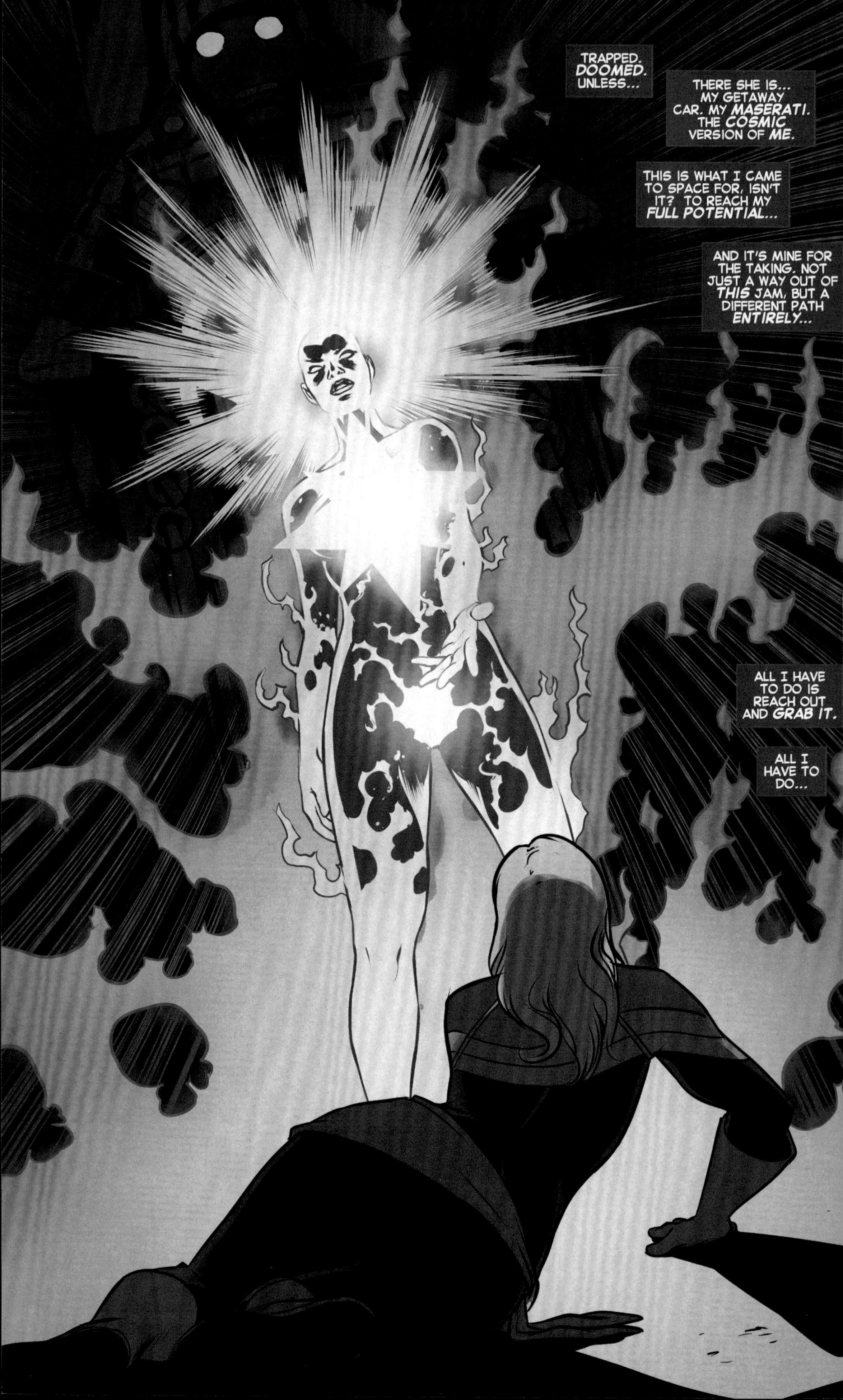
TRAPPED. DOOMED. UNLESS...
THERE SHE IS... MY GETAWAY CAR. MY MASERATI. THE COSMIC VERSION OF ME.
THIS IS WHAT I CAME TO SPACE FOR, ISN'T IT? TO REACH MY FULL POTENTIAL...
AND IT'S MINE FOR THE TAKING. NOT JUST A WAY OUT OF THIS JAM, BUT A DIFFERENT PATH ENTIRELY...
ALL I HAVE TO DO IS REACH OUT AND GRAB IT.
ALL I HAVE TO DO...

...IS
SUBMIT.

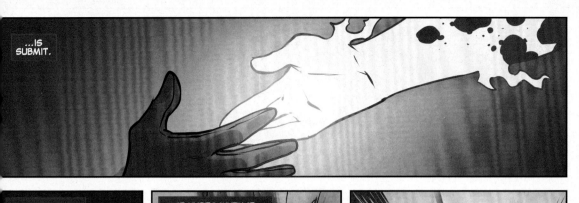

I *KNOW* THIS
FEELING. IF NOT
EXACTLY THIS,
THEN CLOSE...

LIKE GOING
BINARY, BUT
MORE SO...

IT HURTS WHEN IT
REACHES THE HEART.
THERE'S A WEIGHT TO
IT, A BURNING. LIKE
EVERYTHING *EXTRA* IS
BEING SCORCHED OFF...

NO MORE
DOUBTS, NO
MORE *FEARS.* ALL
THAT SURVIVES
IS *FORCE...*

...AND
EGO.

DO YOU
RECOGNIZE
HER, CAROL?

IS SHE WHO
YOU WANT
TO BE?

...NO.

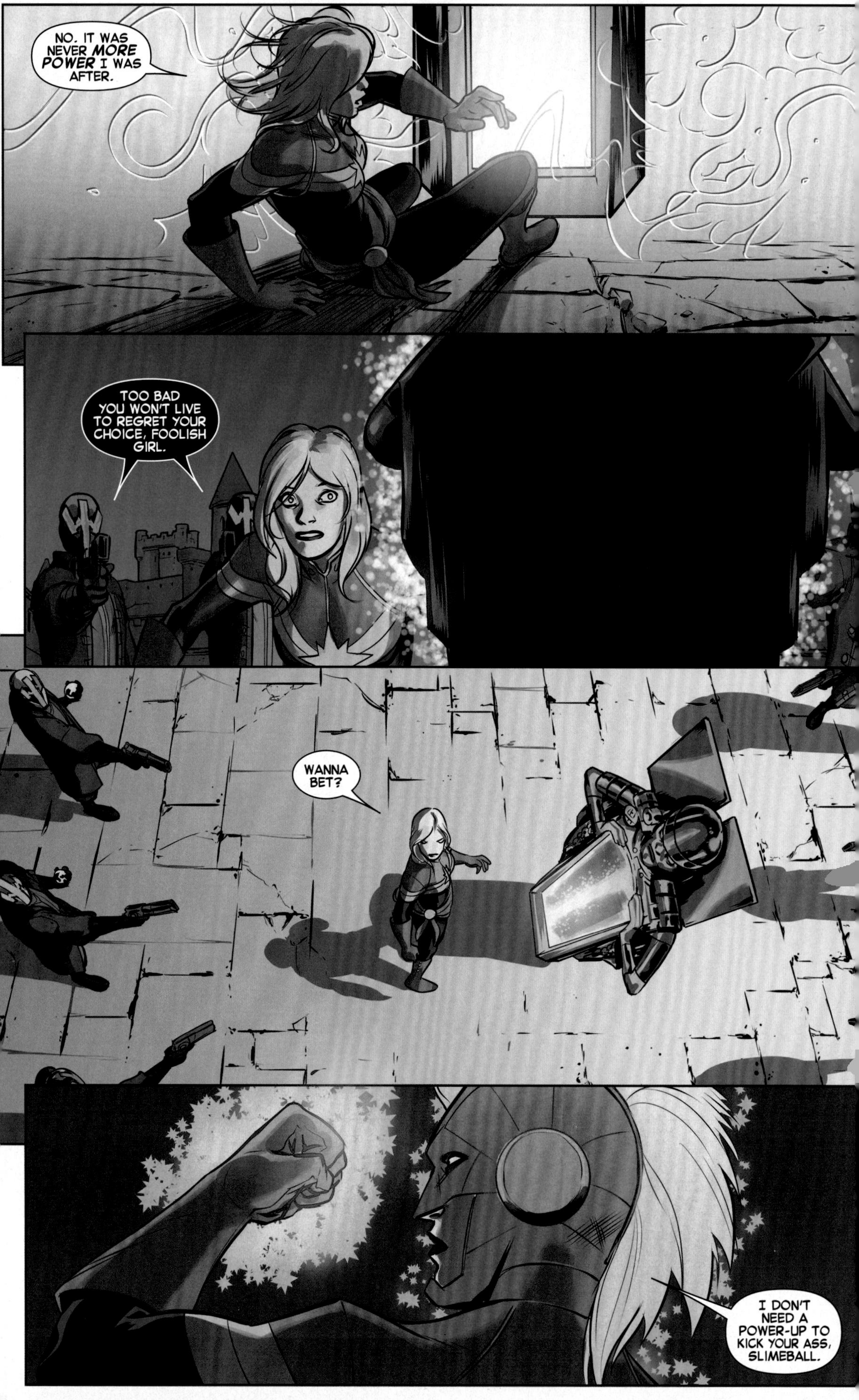
NO. IT WAS NEVER MORE POWER I WAS AFTER.
TOO BAD YOU WON'T LIVE TO REGRET YOUR CHOICE, FOOLISH GIRL.
WANNA BET?
I DON'T NEED A POWER-UP TO KICK YOUR ASS, SLIMEBALL.

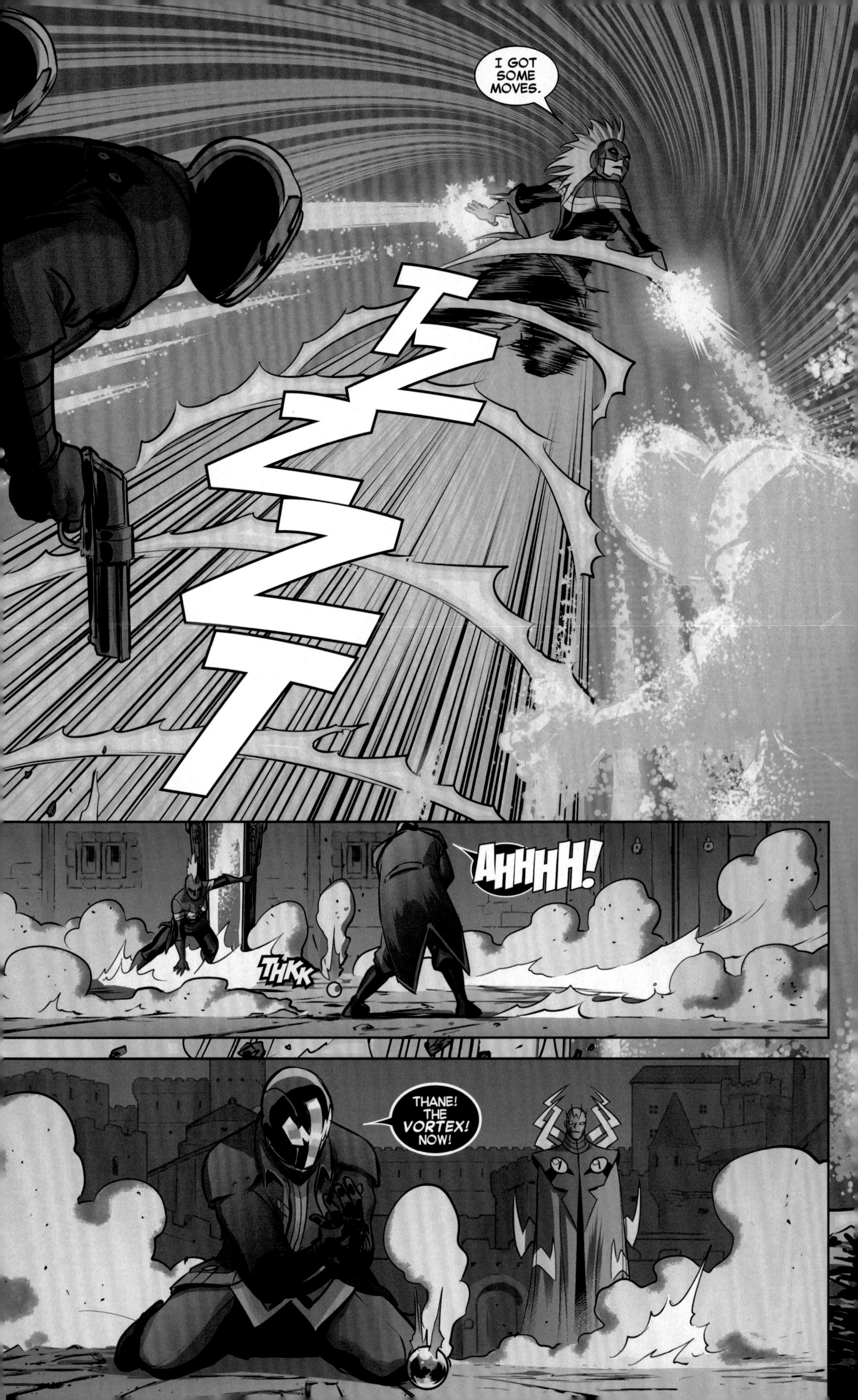
I GOT SOME MOVES.
TZZZZT
AHHHH!
THKK
THANE! THE VORTEX! NOW!

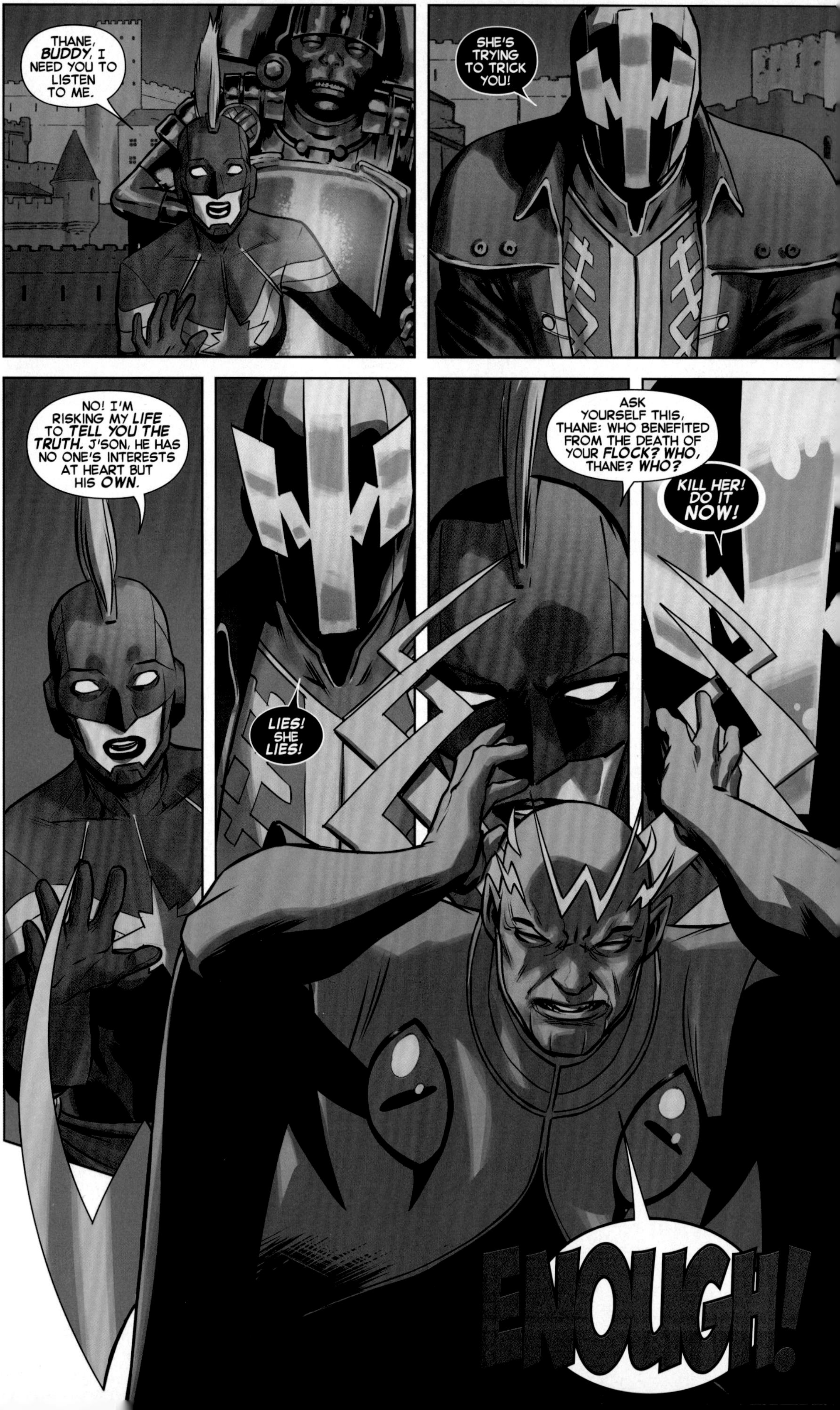
THANE, BUDDY, I NEED YOU TO LISTEN TO ME.
SHE'S TRYING TO TRICK YOU!
NO! I'M RISKING MY LIFE TO TELL YOU THE TRUTH. J'SON, HE HAS NO ONE'S INTERESTS AT HEART BUT HIS OWN.
LIES! SHE LIES!
ASK YOURSELF THIS, THANE: WHO BENEFITED FROM THE DEATH OF YOUR FLOCK? WHO, THANE? WHO?
KILL HER! DO IT NOW!
ENOUGH!

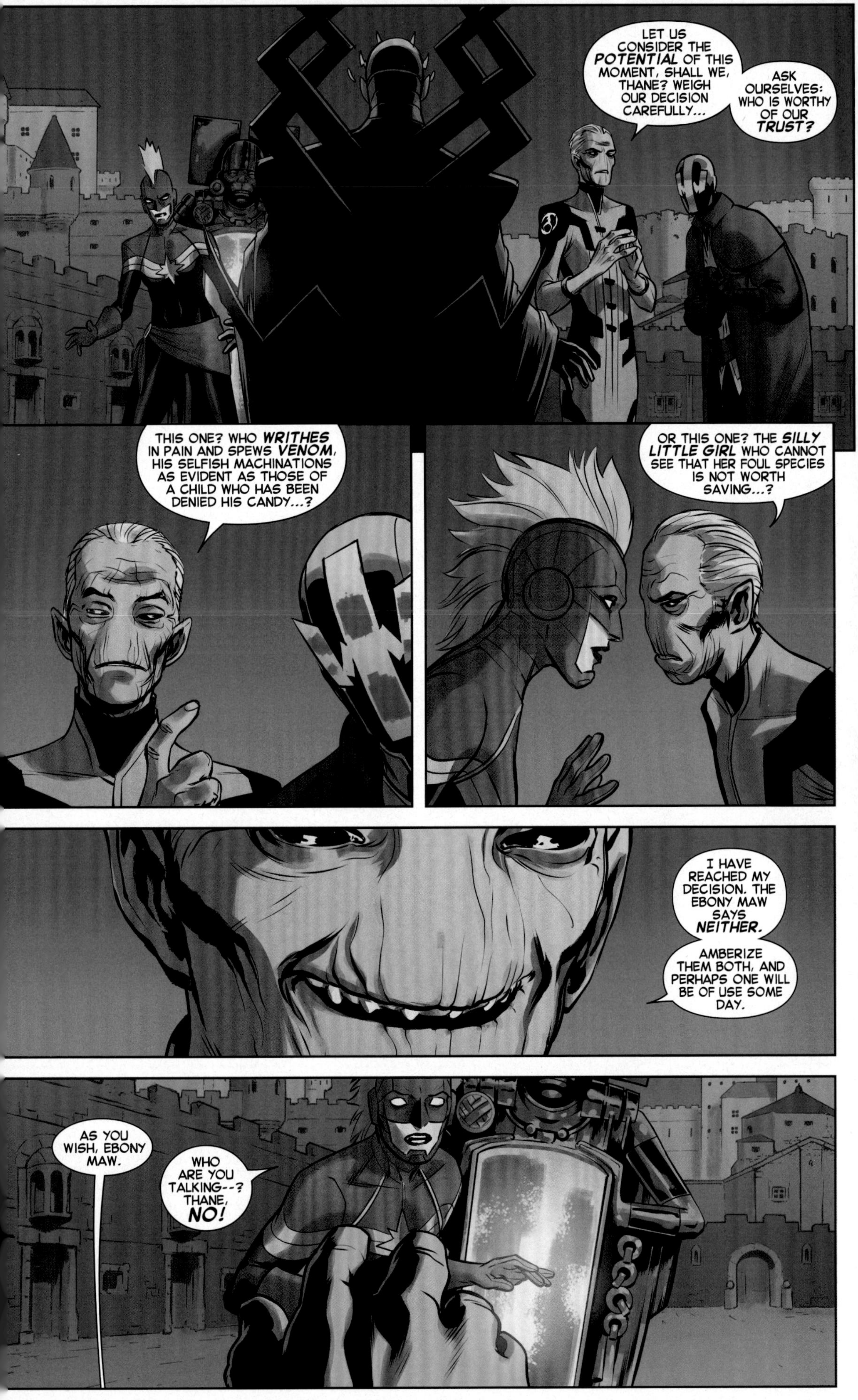
LET US CONSIDER THE POTENTIAL OF THIS MOMENT, SHALL WE, THANE? WEIGH OUR DECISION CAREFULLY...
ASK OURSELVES: WHO IS WORTHY OF OUR TRUST?
THIS ONE? WHO WRITHES IN PAIN AND SPEWS VENOM, HIS SELFISH MACHINATIONS AS EVIDENT AS THOSE OF A CHILD WHO HAS BEEN DENIED HIS CANDY...?
OR THIS ONE? THE SILLY LITTLE GIRL WHO CANNOT SEE THAT HER FOUL SPECIES IS NOT WORTH SAVING...?
I HAVE REACHED MY DECISION. THE EBONY MAW SAYS NEITHER.
AMBERIZE THEM BOTH, AND PERHAPS ONE WILL BE OF USE SOME DAY.
AS YOU WISH, EBONY MAW.
WHO ARE YOU TALKING--? THANE, NO!

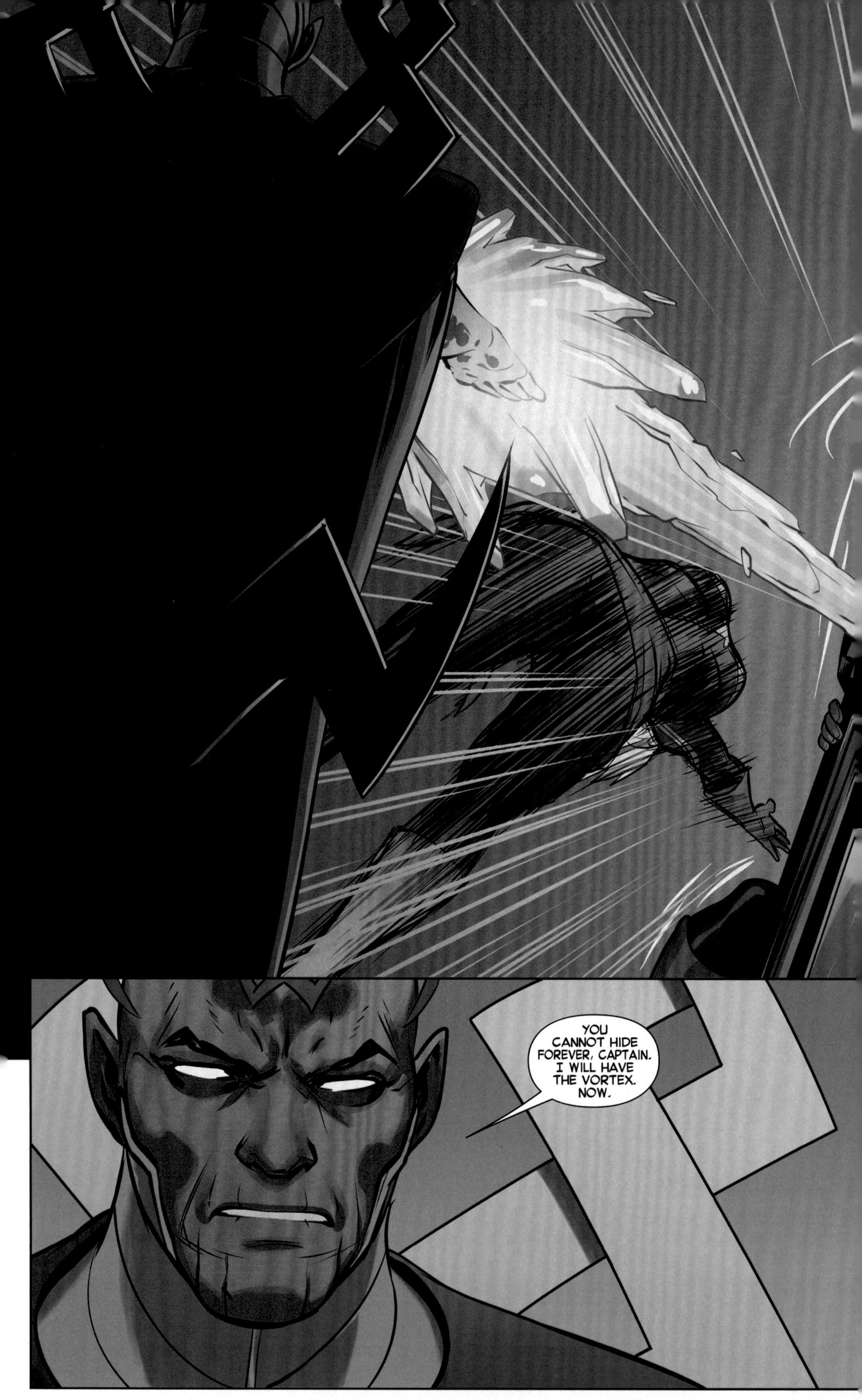
YOU CANNOT HIDE FOREVER, CAPTAIN. I WILL HAVE THE VORTEX. NOW.

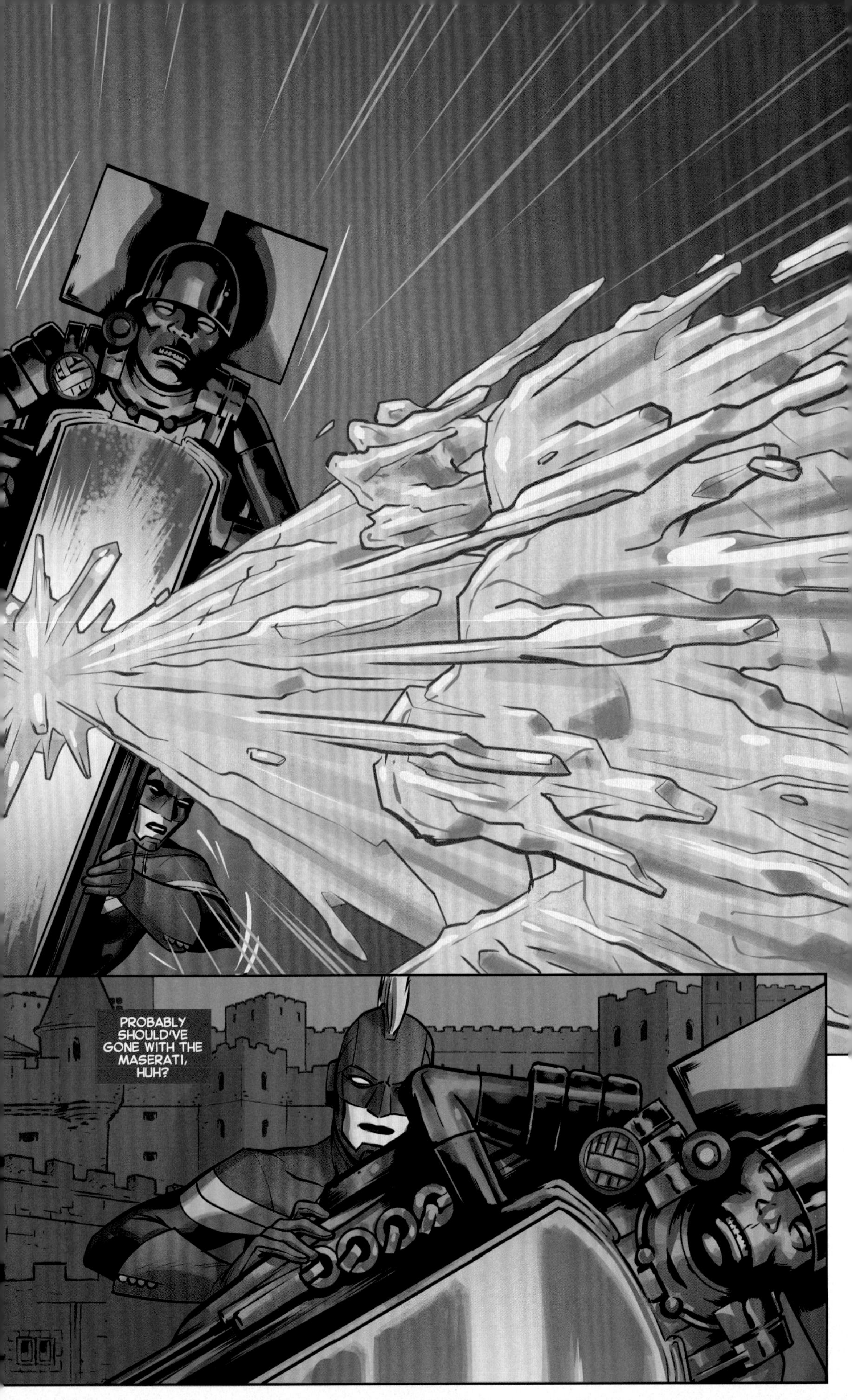
PROBABLY SHOULD'VE GONE WITH THE MASERATI, HUH?

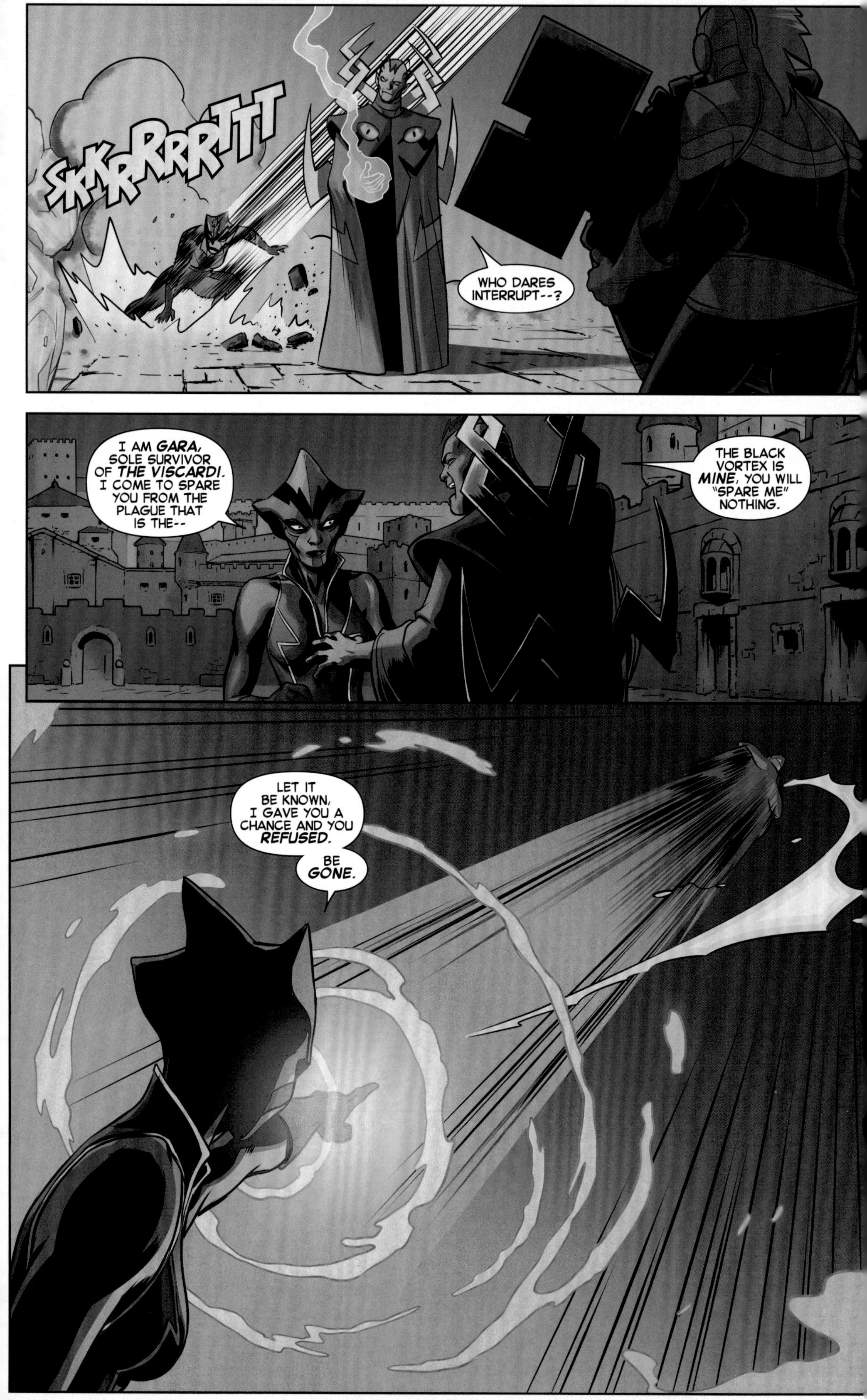
SKKRRRRTTT
WHO DARES INTERRUPT--?
I AM GARA, SOLE SURVIVOR OF THE VISCARDI. I COME TO SPARE YOU FROM THE PLAGUE THAT IS THE--
THE BLACK VORTEX IS MINE, YOU WILL "SPARE ME" NOTHING.
LET IT BE KNOWN, I GAVE YOU A CHANCE AND YOU REFUSED.
BE GONE.

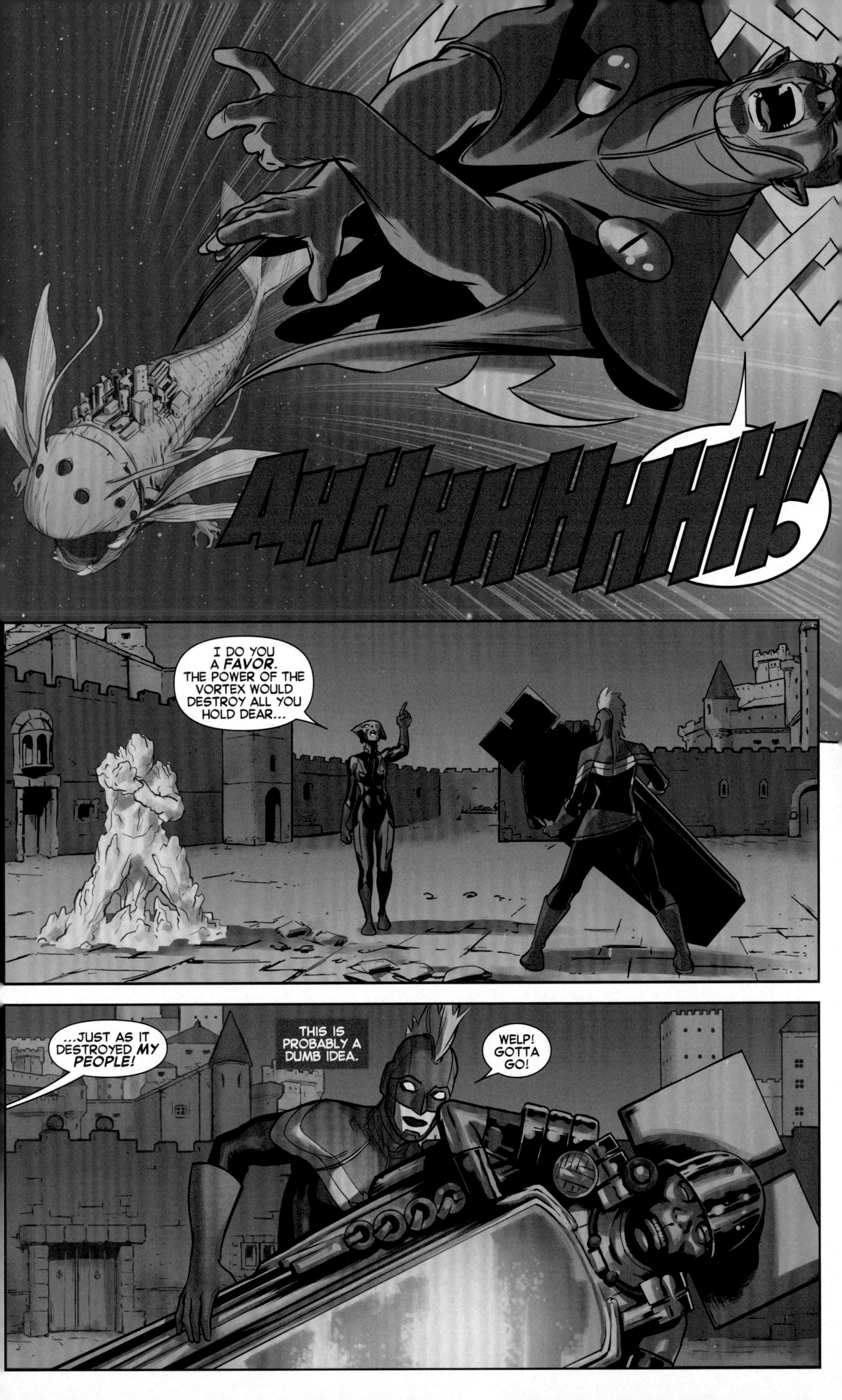
AHHHHHHHHHH!
I DO YOU A FAVOR. THE POWER OF THE VORTEX WOULD DESTROY ALL YOU HOLD DEAR...
...JUST AS IT DESTROYED MY PEOPLE!
THIS IS PROBABLY A DUMB IDEA.
WELP! GOTTA GO!

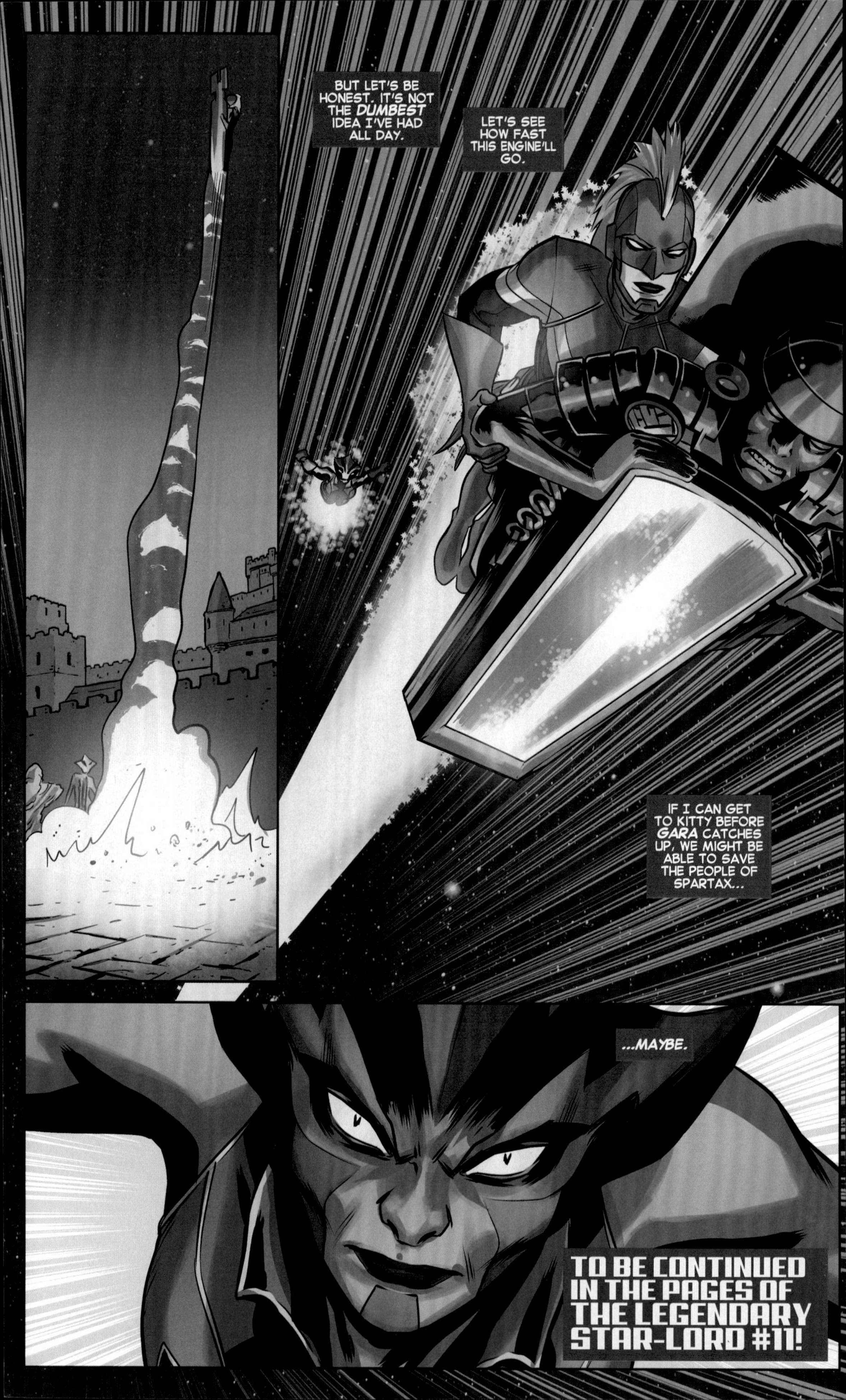
BUT LET'S BE HONEST. IT'S NOT THE DUMBEST IDEA I'VE HAD ALL DAY.
LET'S SEE HOW FAST THIS ENGINE'LL GO.
IF I CAN GET TO KITTY BEFORE GARA CATCHES UP, WE MIGHT BE ABLE TO SAVE THE PEOPLE OF SPARTAX...
...MAYBE.
TO BE CONTINUED IN THE PAGES OF THE LEGENDARY STAR-LORD #11!

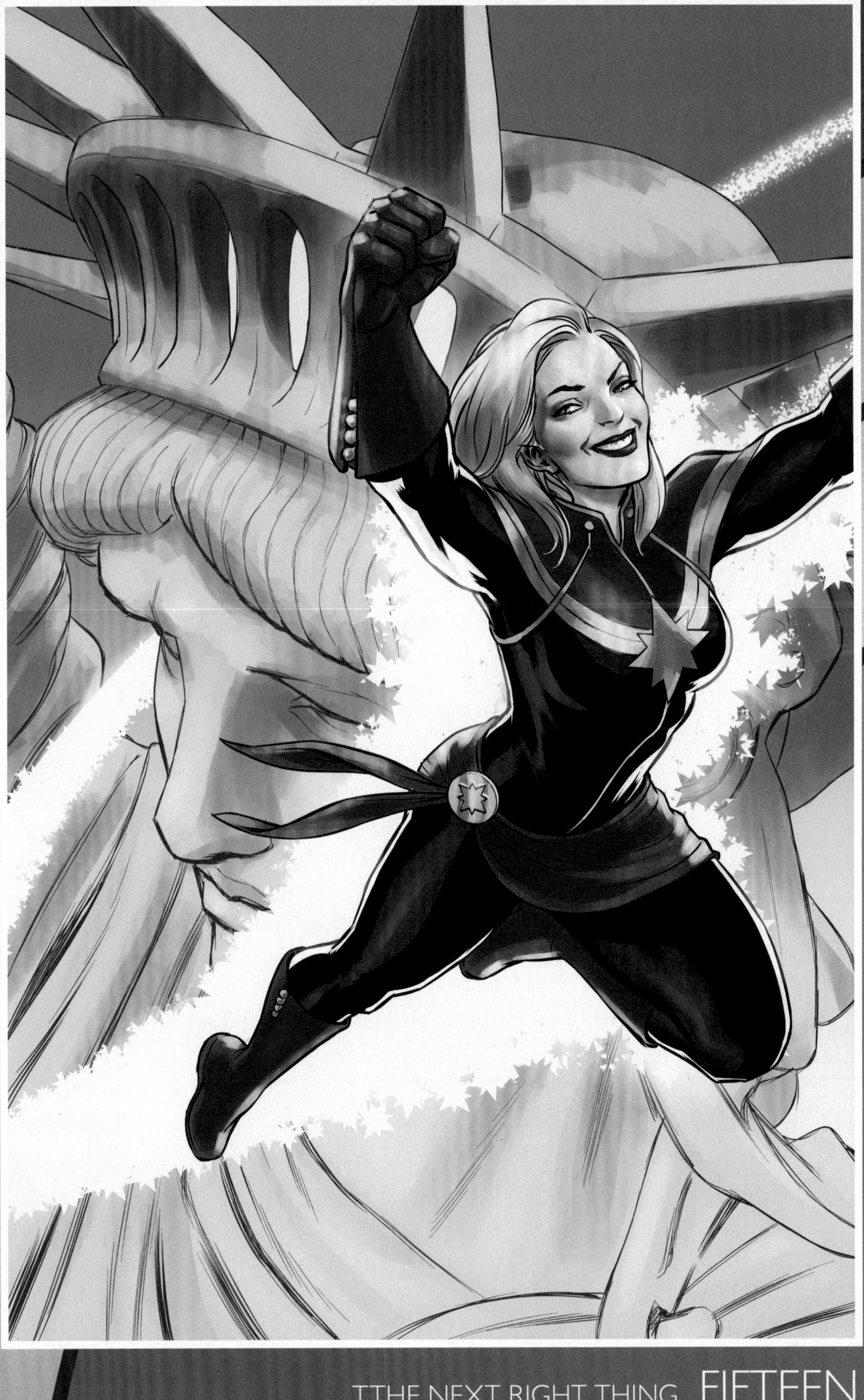

TTHE NEXT RIGHT THING FIFTEEN

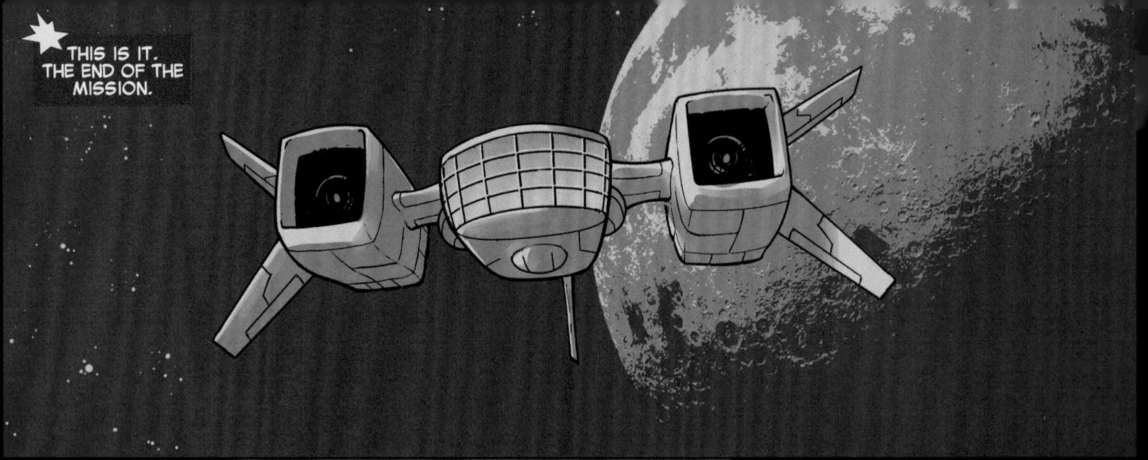
THIS IS IT. THE END OF THE MISSION.
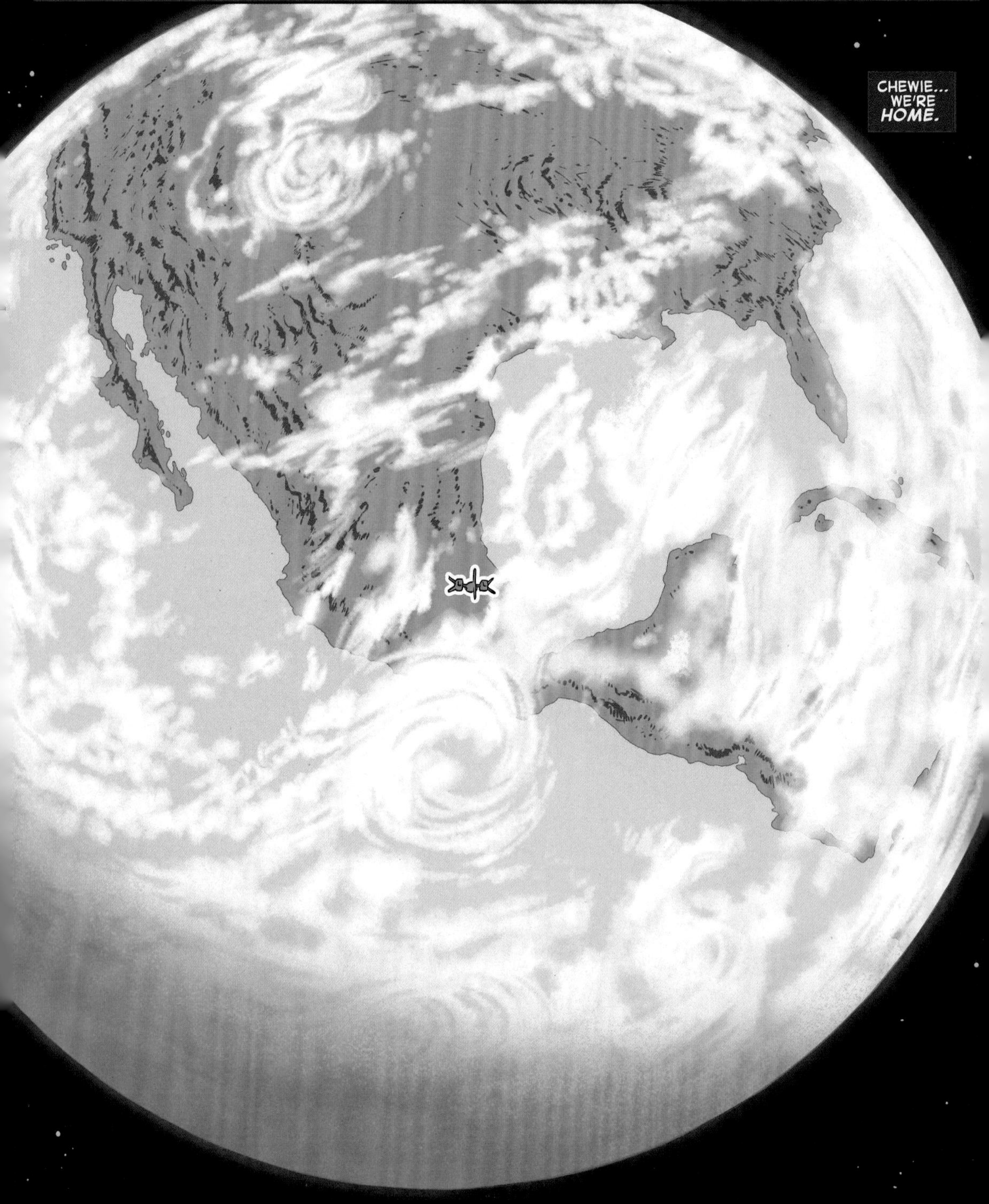
CHEWIE... WE'RE *HOME.*

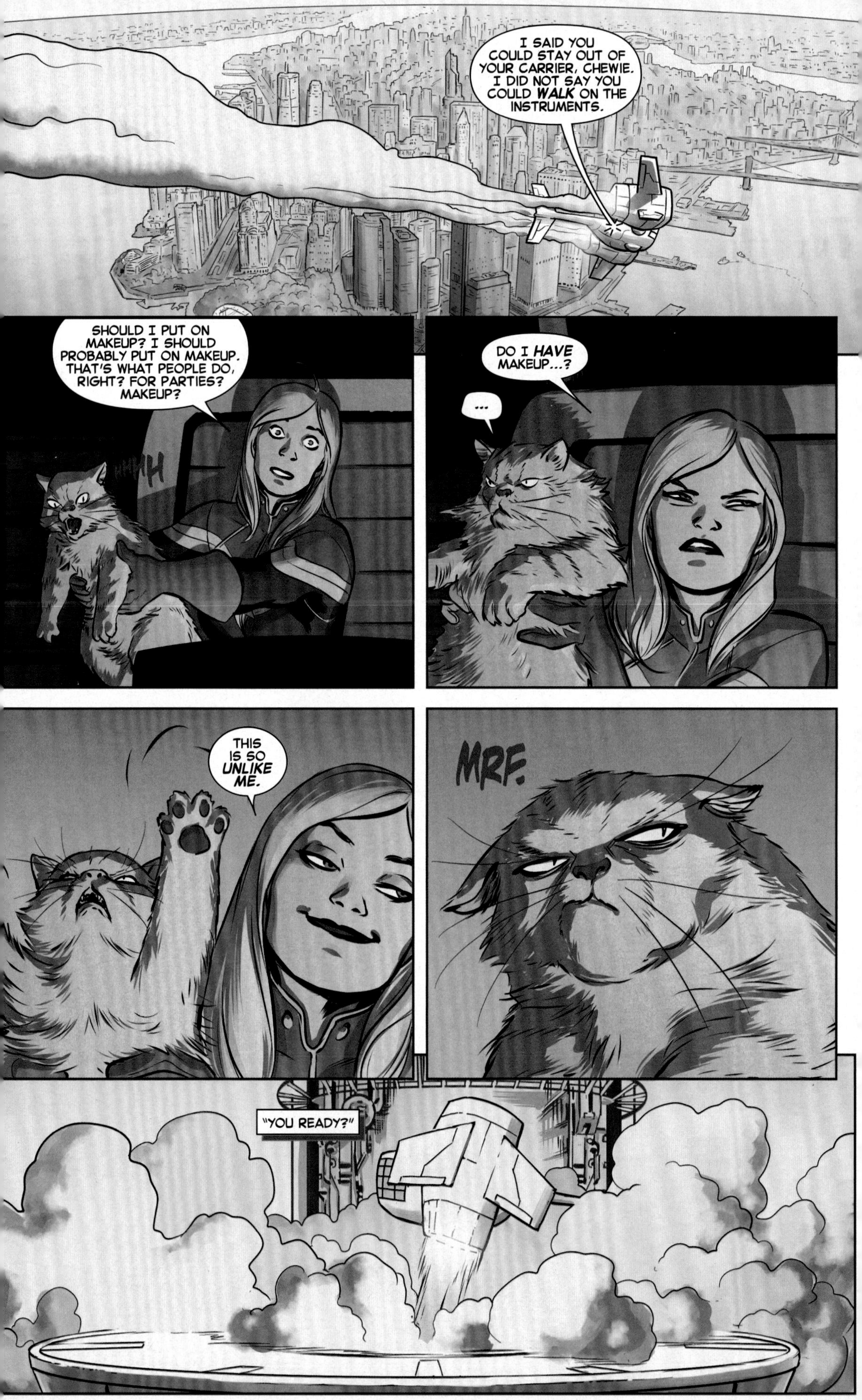
I SAID YOU COULD STAY OUT OF YOUR CARRIER, CHEWIE. I DID NOT SAY YOU COULD WALK ON THE INSTRUMENTS.
SHOULD I PUT ON MAKEUP? I SHOULD PROBABLY PUT ON MAKEUP. THAT'S WHAT PEOPLE DO, RIGHT? FOR PARTIES? MAKEUP?
DO I HAVE MAKEUP...?
...
THIS IS SO UNLIKE ME.
MRF.
"YOU READY?"

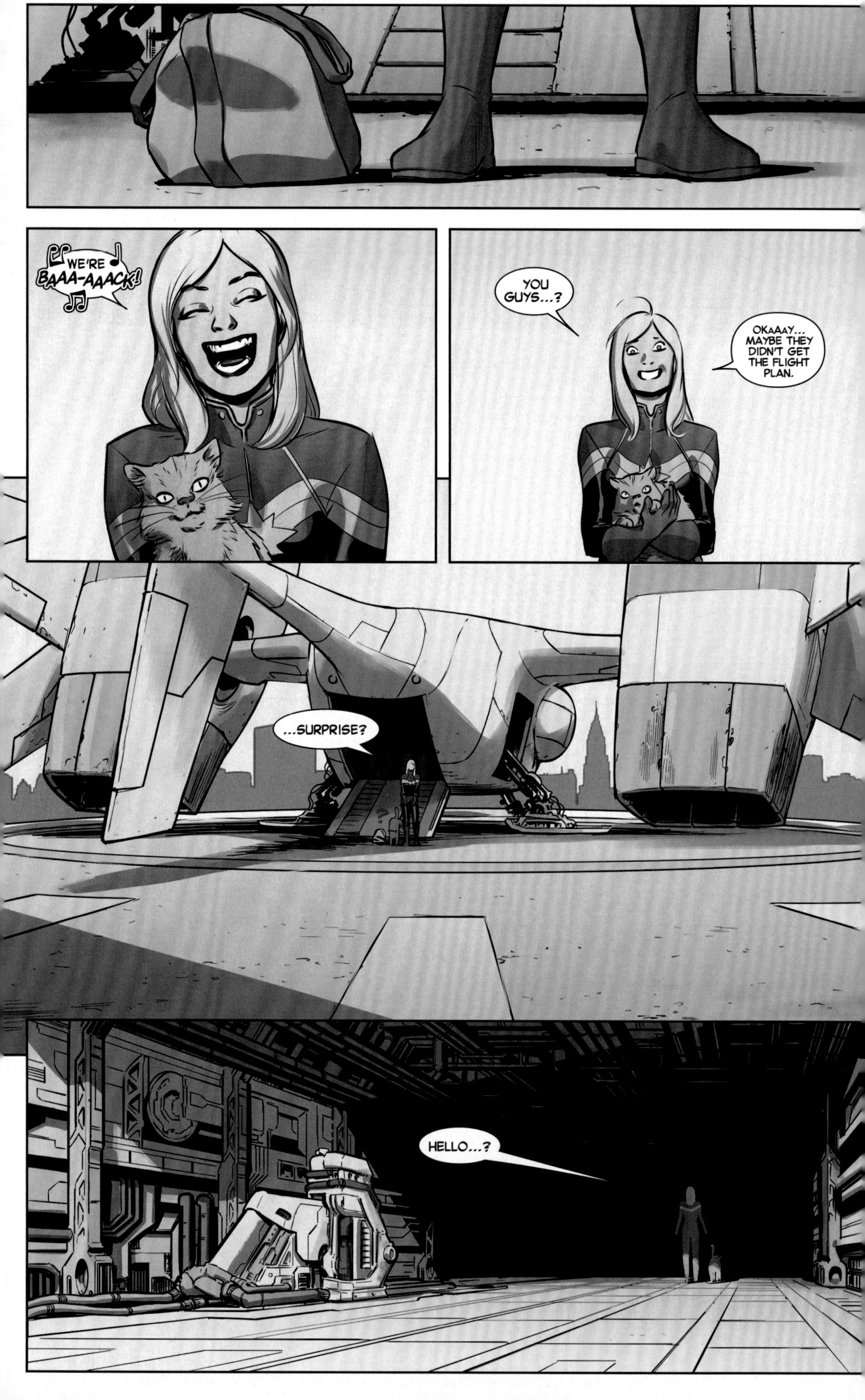
WE'RE BAAA-AAACK!
YOU GUYS...?
OKAAAY... MAYBE THEY DIDN'T GET THE FLIGHT PLAN.
...SURPRISE?
HELLO...?

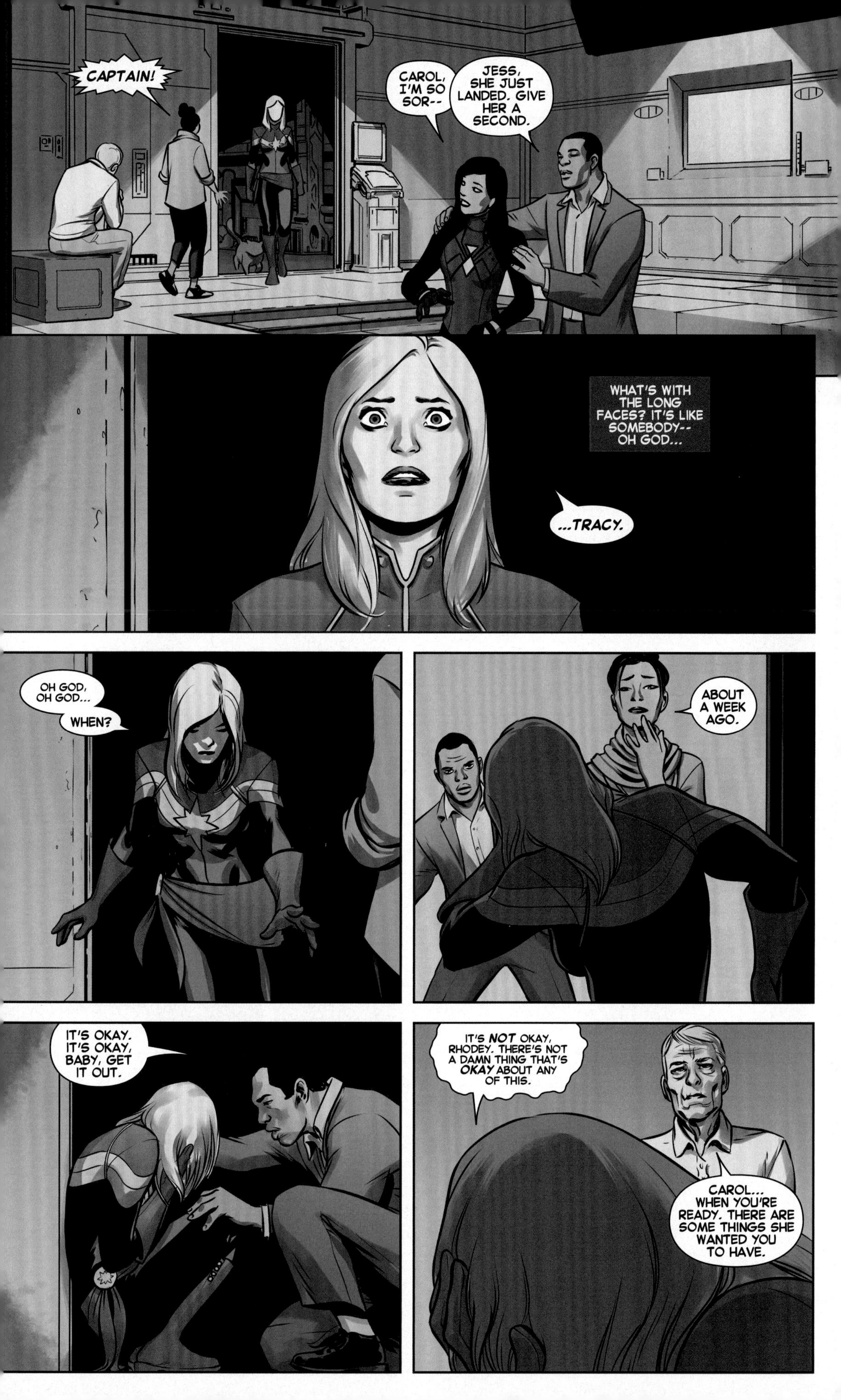

CAPTAIN!
CAROL, I'M SO SOR--
JESS, SHE JUST LANDED. GIVE HER A SECOND.
WHAT'S WITH THE LONG FACES? IT'S LIKE SOMEBODY-- OH GOD...
...TRACY.
OH GOD, OH GOD...
WHEN?
ABOUT A WEEK AGO.
IT'S OKAY. IT'S OKAY, BABY, GET IT OUT.
IT'S NOT OKAY, RHODEY. THERE'S NOT A DAMN THING THAT'S OKAY ABOUT ANY OF THIS.
CAROL... WHEN YOU'RE READY. THERE ARE SOME THINGS SHE WANTED YOU TO HAVE.

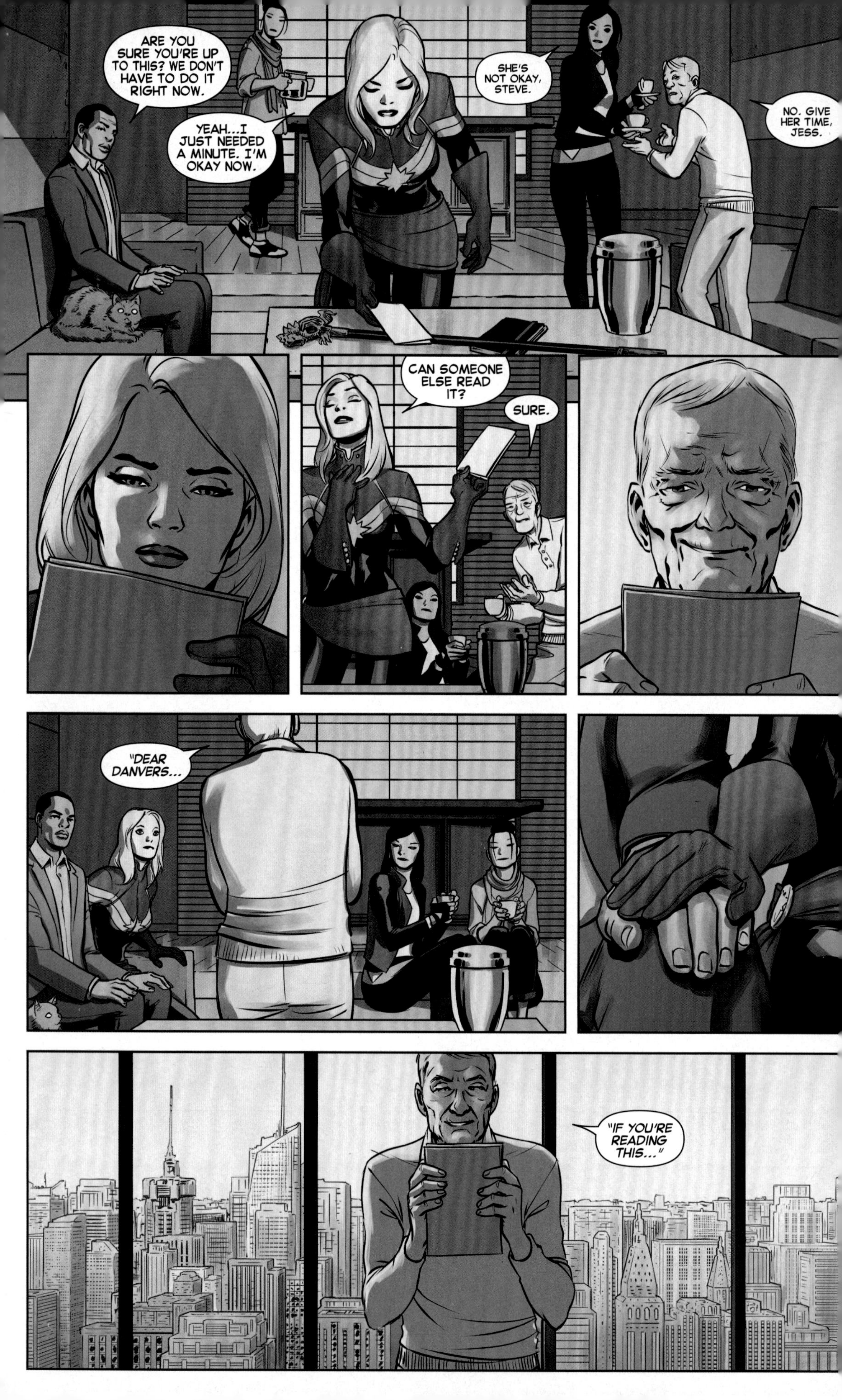
ARE YOU SURE YOU'RE UP TO THIS? WE DON'T HAVE TO DO IT RIGHT NOW.
YEAH...I JUST NEEDED A MINUTE. I'M OKAY NOW.
SHE'S NOT OKAY, STEVE.
NO. GIVE HER TIME, JESS.
CAN SOMEONE ELSE READ IT?
SURE.
"DEAR DANVERS...
"IF YOU'RE READING THIS..."

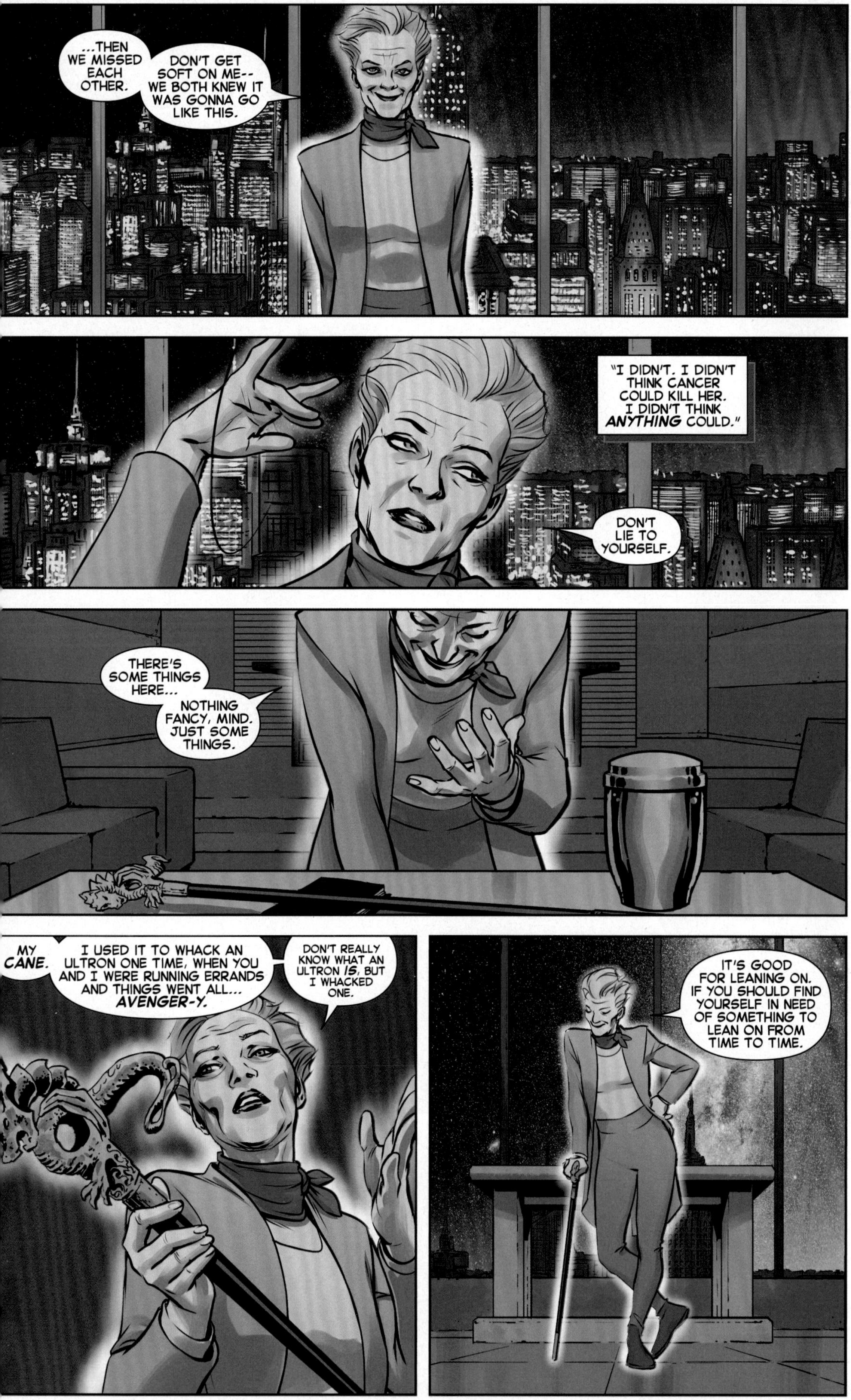

...THEN WE MISSED EACH OTHER.
DON'T GET SOFT ON ME-- WE BOTH KNEW IT WAS GONNA GO LIKE THIS.
"I DIDN'T. I DIDN'T THINK CANCER COULD KILL HER. I DIDN'T THINK ANYTHING COULD."
DON'T LIE TO YOURSELF.
THERE'S SOME THINGS HERE...
NOTHING FANCY, MIND. JUST SOME THINGS.
MY CANE.
I USED IT TO WHACK AN ULTRON ONE TIME, WHEN YOU AND I WERE RUNNING ERRANDS AND THINGS WENT ALL... AVENGER-Y.
DON'T REALLY KNOW WHAT AN ULTRON IS, BUT I WHACKED ONE.
IT'S GOOD FOR LEANING ON. IF YOU SHOULD FIND YOURSELF IN NEED OF SOMETHING TO LEAN ON FROM TIME TO TIME.

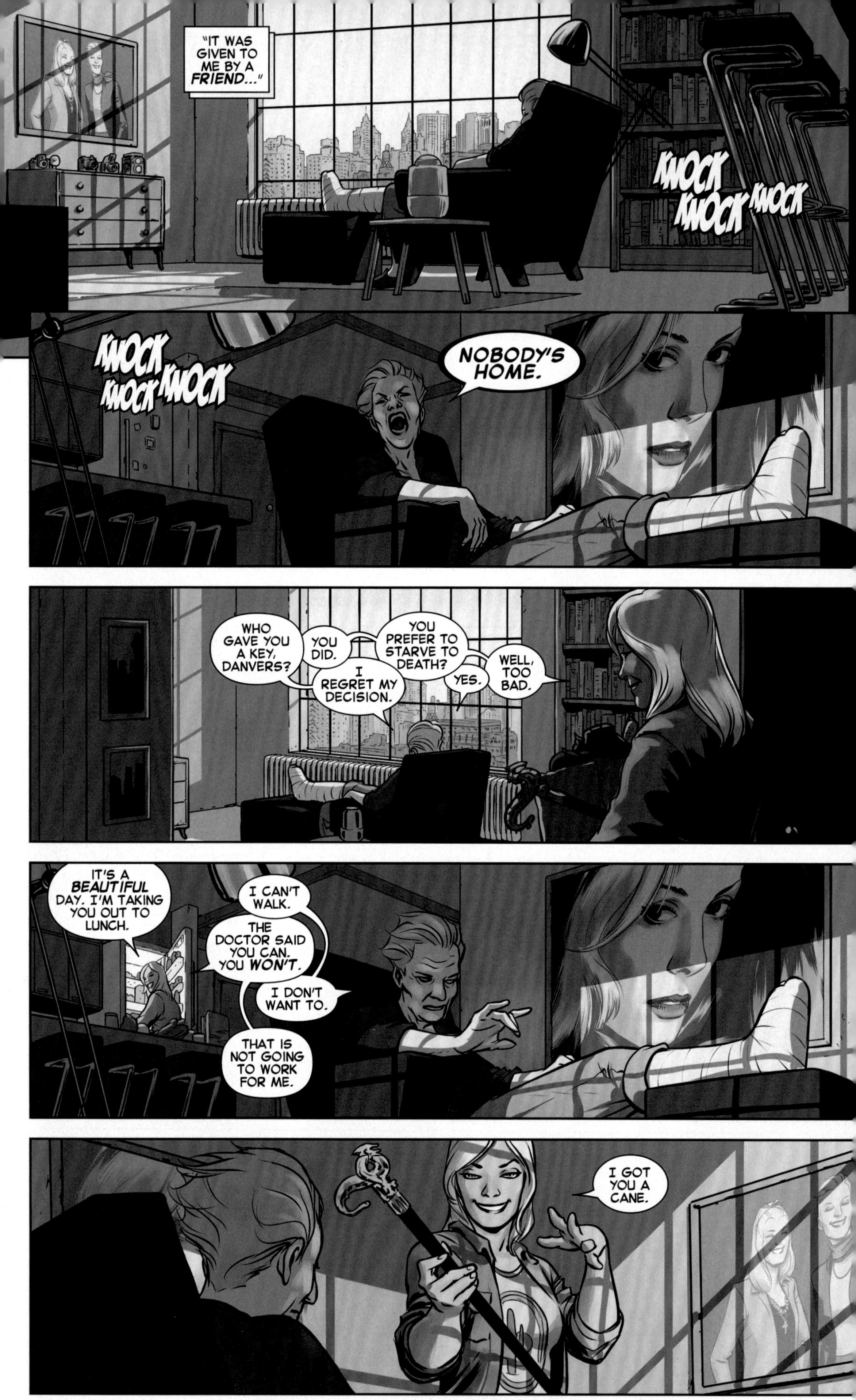
"IT WAS GIVEN TO ME BY A FRIEND..."
KNOCK KNOCK KNOCK
KNOCK KNOCK KNOCK
NOBODY'S HOME.
WHO GAVE YOU A KEY, DANVERS?
YOU DID.
I REGRET MY DECISION.
YOU PREFER TO STARVE TO DEATH?
YES.
WELL, TOO BAD.
IT'S A BEAUTIFUL DAY. I'M TAKING YOU OUT TO LUNCH.
I CAN'T WALK.
THE DOCTOR SAID YOU CAN. YOU WON'T.
I DON'T WANT TO.
THAT IS NOT GOING TO WORK FOR ME.
I GOT YOU A CANE.

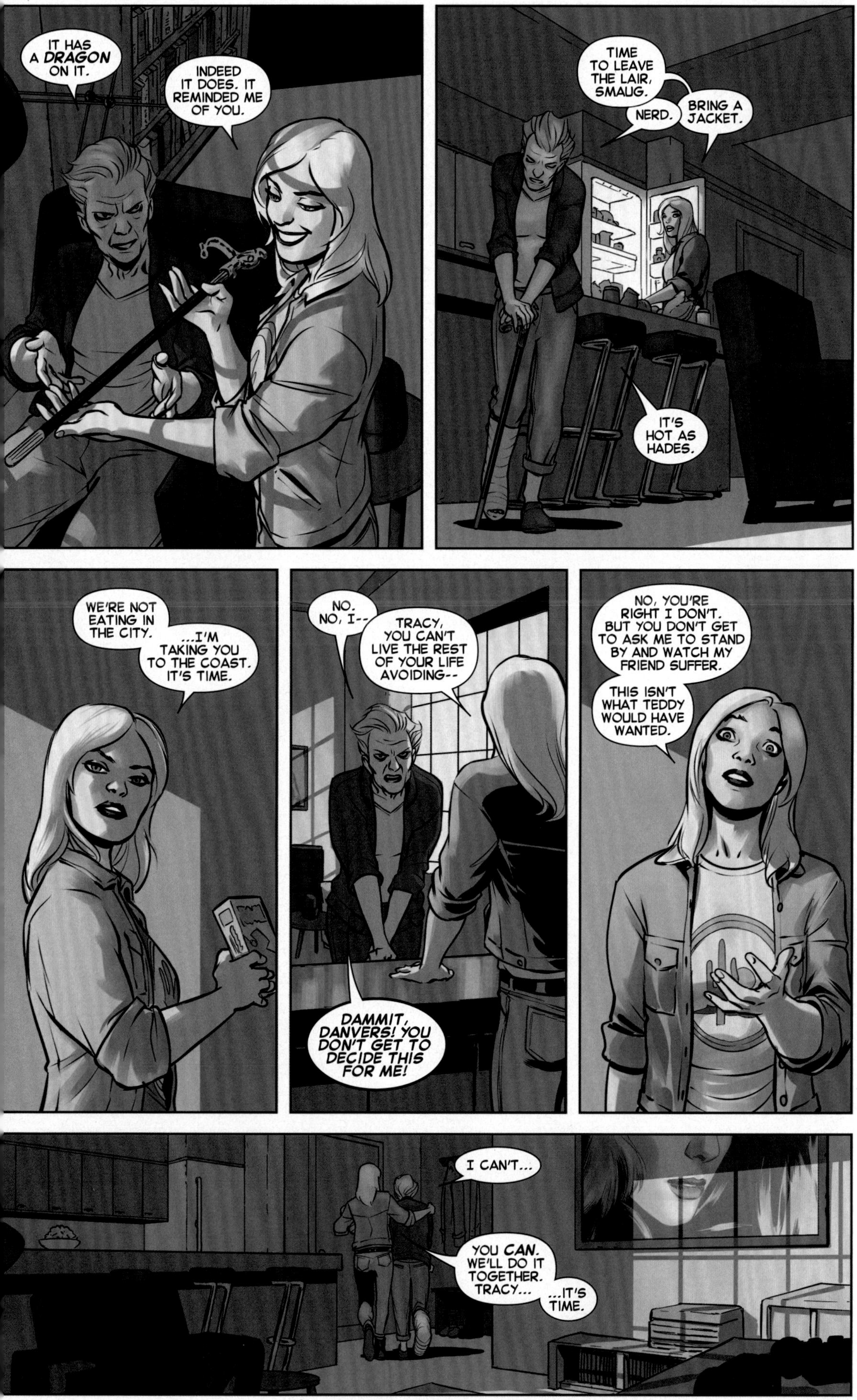

IT HAS A DRAGON ON IT.
INDEED IT DOES. IT REMINDED ME OF YOU.
TIME TO LEAVE THE LAIR, SMAUG.
NERD.
BRING A JACKET.
IT'S HOT AS HADES.
WE'RE NOT EATING IN THE CITY.
...I'M TAKING YOU TO THE COAST. IT'S TIME.
NO. NO, I--
TRACY, YOU CAN'T LIVE THE REST OF YOUR LIFE AVOIDING--
DAMMIT, DANVERS! YOU DON'T GET TO DECIDE THIS FOR ME!
NO, YOU'RE RIGHT I DON'T. BUT YOU DON'T GET TO ASK ME TO STAND BY AND WATCH MY FRIEND SUFFER.
THIS ISN'T WHAT TEDDY WOULD HAVE WANTED.
I CAN'T...
YOU CAN. WE'LL DO IT TOGETHER. TRACY...
...IT'S TIME.

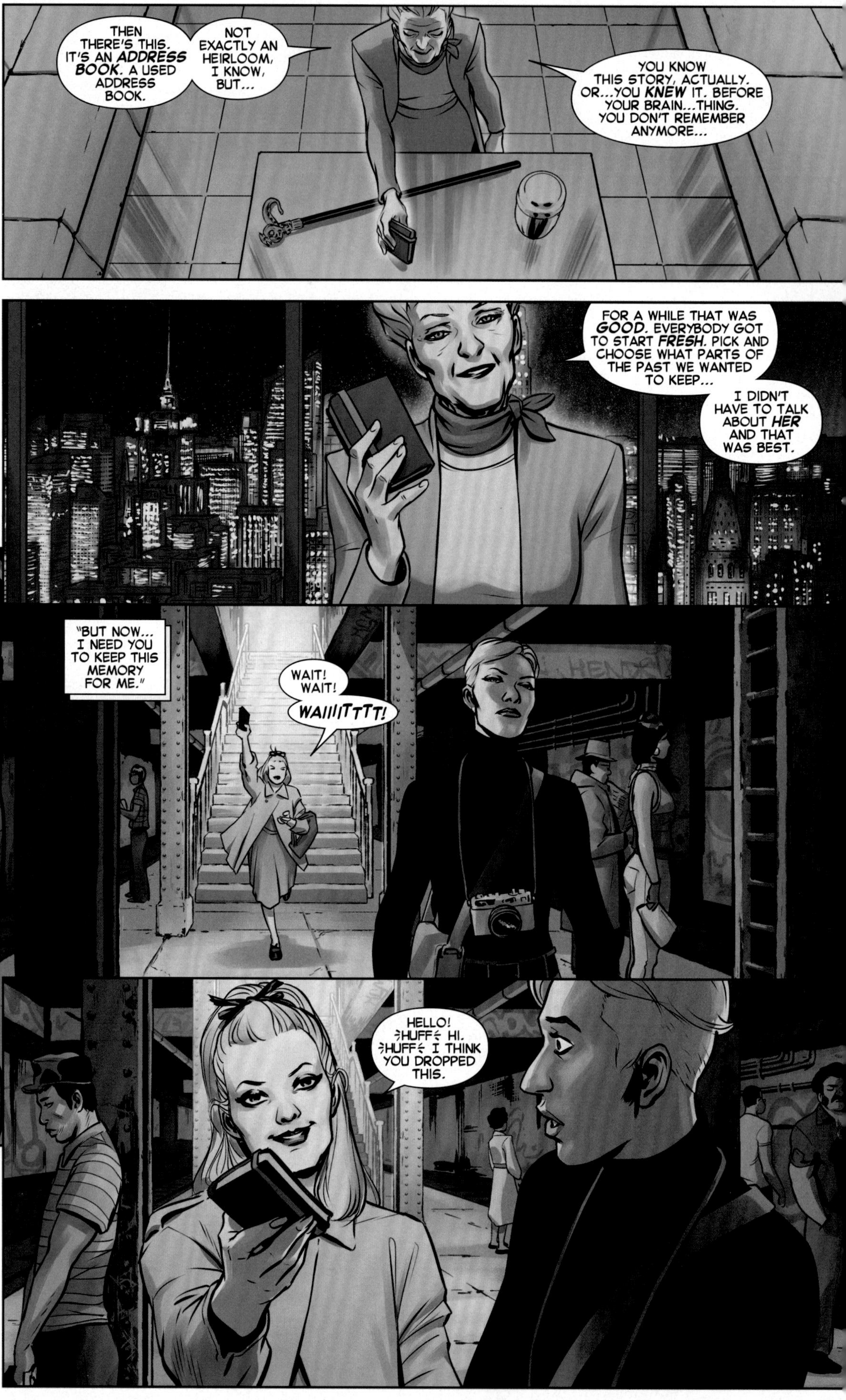

THEN THERE'S THIS. IT'S AN ADDRESS BOOK. A USED ADDRESS BOOK.
NOT EXACTLY AN HEIRLOOM, I KNOW, BUT...
YOU KNOW THIS STORY, ACTUALLY. OR...YOU KNEW IT. BEFORE YOUR BRAIN...THING. YOU DON'T REMEMBER ANYMORE...
FOR A WHILE THAT WAS GOOD. EVERYBODY GOT TO START FRESH. PICK AND CHOOSE WHAT PARTS OF THE PAST WE WANTED TO KEEP...
I DIDN'T HAVE TO TALK ABOUT HER AND THAT WAS BEST.
"BUT NOW... I NEED YOU TO KEEP THIS MEMORY FOR ME."
WAIT! WAIT! WAIIIITTTT!
HELLO! ≡HUFF≡ HI. ≡HUFF≡ I THINK YOU DROPPED THIS.

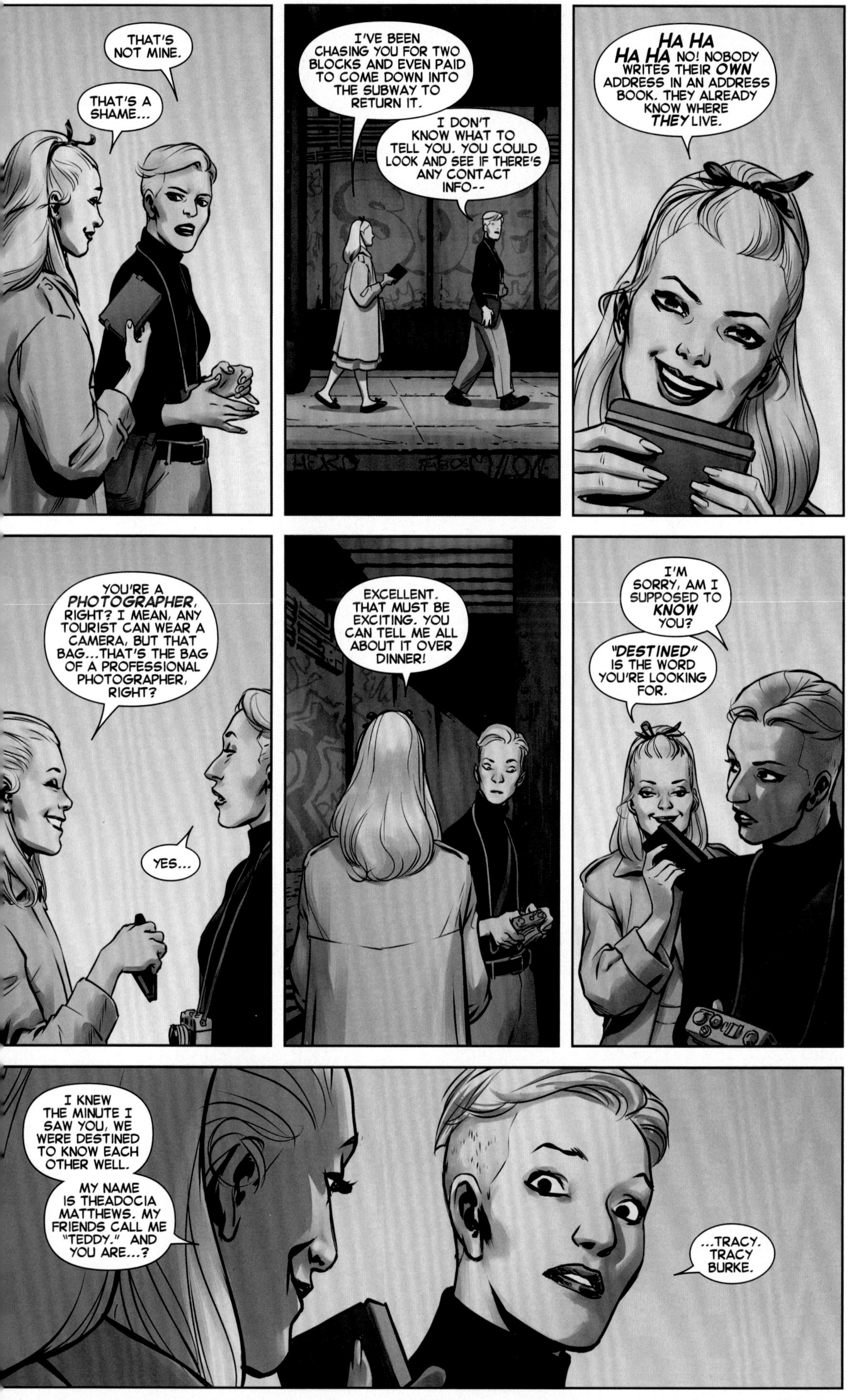
THAT'S NOT MINE.
THAT'S A SHAME...
I'VE BEEN CHASING YOU FOR TWO BLOCKS AND EVEN PAID TO COME DOWN INTO THE SUBWAY TO RETURN IT.
I DON'T KNOW WHAT TO TELL YOU. YOU COULD LOOK AND SEE IF THERE'S ANY CONTACT INFO--
HA HA HA HA NO! NOBODY WRITES THEIR OWN ADDRESS IN AN ADDRESS BOOK. THEY ALREADY KNOW WHERE THEY LIVE.
YOU'RE A PHOTOGRAPHER, RIGHT? I MEAN, ANY TOURIST CAN WEAR A CAMERA, BUT THAT BAG...THAT'S THE BAG OF A PROFESSIONAL PHOTOGRAPHER, RIGHT?
YES...
EXCELLENT. THAT MUST BE EXCITING. YOU CAN TELL ME ALL ABOUT IT OVER DINNER!
I'M SORRY, AM I SUPPOSED TO KNOW YOU?
"DESTINED" IS THE WORD YOU'RE LOOKING FOR.
I KNEW THE MINUTE I SAW YOU, WE WERE DESTINED TO KNOW EACH OTHER WELL.
MY NAME IS THEADOCIA MATTHEWS. MY FRIENDS CALL ME "TEDDY." AND YOU ARE...?
...TRACY. TRACY BURKE.

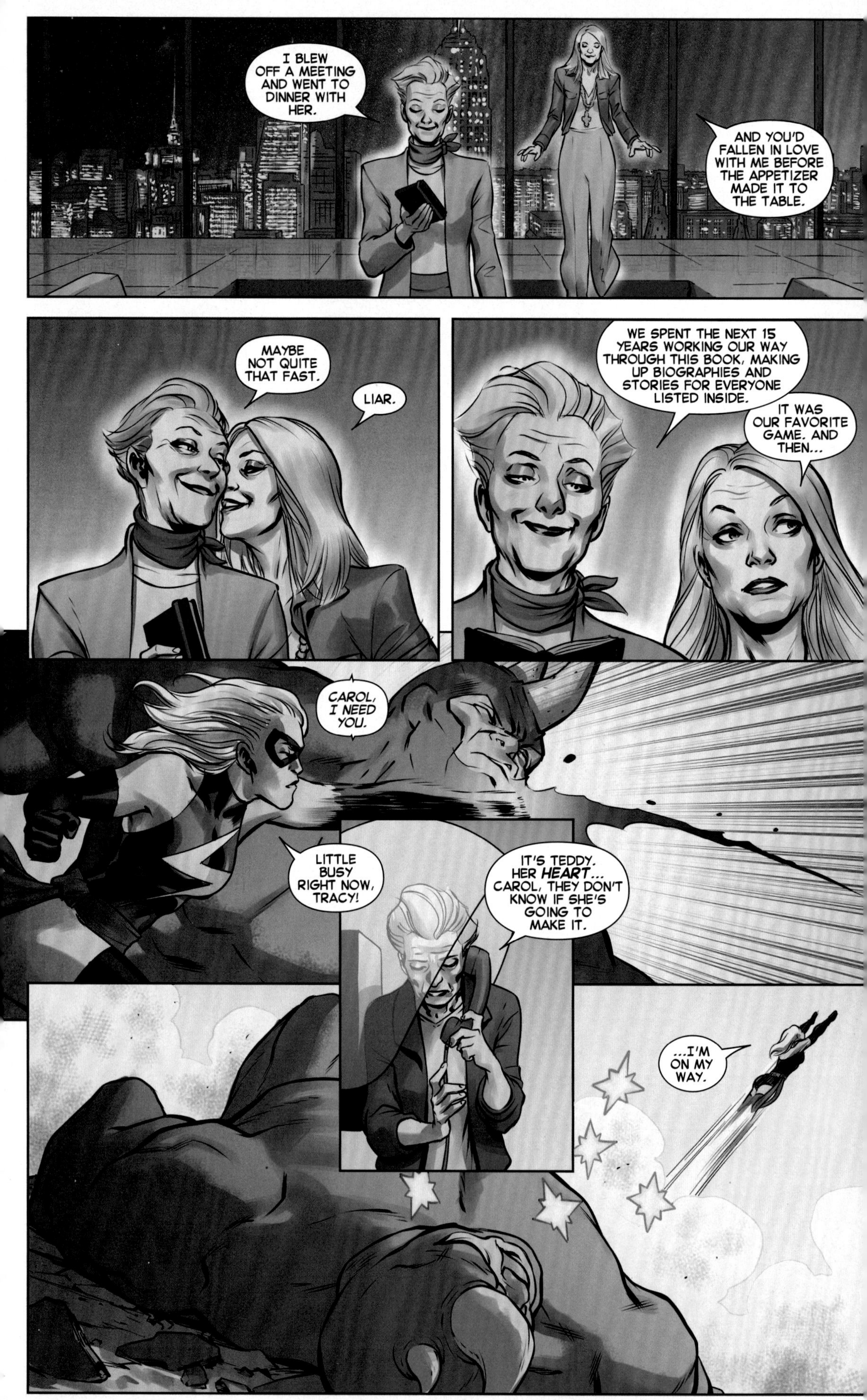
I BLEW OFF A MEETING AND WENT TO DINNER WITH HER.
AND YOU'D FALLEN IN LOVE WITH ME BEFORE THE APPETIZER MADE IT TO THE TABLE.
MAYBE NOT QUITE THAT FAST.
LIAR.
WE SPENT THE NEXT 15 YEARS WORKING OUR WAY THROUGH THIS BOOK, MAKING UP BIOGRAPHIES AND STORIES FOR EVERYONE LISTED INSIDE.
IT WAS OUR FAVORITE GAME. AND THEN...
CAROL, I NEED YOU.
LITTLE BUSY RIGHT NOW, TRACY!
IT'S TEDDY. HER *HEART*... CAROL, THEY DON'T KNOW IF SHE'S GOING TO MAKE IT.
...I'M ON MY WAY.

"YOU WERE THERE WITHIN *MINUTES*...

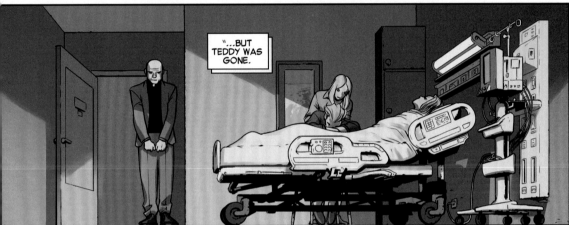

"...BUT TEDDY WAS GONE.

"THEY LET US HAVE THE ROOM FOR A WHILE. TO WORK IT THROUGH, TO SAY GOOD-BYE.

"I WOULD HAVE STAYED THERE WITH HER FOREVER, IF YOU'D'VE LET ME.

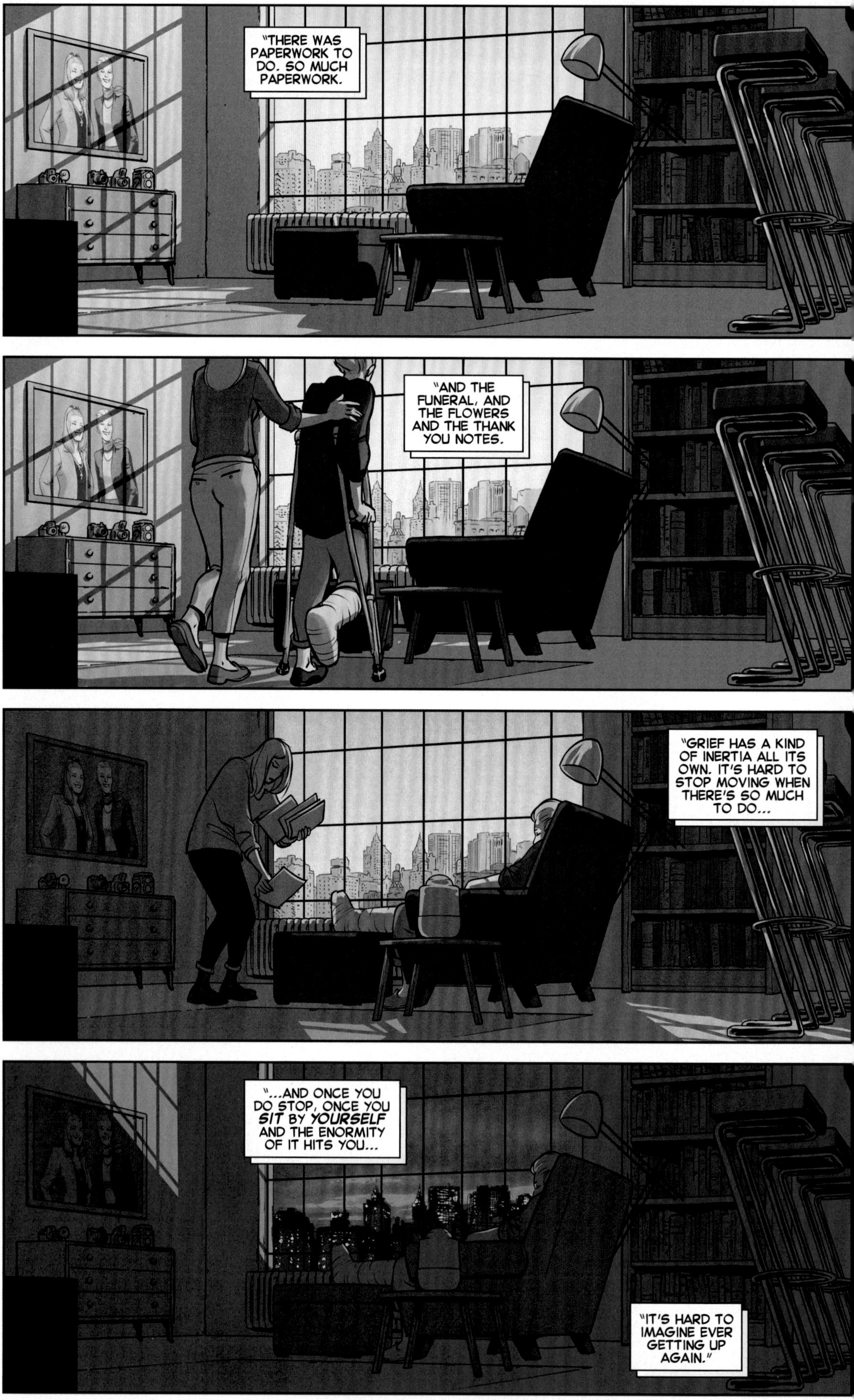
"THERE WAS PAPERWORK TO DO. SO MUCH PAPERWORK.
"AND THE FUNERAL, AND THE FLOWERS AND THE THANK YOU NOTES.
"GRIEF HAS A KIND OF INERTIA ALL ITS OWN. IT'S HARD TO STOP MOVING WHEN THERE'S SO MUCH TO DO...
"...AND ONCE YOU DO STOP, ONCE YOU SIT BY YOURSELF AND THE ENORMITY OF IT HITS YOU...
"IT'S HARD TO IMAGINE EVER GETTING UP AGAIN."

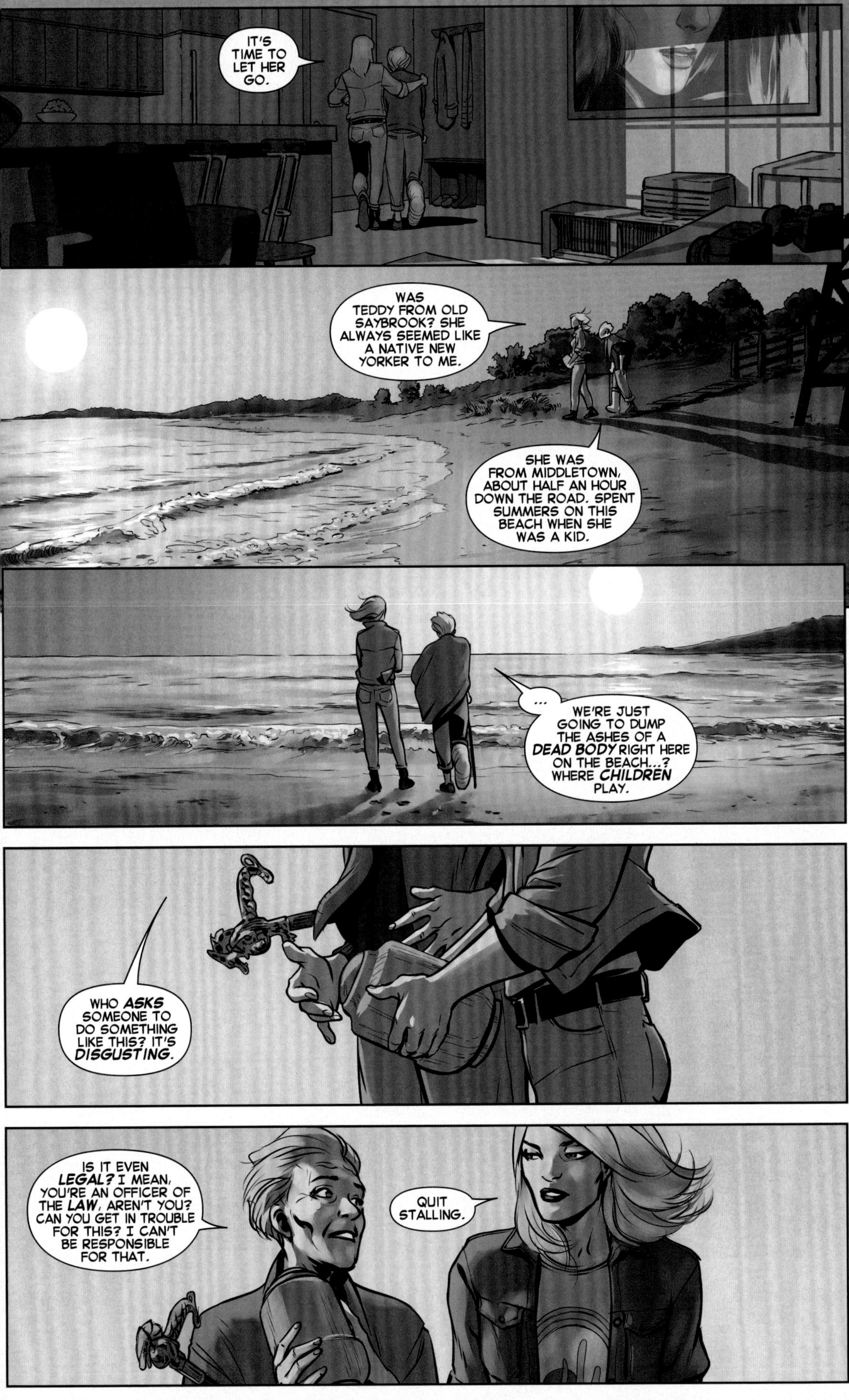
IT'S TIME TO LET HER GO.
WAS TEDDY FROM OLD SAYBROOK? SHE ALWAYS SEEMED LIKE A NATIVE NEW YORKER TO ME.
SHE WAS FROM MIDDLETOWN, ABOUT HALF AN HOUR DOWN THE ROAD. SPENT SUMMERS ON THIS BEACH WHEN SHE WAS A KID.
...
WE'RE JUST GOING TO DUMP THE ASHES OF A DEAD BODY RIGHT HERE ON THE BEACH...? WHERE CHILDREN PLAY.
WHO ASKS SOMEONE TO DO SOMETHING LIKE THIS? IT'S DISGUSTING.
IS IT EVEN LEGAL? I MEAN, YOU'RE AN OFFICER OF THE LAW, AREN'T YOU? CAN YOU GET IN TROUBLE FOR THIS? I CAN'T BE RESPONSIBLE FOR THAT.
QUIT STALLING.

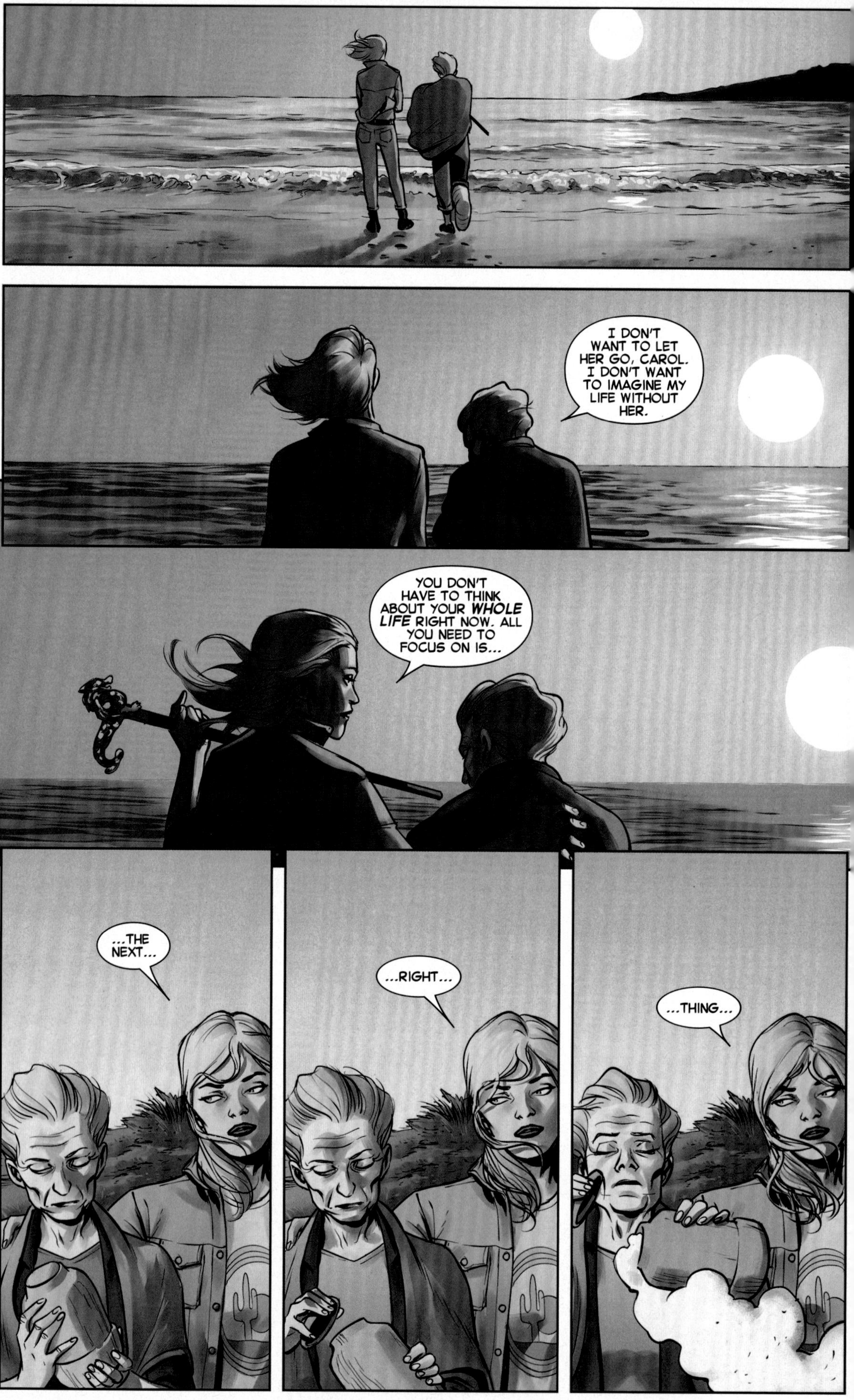
I DON'T WANT TO LET HER GO, CAROL. I DON'T WANT TO IMAGINE MY LIFE WITHOUT HER.
YOU DON'T HAVE TO THINK ABOUT YOUR *WHOLE LIFE* RIGHT NOW. ALL YOU NEED TO FOCUS ON IS...
...THE NEXT...
...RIGHT...
...THING...

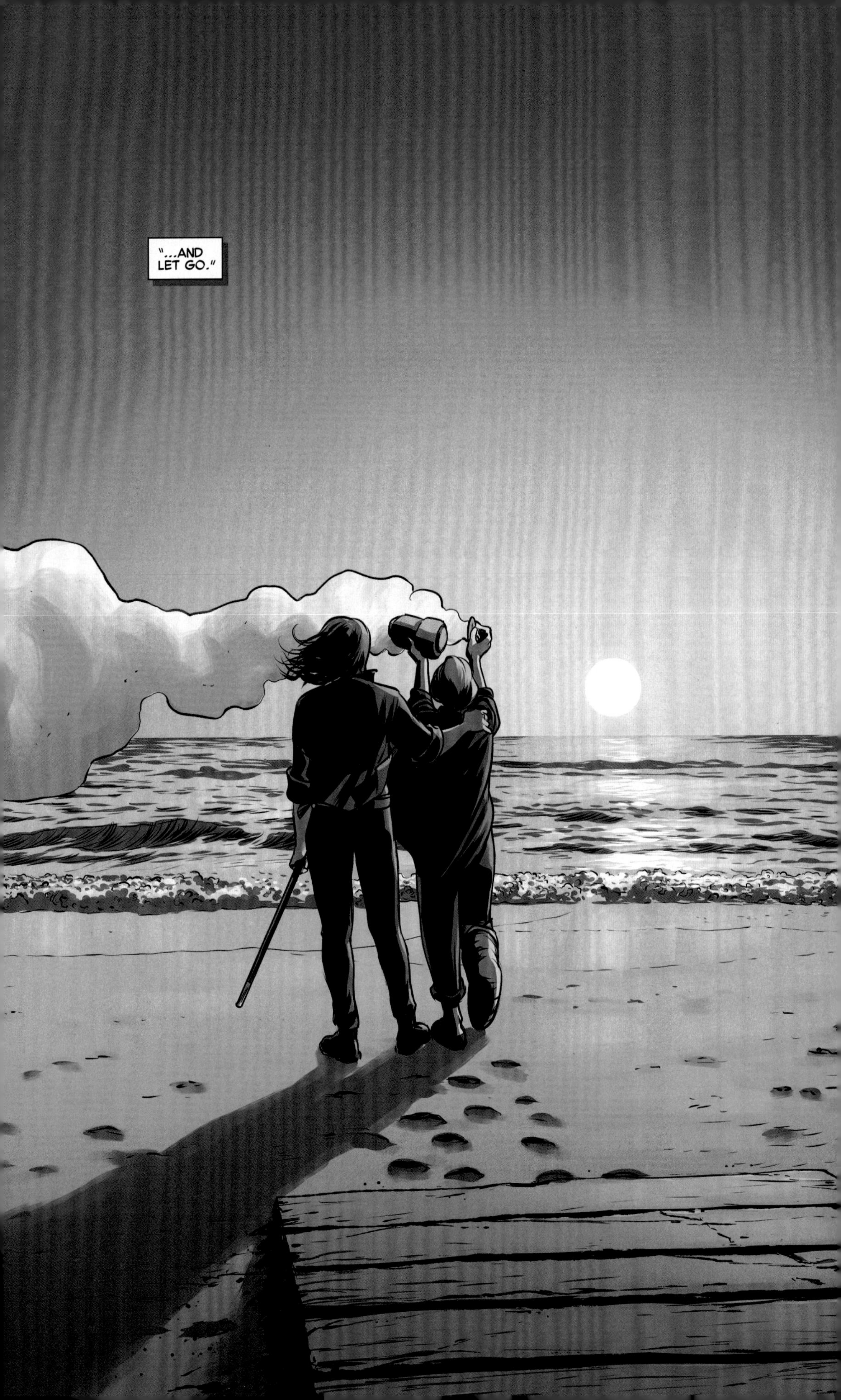
"...AND LET GO."

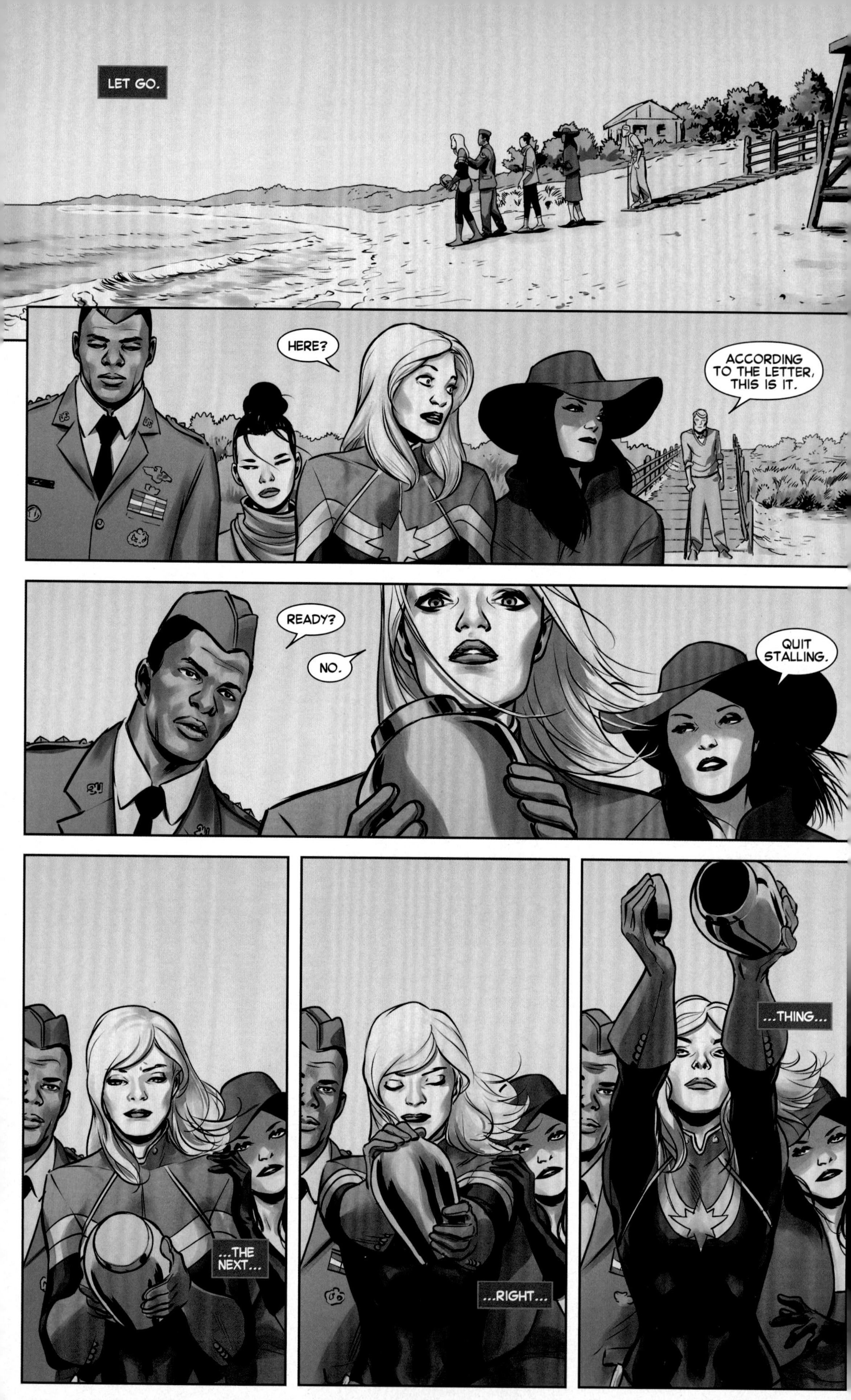
LET GO.
HERE?
ACCORDING TO THE LETTER, THIS IS IT.
READY?
NO.
QUIT STALLING.
...THE NEXT...
...RIGHT...
...THING...

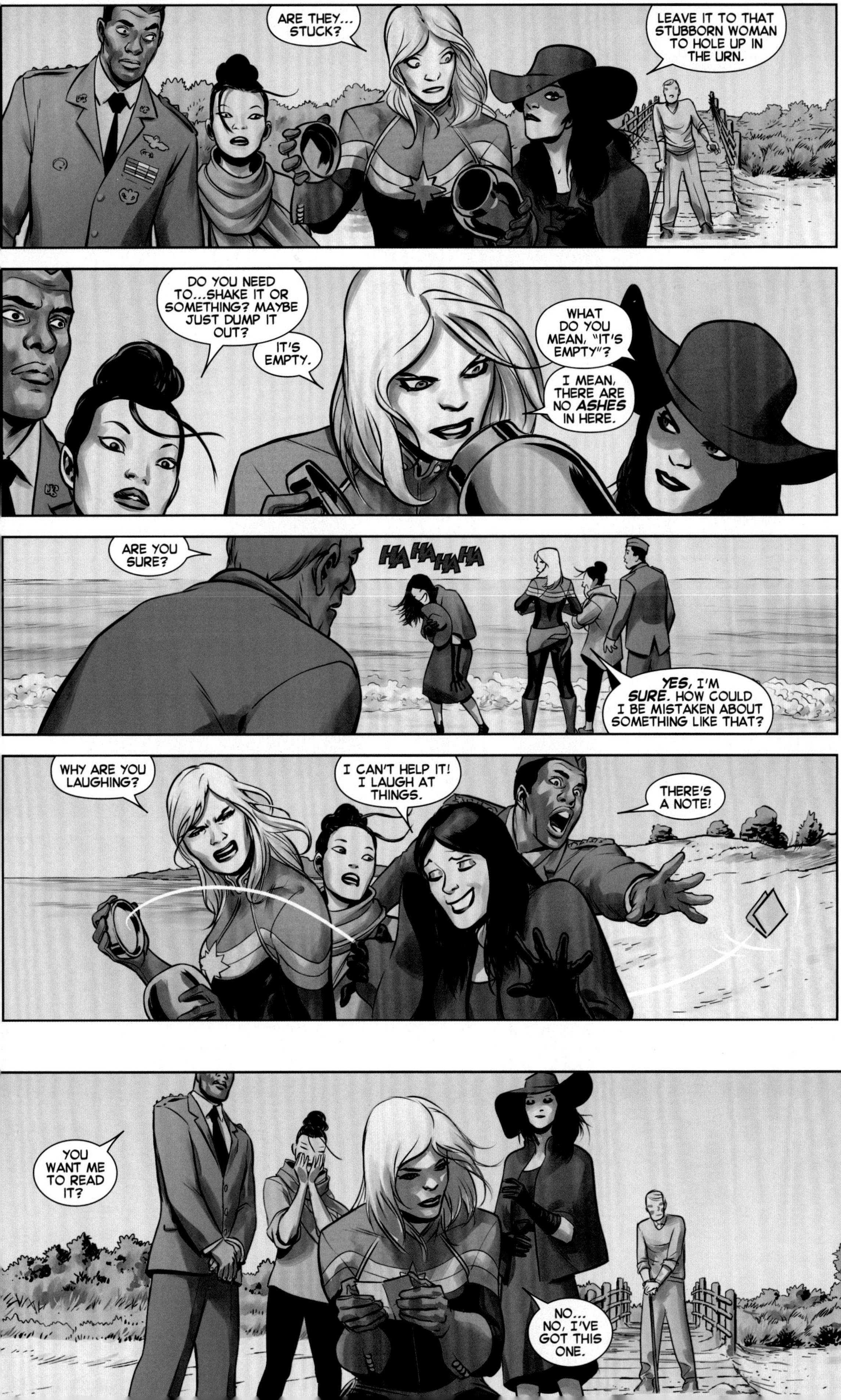
ARE THEY... STUCK?
LEAVE IT TO THAT STUBBORN WOMAN TO HOLE UP IN THE URN.
DO YOU NEED TO...SHAKE IT OR SOMETHING? MAYBE JUST DUMP IT OUT?
IT'S EMPTY.
WHAT DO YOU MEAN, "IT'S EMPTY"?
I MEAN, THERE ARE NO ASHES IN HERE.
ARE YOU SURE?
HAHAHAHA
YES, I'M SURE. HOW COULD I BE MISTAKEN ABOUT SOMETHING LIKE THAT?
WHY ARE YOU LAUGHING?
I CAN'T HELP IT! I LAUGH AT THINGS.
THERE'S A NOTE!
YOU WANT ME TO READ IT?
NO... NO, I'VE GOT THIS ONE.

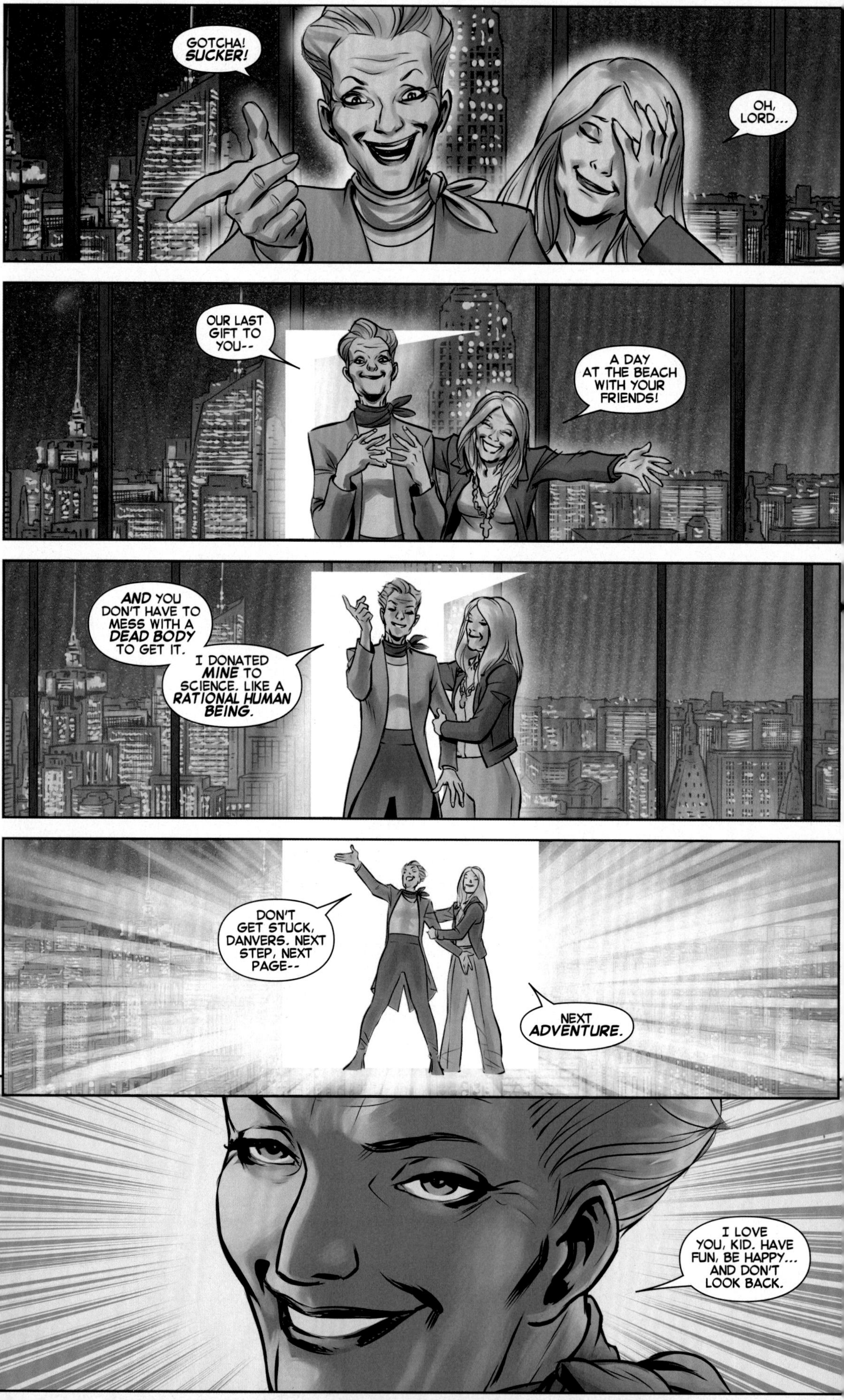
GOTCHA! SUCKER!
OH, LORD...
OUR LAST GIFT TO YOU--
A DAY AT THE BEACH WITH YOUR FRIENDS!
AND YOU DON'T HAVE TO MESS WITH A DEAD BODY TO GET IT.
I DONATED MINE TO SCIENCE. LIKE A RATIONAL HUMAN BEING.
DON'T GET STUCK, DANVERS. NEXT STEP, NEXT PAGE--
NEXT ADVENTURE.
I LOVE YOU, KID. HAVE FUN, BE HAPPY... AND DON'T LOOK BACK.

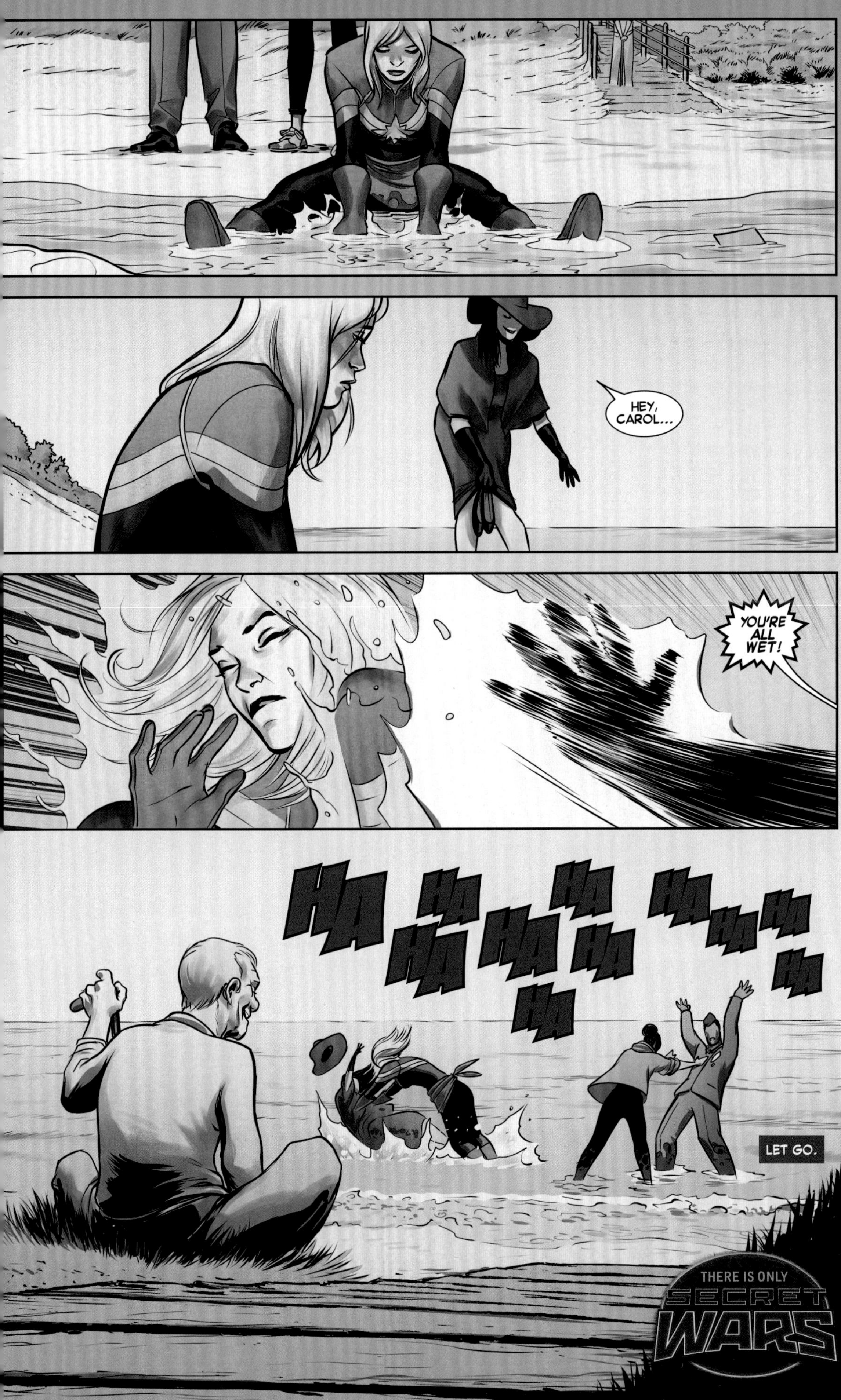
HEY, CAROL...
YOU'RE ALL WET!
HA HA HA HA HA HA HA HA HA HA HA HA HA
LET GO.
THERE IS ONLY SECRET WARS

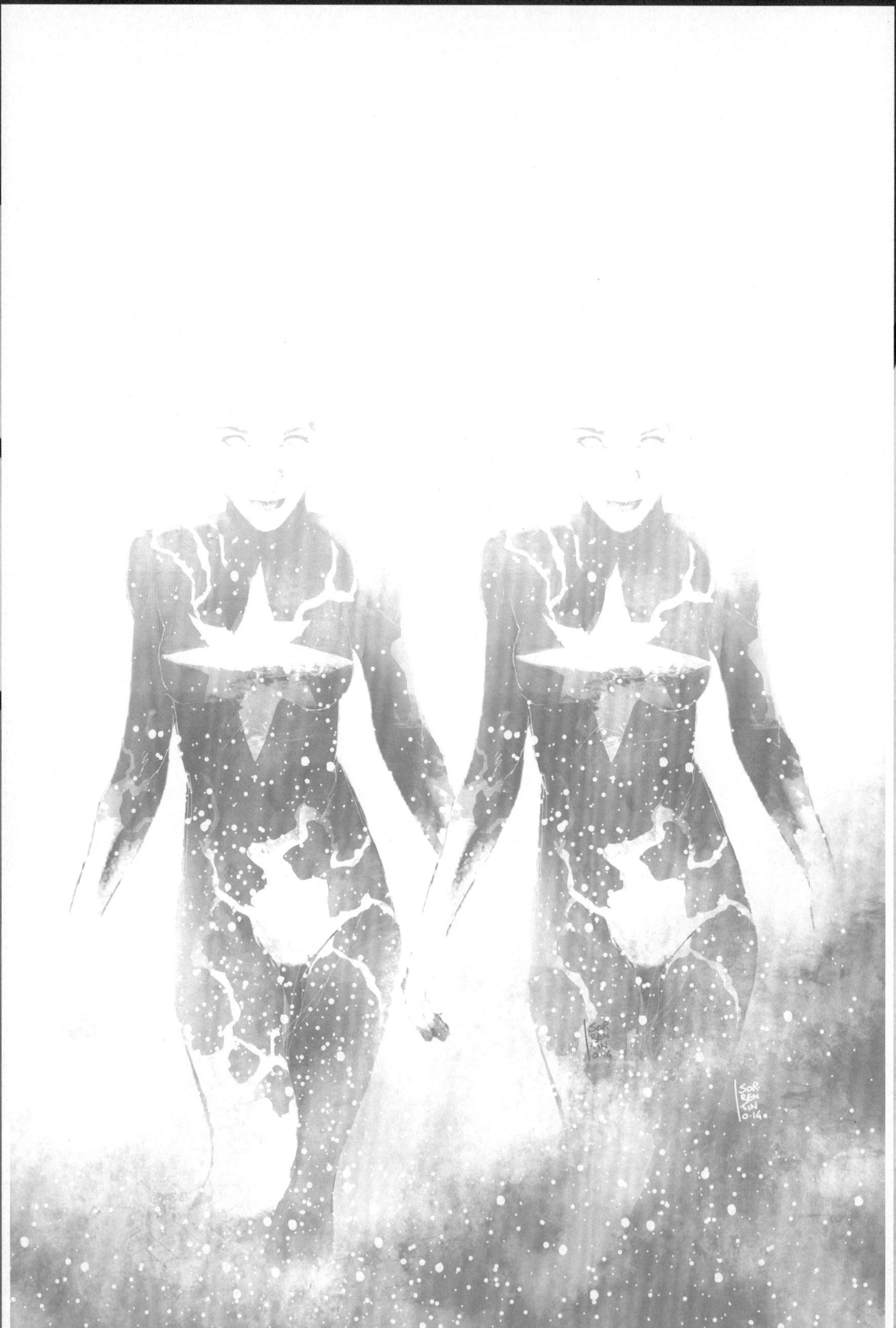

CAPTAIN MARVEL FOURTEEN
COSMICALLY ENHANCED VARIANT BY ANDREA SORRENTINO

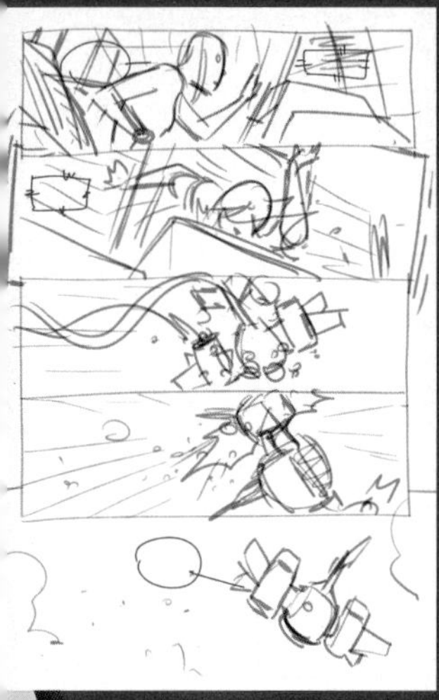

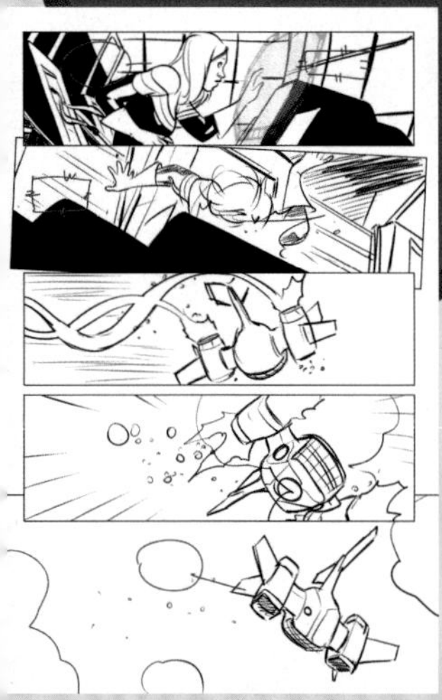

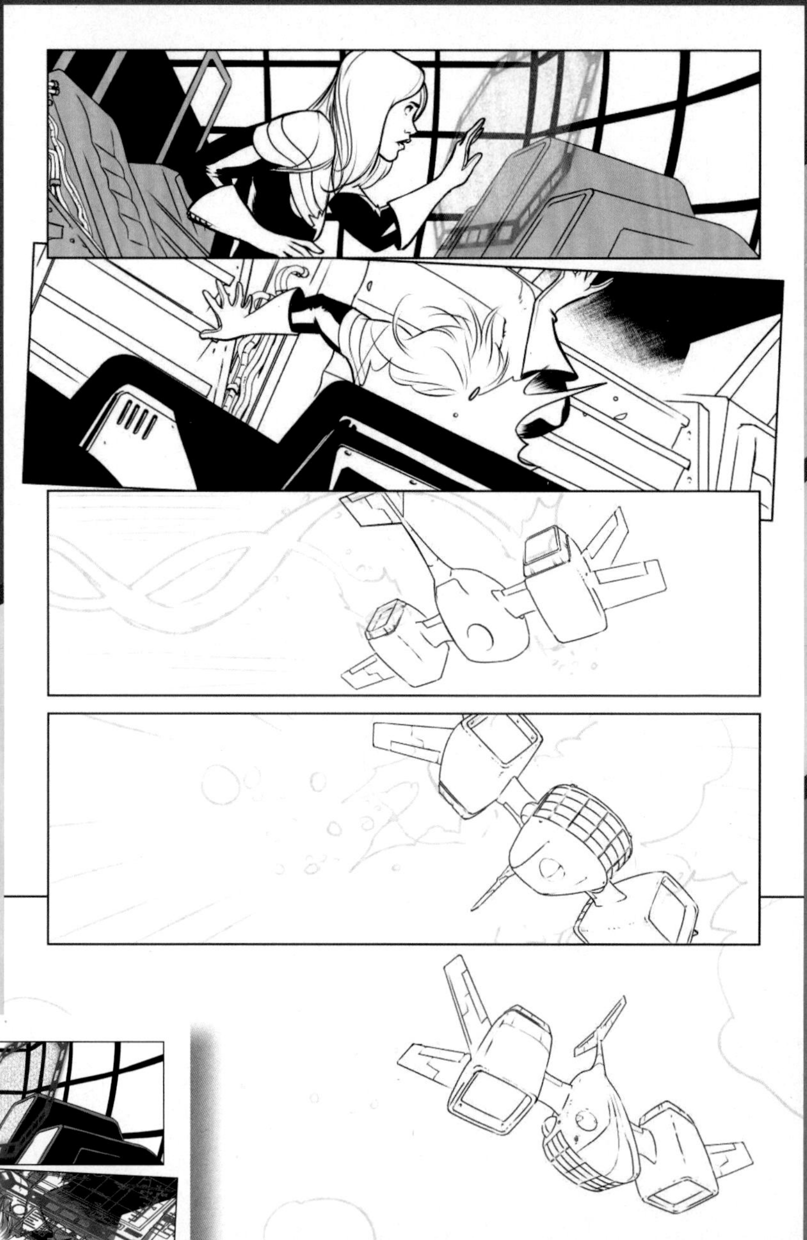

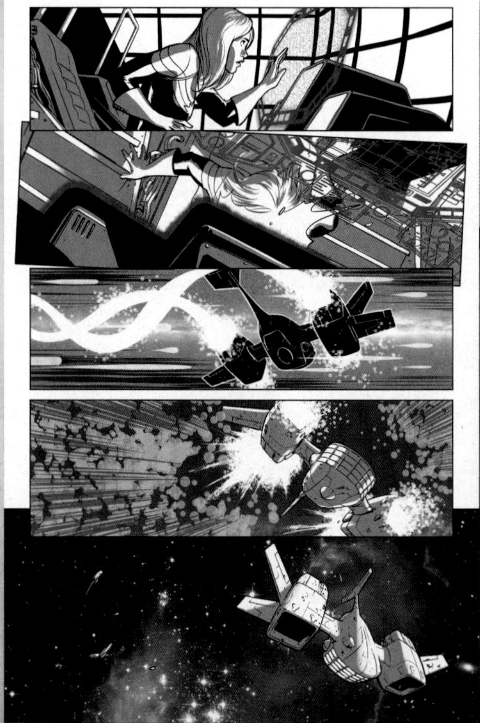

CAPTAIN MARVEL TWELVE, PAGE 13
ART PROCESS BY DAVID LOPEZ

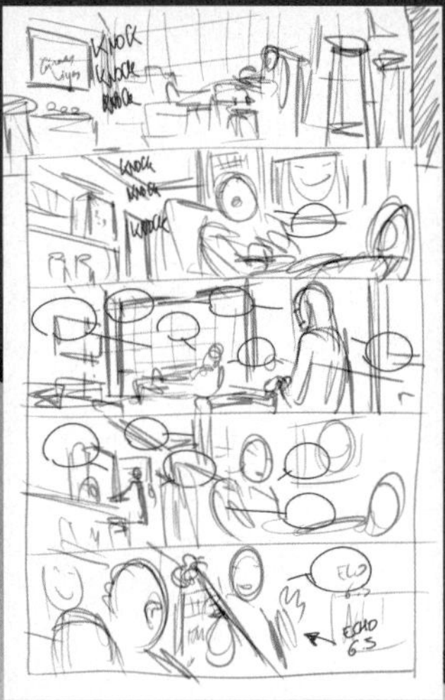

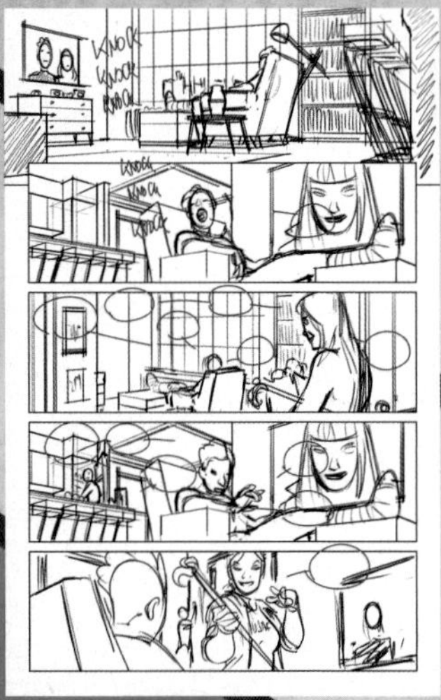
KNOCK
KNOCK
KNOCK

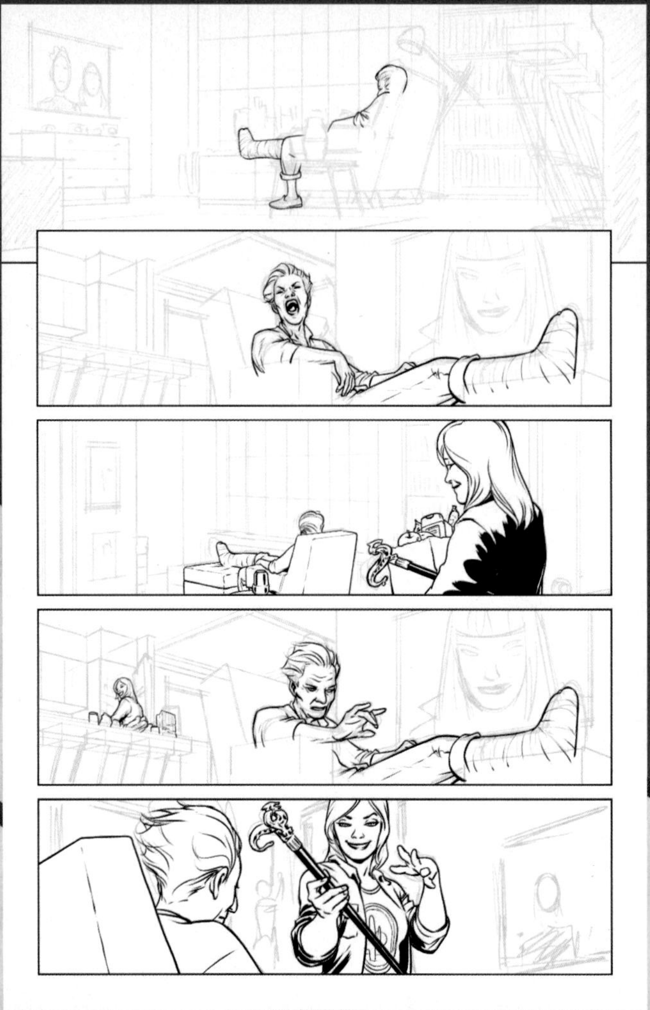

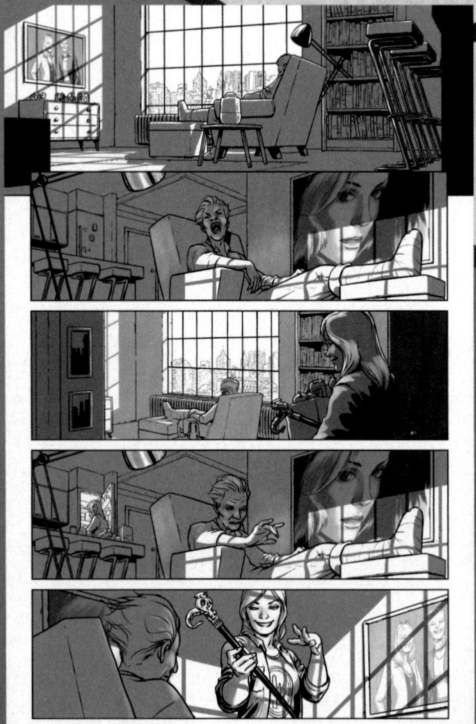

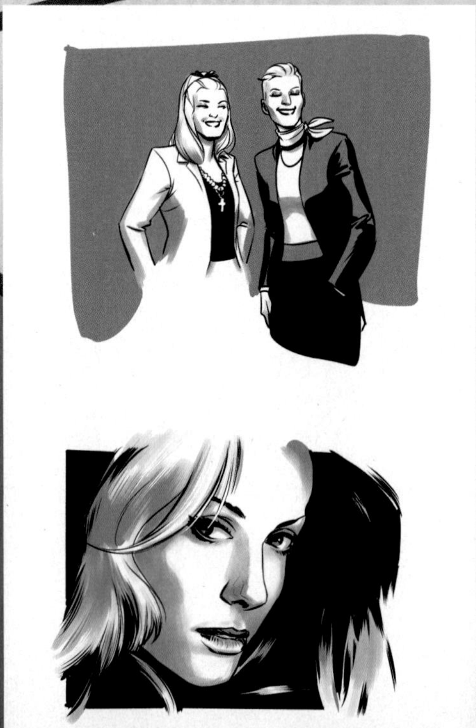

CAPTAIN MARVEL FIFTEEN, PAGE 7
ART PROCESS BY DAVID LOPEZ

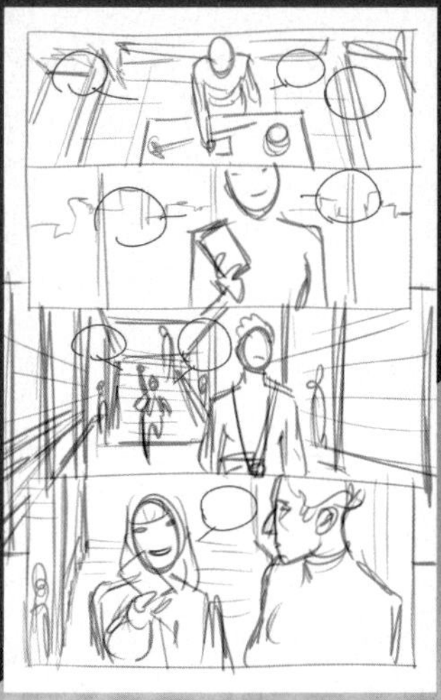

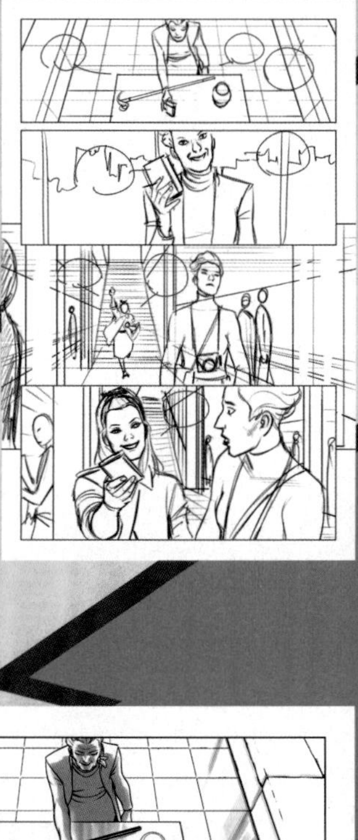

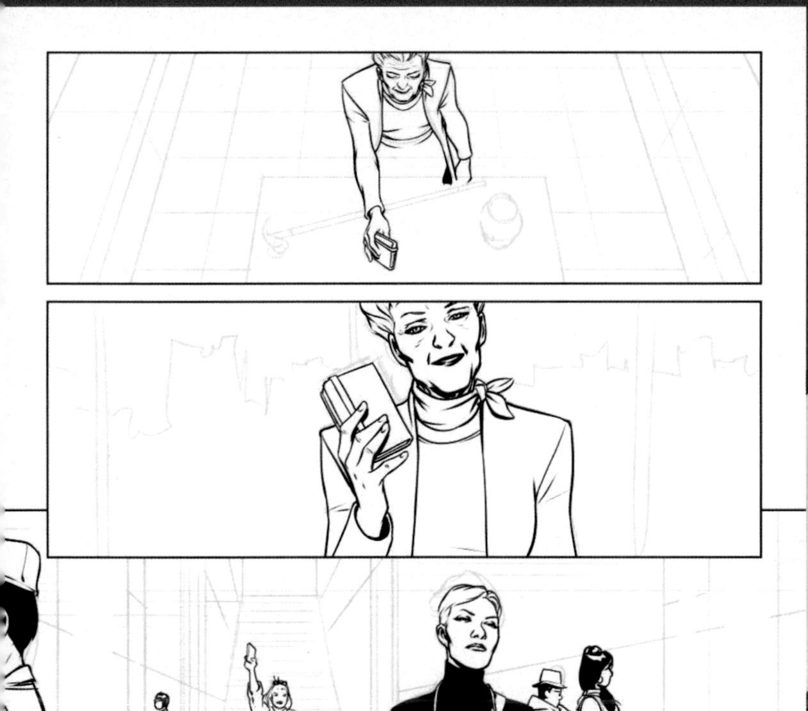

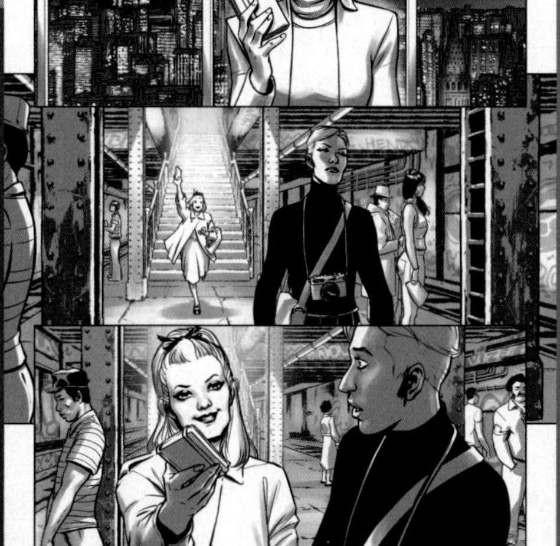

CAPTAIN MARVEL FIFTEEN, PAGE 9
ART PROCESS BY DAVID LOPEZ

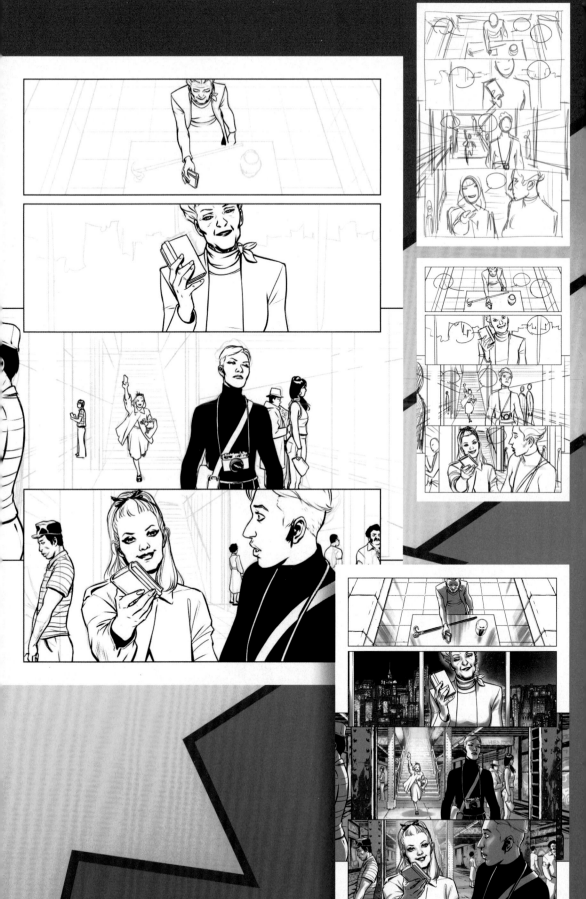

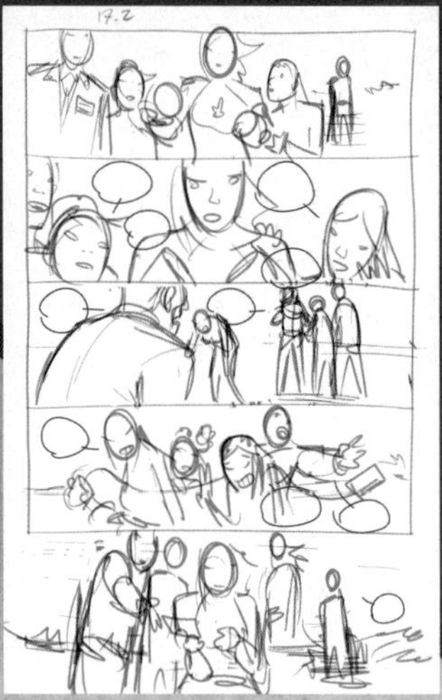

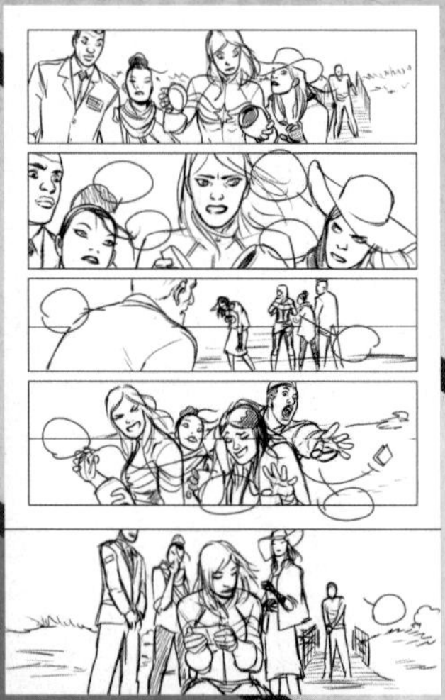

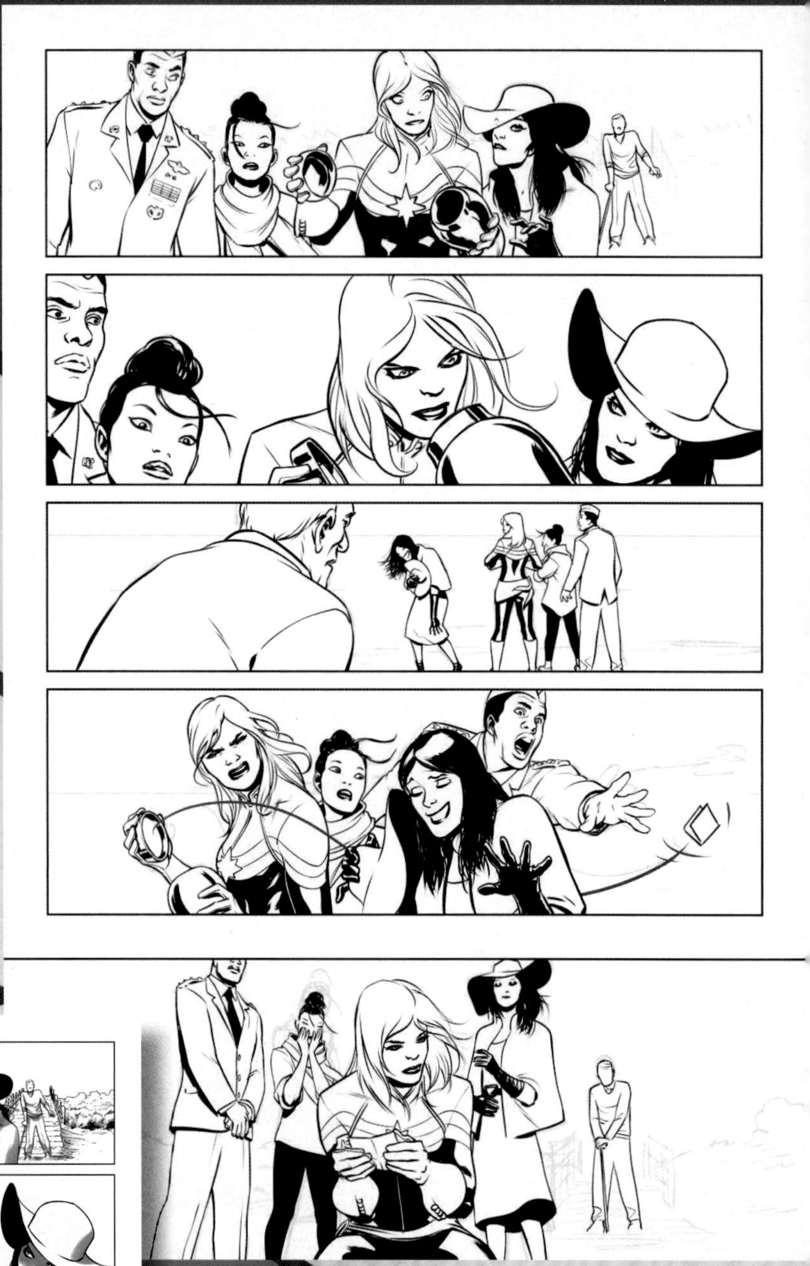

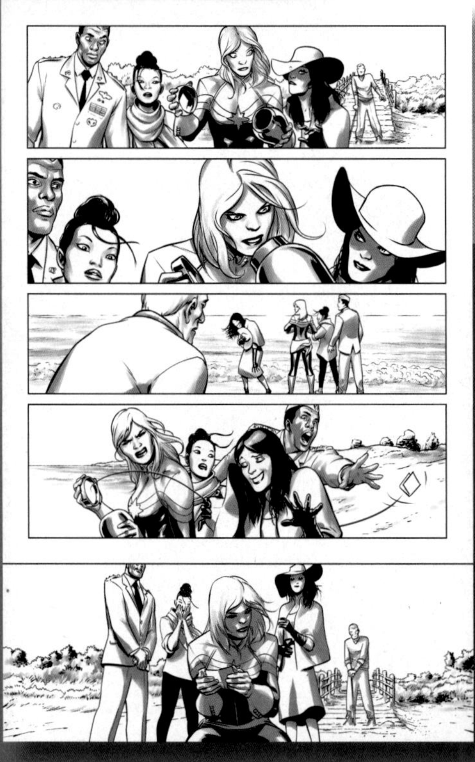

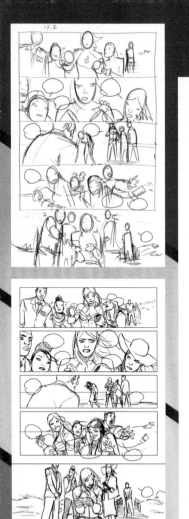

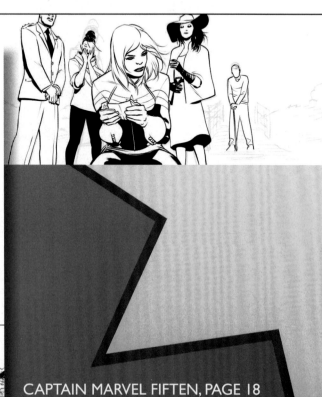

CAPTAIN MARVEL FIFTEN, PAGE 18
ART PROCESS BY DAVID LOPEZ